Mission, Communion and Relationship

AMERICAN
UNIVERSITY
STUDIES

SERIES VII
THEOLOGY AND RELIGION

VOL. 283

PETER LANG
New York • Washington, D.C./Baltimore • Bern
Frankfurt am Main • Berlin • Brussels • Vienna • Oxford

Peter Addai-Mensah

Mission, Communion and Relationship

A Roman Catholic Response to the Crisis of Male Youths in Africa

PETER LANG
New York • Washington, D.C./Baltimore • Bern
Frankfurt am Main • Berlin • Brussels • Vienna • Oxford

Library of Congress Cataloging-in-Publication Data

Addai-Mensah, Peter.
Mission, communion and relationship: a Roman Catholic response
to the crisis of male youths in Africa / Peter Addai-Mensah.
p. cm. — (American university studies. VII, Theology and religion; v. 283)
Includes bibliographical references (p.   ).
1. Church work with youth—Ghana. 2. Young men—Religious life—
Ghana. 3. Problem youth—Religious life—Ghana. 4. Church work
with youth—Catholic Church. I. Title.
BX1682.G5A33   259'.2308109667—dc22   2008053494
ISBN 978-1-4331-0498-5
ISSN 0740-0446

Bibliographic information published by **Die Deutsche Bibliothek**.
Die Deutsche Bibliothek lists this publication in the "Deutsche
Nationalbibliografie"; detailed bibliographic data is available
on the Internet at http://dnb.ddb.de/.

CONTENTS

PREFACE

This book is a revised version of a dissertation submitted for a doctoral degree in Sacred Theology.

From September, 1995-June, 2005, I served as a formator at St. Peter Regional Seminary, Cape Coast, Ghana. In addition to my responsibilities as a Spiritual Director and a Lecturer, I was also the priest-in-charge of students' medicare. I had the opportunity to minister to a greater number of seminarians on one-on-one basis.

As a Regional Seminary, St. Peter's had seminarians from other countries in the sub-region of West Africa as well as India. During the Liberian civil wars (1989-1996 and 1999-2003),[1] students from Liberia came to St. Peter Regional Seminary because their seminary was ran over and became the headquarters of the rebel forces of Charles Taylor.[2] In my encounter with the Liberia students, I had some eye-witness accounts of the brutalities of the civil wars. Unfortunately, two of them died of cancer in the course of their studies at the seminary.

After serving for ten years, the board of governors of the seminary offered me a sabbatical with a study-leave. When I arrived in the United States of America, one day, a friend of mine invited me to go and see a movie. It was *Blood Diamonds*.[3] The movie was about the Sierra Leone civil war (1991-1999) which was fought because some rebels wanted to take control of the rich diamonds in the country. In this movie, teenagers were recruited as soldiers to cause mayhem in Sierra Leone. They raped women, "chopped-off" people's

---

[1] Wikipedia, "Liberia Civil War", http://en.wikipedia.org/wiki/Liberia_Civil_War (accessed November 27, 2007).

[2] For more on Charles Taylor see, BBC News, "Charles Taylor—Preacher, Warlord and President", http://news.bbc.co.uk/2/hi/africa/2963086.stm (accessed November 27, 2007).

[3] The story of the film is about a fisherman, a smuggler and a syndicate of businessmen struggling over the possession of a priceless diamond. This film is about the civil war in Sierra Leone and attempts to control the diamonds in that country. During the war teenagers were recruited and indoctrinated that the elders did not respect them. They had no voice. They had no future. However, with guns in their hands, they would be respected. They would have whatever they wanted. The teenage-soldiers in the Sierra Leone and Liberia civil wars were the most brutal. They were the most feared. Their commanders had told them that they had no money to pay them, so they had to finance themselves. For more on the film, see Wikipedia, "Blood Diamond Film", http://en.wikipedia.org/wiki/Blood_Diamond_(film) (accessed August 19, 2007).

arms and legs and killed others. They really caused terror and traumatized many people. Some inhabitants fled for their lives and settled as refugees in other countries in the sub-region.[4] In the course of the civil wars in Sierra Leone and Liberia, Ghana hosted about 40, 000 refugees. The experiences with the Liberian seminarians at St. Peter Regional Seminary and the movie, *Blood Diamonds*, touched me very much. I began to wonder, what would I have done, if it had happened in Ghana? How would I have reacted? Where would I have fled to? What would have been my future?

The Akans of Ghana say, *se wohunu se egya erehye wo yonko abodwese a, na wo asa nsuo asi wo dee ho*—If you see that your neighbor's beard is on fire, you must provide water as a stand-by against yours. It is also said that "it is better to light a candle than to curse the darkness." As a priest and a theologian, I may not be part of the problems that had beset some countries like Sierra Leone and Liberia and others in Africa but I can become part of the solution. My humble part of the solution is offering a proposal for the proper formation of youth with particular reference to male youth in Africa in order that:

1. They are not easily manipulated and recruited as child and teenage-soldiers to cause mayhem.[5]

2. They become ambassadors and messengers of peace in the sub-region of West Africa in particular and African continent in general.

It is for these reasons that I have chosen to reflect on this topic, *Mission, Communion and Relationship: A Roman Catholic Response to the Crisis of Male Youth in Africa.*

---

[4] BBC News, "Special Report on Sierra Leone", http://news.bbc.co.uk/2/hi/special-report/1999/01/99/Sierra-Leone/251286.stm (accessed November 27, 2007).

[5] Liberian Embassy, "Child Soldiers of Liberia", http://www.liberia-leaf.org/reports/trials/childsoldiers/index.htm (accessed November 27, 2007).

ACKNOWLEDGMENTS

Now to him who by the power at work within us is able to accomplish abundantly far more than all we can ask or imagine, to him be glory in the church and in Christ Jesus to all generations, forever and ever. Amen

Eph. 3: 20-21

This work has been some years of hard and painstaking experience. I could not have accomplished it without the help of others. I would like first and foremost to offer thanks and praise to the Almighty God through whose grace and assistance I was able to bring this work to fruition.

Secondly, I would like to thank the Board of Governors of St. Peter Regional Seminary, Cape Coast, Ghana for granting me a sabbatical with a study-leave after serving in the seminary for ten years to do further studies.

My next thanksgiving goes to Prof. Margaret Eletta Guider, O.S.F. the former Director of the Doctoral Program at Weston Jesuit School of Theology, Cambridge, MA. who doubled up as my advisor when I was writing my dissertation which has been revised into this book. I would like to thank Prof. John Baldovin, SJ of Weston and Prof. Pashington Obeng of Harvard Divinity School and Wellesley College, MA who were my first and second readers respectively of my dissertation for their constructive critiques, guidance and suggestions.

Many family friends made my stay in Boston a very happy one and they need to be acknowledged. I would like to single out Dr. and Mrs. Robert and Joanne Paone and the late Mrs. Anne Schuler (Holy Cow). I would like also to mention Mr. Jerry Hubbard and his mother, David Porper, Rev. Fr. Richard Conway (DOC) and his family and Dolly St. Andre and her late husband, Edward St. Andre.

Ms. Sue Branker and her son Jared Julian are people I cannot forget. They took me into their lives and made sure that I was okay during my stay in Somerville, MA. May God bless all of you for me.

Finally, I would like to thank SIL International and David Irvin, the administrator of Copyright Permissions of www.ethnologue.com for the permission to use the map on languages in Ghana.

INTRODUCTION

"Se wohunu se egya erehye wo yonko abodwese a, na wo asa nsuo asi wo dee ho."—
"When you see that your neighbor's beard is on fire, you must provide water as a stand-by in case yours also catches fire."

"Lord, when did we see you hungry, or thirsty, or a stranger, or naked, or sick, or in prison, and did not minister to you?"

Matt. 25: 44[1]

Africa, as a continent, is not poor by nature. It is endowed with many gifts including its peoples and cultures, its lands and nations, and its abundant natural resources such as oil, precious metals, and diamonds. As Josephat Juma notes,

> Africa is endowed with a good climate, vast expanses of natural resources, scenic grandeur and a big population. Africans are a hardworking and creative people. Their resilience has made them withstand oppressive regimes; dangerous diseases and international development experiments. Africans are landing top jobs in international fora and global agencies. In spite of all this, the continent remains chronically poor.[2]

Tragically, the majority of Africa's people live in abject poverty. Many have no experience of a peaceful social order that is necessary for human beings to flourish. Beset by civil wars and diseases, the crises of Africa have raged on throughout the continent in Angola, the Democratic Republic of Congo (formerly Zaire), Mozambique, Rwanda, Sierra Leone, Uganda, Darfur and Somalia and recently in Kenya, following the 2007 elections. Civil strife, disease and economic impoverishment have claimed the lives of countless people. Currently, millions of displaced persons are living in refugee camps far away from their homes. Most of these refugees are women and children. In the midst of these dehumanizing realities, people's human rights are repeatedly violated. Women are raped. Many have their hands 'chopped' off. Children

---

[1] The scriptural references in this book are from *The New Revised Standard Bible*, (New York: Oxford University Press, 1989).

[2] Josephat Juma, "Africa: Poor by Choice",
http://www.africanexecutive.com/modules/magazine/articles.php?article=1091&magazine (accessed February 18, 2007).

and teenagers, especially boys and young men, are recruited by militia against their wills. Coerced to use drugs like marijuana and cocaine, they become addicted and as agents of mindless violence set out to harm and kill those whom they have been indoctrinated to believe as the 'enemy'. For example, in Liberia, about 20% of all the combatants in the devastating civil war were children and youth who were seen to be the most brutal among the fighters as they tortured, raped and killed innocent people. Some were even said to have been engaged in cannibalism.[3] Out of a population of 2.8 million, 150,000 died because of the conflict; 750,000 fled the country and over 1.2 million were displaced internally.[4] During the nine-year civil war in Sierra Leone, aid workers and government officials reported that among the worst of human rights abuses such as rape, abductions, murders, mutilations, forced labor, massive looting, and ambushes, were those carried out by trained child combatants and teenage rebels.[5] "The panic in Freetown when they appeared clearly showed the fear these youngsters, with matted locks and dressed in tatters, inspired in the adult civilian population."[6] The degree of cruelty carried out by male youth against other human beings remains a devastating commentary on humanity's prospects for the future.

Indeed, human beings are complex and unpredictable creatures. As Africans, such realities challenge us in our attempts to respond to the perennial questions: who are we? where do we come from? what are we doing here? where are we going? Those of us who believe in God are constantly reminded that we are not alone. We are in relationship with God. Seen from this perspective, any attempt to understand humanity without reference to God will be an exercise in futility. The reason is a simple one: as human beings, each one of us comes from God and through relationship we hope to return to God one day. Mindful of this faith horizon, the Church cannot neglect the youth crisis confronting the African continent.

---

[3]   Liberian   Embassy,   "Child   Soldiers   of   Liberia",   http://www.liberia-leaf.org/reports/trials/childsoldiers/index.htm   (accessed March 10, 2007).

[4] Liberia Embassy, "Liberia at War", http://www.liberia-leaf.org/reports/trials/war/index.htm (accessed January 7, 2007).

[5] For more information see BBC News, "Special Report: Sierra Leone's Civil War" http://news.bbc.co.uk/2/hi/special-report/1999/01/99/Sierra-Leone/251286.stm   (accessed March 10, 2007).

[6] Ibid.

The Church by its very nature is missionary. (AG. 2)[7] Sent to all nations and to people of all ages (Mt. 28: 19-20; Mk. 16: 19-20),[8] the Church's participation in God's mission involves proclaiming the good news of Jesus Christ and listening to the ways in which the Spirit is speaking to the churches. (Rev 2-3) As leaders of the Roman Catholic church in Ghana endeavor to foster communion, they must be mindful of the signs of the times. Given the realities of Ghanaian history, society and culture, I argue in this book that precisely because of the Church's participation in the *missio Dei* it bears an ecclesial responsibility for the integral human development of *all* people. Essential to this process is the promotion of inter-religious understanding, beginning with the tenets and traditions of Africa Traditional Religion (ATR)—the indigenous religion of Ghana, continuing with the teachings and practices of Islam—the dominant religion that preceded Roman Catholicism in Ghana, and attending to the polity and piety of other Christian churches—both historical and independent.

Conscious of the profoundly 'spiritual' nature of the post-colonial and post-modern crises that have contributed to the breakdown of community, the loss of cultural identity, the corruption of moral integrity, and the neglect of relational duty, my specific interest in this book is the plight of growing numbers of male youth in Africa, especially the young men of Ghana. It is my conviction that responses on the part of the Roman Catholic church to this crisis cannot be undertaken in isolation. As a 'church in mission', the church in Ghana must endeavor to be 'a church in relationship.' By embracing the ecclesial model of 'church as communion', church leaders and ministers must work intentionally and creatively to become a community of disciples capable of seriously engaging the religious sensibilities, moral imagination and social consciousness of all Ghanaian people.

Thesis Statement

We read in the scriptures that the purpose of Jesus' coming into the world was to preach the Reign of God. (Mk.1:14-15) According to Paul, the Reign of God is not a matter of eating and drinking, but a matter of sharing in the justice, peace and joy of the Holy Spirit. (Rom. 14:17) The Church as the sacrament of Christ participates in God's mission. In doing so the church's mission cannot

---

[7] *Ad Gentes*, 2, *The Documents of Vatican II,* ed. Austin P. Flannery (Grand Rapids: W.B. Eerdmans, 1975), 814.

[8] *Gaudium et Spes*, 58. *The Documents of Vatican II*, 962.

be uncoupled from the mission of Christ. By his coming into the world, Jesus pitched his tent among us (Jn 1:14), so that we, human beings, would have life and have it to the full. (Jn 10:10b) Consequently, as a church that understands its twofold responsibility for being a sacrament of salvation as well as integral liberation, it cannot neglect its responsibility for the development and progress of human beings,[9] whether male or female, young or old, rich or poor, Catholic or not.

Ecclesiology cannot be done in the abstract. It requires a context, a warrant, and a focus. To these ends, I have chosen to write on the topic: MISSION, COMMUNION AND RELATIONSHIP: A ROMAN CATHOLIC RESPONSE TO THE CRISIS OF MALE YOUTH[10] IN AFRICA. From the outset, let me be very clear that my focus on male youth does not represent any bias against or lack of regard for the equally important challenges confronting female youth. It simply is my conviction that in recent decades advocacy for the integral development of male youth is rarely reflected upon by the church *or* society with any specificity or urgency. The following two observations inform this conviction:

1. In recent times, Ghana has been described as an oasis of peace, notwithstanding some conflicts that once in a while occur in some communities in Northern Ghana. While neighboring countries like the Ivory Coast, Liberia, Sierra Leone and Togo have been affected by warfare and political conflicts, Ghana has enjoyed a relative peace. These wars have claimed thousands of human lives by death, trauma and injury. Countless properties have been confiscated or destroyed. In these wars as well as those that have taken place in Angola, Uganda, Congo and Rwanda, the use of teenage-soldiers was widespread. Invariably, they were mostly male youths. Many lost their lives. For those who lost parts of their bodies, minds and spirits, the cost of rehabilitating them into the society after the wars has proven to be enormous. The trauma of being soldiers as children and adolescents will affect them for the rest of their lives. The Akans of Ghana say, *se wohunu se egya erehye wo yonko abodwese a, na wo asa nsuo asi wo dee ho*—when you see that your neighbor's beard is on fire, you must provide water as

---

[9] Jean-Marc Ela, *My Faith as an African*, trans. John Pairman Brown and Susan Perry (Maryknoll, NY: Orbis Books, 1988), 149

[10] The category of 'male youth' includes teenage boys and young men between the ages of 16– 30.

a stand-by in case yours also catches fire. Abundant evidence suggests that male youth in Africa need to be formally educated, adequately formed, and entrusted with a hopeful vision for the future. In the absence of these conditions, many will easily fall prey to opportunists. As Proverbs say, 'a nation or a people without a vision perish.' (Prov. 29:18)

2. In recent years, Ghana has put in place numerous programs for women and girls. When the New Patriotic Party (NPP) government under President John Agyekum-Kuffour assumed office in 2001, the Ministry for Women and Children Affairs was established and headed by a woman director.[11] The rationale for this Ministry was to promote and maintain both the dignity and empowerment of women and children. In addition to this initiative, ever greater emphasis has been placed on the education of girls in this new era of educational reform. Also, special units have been set up in the Police Administration to address issues impacting lives in domestic violence victims (DOVVSU).[12] Though much more needs to be done, these programs are demonstrating some positive results. Rape cases are dealt with immediately and perpetrators are punished under the law. Cases of teenage pregnancy are in decline. The number of girls and young women in educational institutions has increased significantly. The incidence and root causes of domestic violence and abuse are being brought to the attention of society.

As a priest and theologian, I am of the view that through collaboration and cooperation with the broader society, the church has much to contribute to the country's desire for peace and harmony. This being said I want to emphasize in the strongest terms possible that just as girls and young women are being helped to live their lives in ways that enable them to discover the fullness of what it means to be human, boys and young men cannot be left behind by the society or the church. I would argue further that the well-being, safety, and security of women cannot be advanced in the absence of effective initiatives

---

[11] For more information, see Ministry of Women and Children Affairs, "Ghanaian Parliament passes the Domestic Violence Bill" http://www.mowac.ghana.net (accessed January 10, 2007).

[12] For more information on Domestic Violence and Victims Supporting Unit (DOVVSU) see Ghana Police, "What is DOVVSU?" http://www.ghanapolice.org (accessed January 10, 2007),

and programs designed to address the many problems facing male youth. Some of these problems include:

1. "Streetism" is the description given to the reality of young boys and adolescents living on the streets of the cities without any connection to their families. Unheard of some years ago, one attribution for the phenomenon is the absence of responsible and runaway fathers.

2. male youth becoming drug addicts and serving as couriers for drug barons.

3. a rampant increase in armed robberies, home invasions and highway assaults by adolescents.

4. an increasingly high unemployment among male youth, and

5. a prevailing tendency to look down on African (Ghanaian) culture and become enchanted by foreign ones. The erosion of a positive cultural identity has potentially tragic consequences for male youth.

I am of the view that there should not be competition between the sexes for social services and access to human development opportunities in Ghana. However, for the sake of the nation, and moreover, the sake of the Gospel, I have chosen to make the focus of my discussion on the particular *ecclesial* responsibility of the Roman Catholic church to realize its mission of building communion and relationship through multidimensional efforts to promote the integral human development of male youth throughout Africa, and especially, in my homeland of Ghana.

Aims

My aims in writing this book are the following:

1. To explain more fully the permanent validity of the missionary dynamics of the Roman Catholic church in Africa by drawing upon historical insights from the past and contextual insights from the present and to deal with the issues and concerns raised in selected documents of the United Nations and the African Union.

2. To provide a social analysis of the plight of male youth in Ghana and sub-Saharan Africa so as to enable church leaders to be more critically

conscious of the interactive dynamics of history, religious pluralism and globalization as well as the socio-cultural and political realities of sub-Saharan Africa.

3. To identify the strengths and limitations of the model of 'church as communion' by setting recent documents of the Roman Catholic church, including those of the bishops of Africa and Ghana.

4. To set in dialogue selected traditional proverbs and biblical texts pertaining to male youth, as foundational theological starting points for reflection on the timeless and contemporary challenges facing male youth and significance of moral development and spiritual transformation in male development and religious maturity.

5. On the basis of this research, to provide the Roman Catholic church in Ghana with an innovative theological vision to support and sustain pastoral outreach to and with male youth in Ghana and Africa.

Audience

Inasmuch as the bishops of the Roman Catholic church exercise the role and function of teachers and shepherds in the Church, this book is addressed first and foremost to the Roman Catholic Bishops of Ghana and sub-region of Africa. At the same time, I acknowledge the fact that responsibility for the day-to-day implementation of any theological and pastoral proposals will be assumed by priests, religious, catechists and lay-leaders. Secondly, given the importance of ecumenical collaboration, I also write for the sake of pastors and leaders of other Christian denominations in Africa. Thirdly, mindful of the importance of religion and culture, I write for the spiritual leaders of Islam. Fourthly, I write for the "abusua-panin"—the clan heads. In Ghana, the human being is always seen as a member of a clan. Whatever one does cannot be inimical to the clan. Since the authority of the clan head is highly respected in Ghana, I believe that mindfulness of the "abusua-panin" is critical for any Roman Catholic effort to contribute to the integral development of male youth. Finally, I write for the sake of male youth: students, laborers, soldiers, seminarians, migrants, refugees, artists, entrepreneurs, prisoners, brothers, sons, fathers, uncles, cousins—the young 'bearded-ones'.

Focus

This work holds together insights from ecclesiology, church history, theological-anthropology, the social sciences as well as African and Western philosophy with concrete ecclesial and human experiences. Some of the questions this discussion endeavors to answer include:

1. What kind of influence (positive and/or negative) does the Roman Catholic church currently exercise in Africa with regard to male youth?

2. What lessons can be learned from history—both ecclesial and social—with regard to the Roman Catholic church's outreach to male youth?

3. In the light of the two questions, how do the realities facing the Roman Catholic church in Africa speak to the Universal Church (and *vice versa*) with regard to the adequacy and appropriateness of communion ecclesiology *and* the permanent validity of missionary activity, especially among youth?

4. What can the Roman Catholic church in Africa learn through dialogue with other Christian churches, African Traditional Religion, and Islam, with regard to a more comprehensive inter-religious understanding of the formation and identity of male youth in a postcolonial, postmodern, and religiously pluralistic world reality?

5. What resources from scripture and tradition can be used in the construction of a foundational theological vision for ecclesial engagement of male youth?

6. What are the immediate pastoral challenges ahead for the church in Ghana and Sub-Saharan Africa with regard to male youth?

Methodology

The method of this discussion is interdisciplinary. Rooted in the scripture and tradition, the method is constructive and contextual. It makes use of approaches that are historical–critical, narrative, analytical, descriptive and prescriptive. As an expression of its 'African-ness', the work gives particular attention to the significance of oral tradition for teaching and learning. In so doing, I hope to draw upon the wisdom that is at the core of African philosophy and theological imagination.

Overview: The History of Ghana

Ghana is in West Africa. It was formerly called the Gold Coast. This name was given to the country by Portuguese sailors in 1471. Upon setting foot on the land, they found an abundance of minerals and started trading with the inhabitants. This trade soon attracted other Europeans. Among them were the English, the Dutch, the Swedish, the Danish and the French. This led to a series of conflicts over land and mineral resources. In 1820, the British took control of the region and imposed colonial rule. After 130 years of British rule, Ghana gained independence on March 6th, 1957. Kwame Nkrumah became the country's first president. The name "Ghana" was chosen at independence. It referred to the ancient Ghana Empire that existed from the ninth until the thirteenth century. After a series of military interventions since independence, Ghana is now under a democratically elected government, having changed successfully from one civilian government to another. It has a population of about 20 million according to the National Census of 2000. The major ethnic groups in Ghana are: Akan (44%); Moshi-Dagomba (16%); Ewe (13%); Ga (8%) and others.[13] The country is organized politically into 10 administrative regions and 169 districts.

The History of Roman Catholic Church in Ghana

The beginning of Roman Catholic Church in Ghana was not well-planned. Merchants were on their way to India to buy spices. They had to make their way by the Atlantic Ocean due to the fact that the earlier and shorter route through the Mediterranean Sea had fallen to Muslim conquests. According to historians such as Helene M. Pfann, it was the need for fresh water that caused Portuguese merchants and sailors to land on the shores of Ghana.[14] Though Portuguese chaplains accompanied the merchants and sailors, they too became caught up in the gold trade and did not make any serious attempts at evangelization.

---

[13]Info please, "Ghana-Ethnicity Race" http://www.infoplease.com/ipa/A0107584.html (accessed January 4, 2007).
[14] Helene M. Pfann, *A Short History of The Catholic Church in Ghana*, Cape Coast (Ghana: Catholic Mission Press, 1965), 5.

The Roman Catholic Church in Ghana Today

After more than one hundred and thirty years, Roman Catholicism has taken root in Ghana. The Church can be found in the four corners of the country. It exists in all the ten administrative regions of Ghana. The Roman Catholic Church map has four ecclesiastical provinces made up of four Archdioceses, fifteen Dioceses and an Apostolic Vicariate.[15] It has produced two cardinals and all the local ordinaries are Ghanaians. About 90% of the priests and religious sisters and brothers engaged in the missionary activity of the Church are indigenous people.

The Church in Ghana and Its Relationship with the Universal Church

The Roman Catholic church in Ghana is in communion with the Church of Rome. The Vatican has a papal nuncio resident in Ghana. The archdioceses and dioceses of Ghana are not closed to themselves. Meetings occur at the provincial level and bishops come together as the Bishops' Conference of Ghana. At the sub-regional level, the Ghanaian bishops are members of Anglophone Episcopal Conferences of West Africa (AECAWA). Attempts have been made to merge with their Francophone counterpart. At the continental level, the bishops of Ghana are members of the Symposium of Episcopal Conferences of Africa and Madagascar (SECAM).

The Roman Catholic Church in Ghana and Its Relationship with other Christian Churches, Islam and African Traditional Religion (ATR)

Ghana is not a predominantly Roman Catholic country. According to the National Census of 2000, Christians constitute about 63%. Out of this number, Catholics are about 20%. Other religious groups found in Ghana are believers in ATR (21%) and Islam (16%). The Akans say, T*e koro ngo agyina*—one head does not take counsel. Since the Roman Catholic church exists with other Christian denominations, I argue in this book that it must work in concert and partnership with them in responding to the plight of male youth. To this end, it is critical that Christians work together in developing joint programs to form and train the young men to be patriotic, responsible and resourceful citizens of the country.

---

[15]   David   M.   Cheney,   "Catholic   Church   in   Ghana"   http://www.catholic-hierarchy.org/diocese/daco.html (accessed January 10, 2008).

In a similar fashion, Christians also must find ways of working with Muslims. Islam has been in Ghana for a very long time. As noted previously, it accounts for about 16% of the population in Ghana. Though the majority of the Muslims in Ghana are Sunnis, there also are some who are members of the Ahamadiyah movement. Historically speaking, there has been relative peace among Christians and Muslims in Ghana. However, the same cannot be said of other countries in the sub-region like Nigeria and Chad as well as countries like Sudan and Somalia. In a number of African countries, clashes between Christians and Muslims have led to wars and great devastation. When extremists use Islam as a justification for engaging in violent actions,[16] it is often male youth who are involved in carrying out such activities. Efforts on the part of the Roman Catholic church in the sub-region to enter into dialogue with Muslim leaders could contribute positively to the interruption and prevention of tensions and hostilities that manipulate religion to political ends.

Finally, for the sake of male youth—both Christian and non-Christian, the Roman Catholic church in Ghana must engage in dialogue with the leaders of African Traditional Religion. The wisdom present in ATR cannot be neglected or minimized inasmuch as it holds the key to understanding the deep spiritual roots of the cultures of Ghana. If the mission of the church is to be carried out in the spirit of the Second Vatican Council, such dialogue is an imperative. In an effort to restore to male youth a sense of pride and integrity, such efforts are critical to the social process of cultural identity formation and the ecclesial process of inculturation.

Contributions of the Roman Catholic Church to Ghanaian Society

The Roman Catholic church in Ghana has tended to have a holistic approach towards the development of the human person. The contributions of the church have been felt in all aspects of human endeavors: cultural, economic, political, religious and social. The church has been the voice of the voiceless. It has championed the course of participatory democracy particularly during military interventions in Ghana. On the economic front, the church has established credit unions in order to help people acquire loans in order to establish and expand small and medium scale enterprises. Socially, the church in Ghana has promoted healthcare through its sponsorship of hospitals, clinics and health posts that are designed mostly to serve the rural poor.

---

[16] John L. Esposito, *Unholy War: Terror in the Name of Islam* (Oxford: University Press, 2002)

Educationally, the church has its own elementary, secondary, vocational and technical schools as well as training colleges and a recently established Roman Catholic University. The power of these many endeavors to promote and develop the dignity of the human person cannot be under-estimated. Yet the social question regarding the plight of so many young people remains as does the question: what can the church do to be more effective in fulfilling its missionary mandate among male youth of Ghana?

Challenges Ahead

There is no doubt that the Roman Catholic church has achieved much in the course of about hundred and thirty years of its existence in Ghana. However, there is more to be done. Among these challenges is the articulation of an adequate theological understanding of mission, communion and relationship that draws upon diverse foundations upon which pastoral initiatives and social strategies for responding to the plight of male youth strategies may be built and sustained. The desire to form young men for authentic Christian life and social responsibility means that the church must commit itself to providing alternatives to the seduction of negative cultural practices represented in the globalizing forces of violence, drugs, promiscuity, irresponsibility, escapism, consumerism that prevent young men from becoming resourceful, respected, and responsible human beings. To the extent that they are our future, ecclesially and socially, Church leaders must do all that we can in order to put out the fire in their beards—for our sakes as well as their own.

Contents of Chapters

Chapter One —The Missionary Dynamics of the Church in Ghana: Historical Background and Contemporary Context: A Roman Catholic Perspective with Emphasis on Ministry to Male Youth

This chapter surveys the historical origins of Christian missionary activity in Ghana and provides an analysis of the current ecumenical reality. I begin the chapter by reviewing of the historical observations and missiological insights made by Lamin Sanneh in his book, *West African Christianity: The Religious Impact.* In an effort to focus my study of Christianity in the sub-region and its impact on the people, I draw upon the works of Pashington Obeng, G. C. Baeta and Brigid M. Sackey. My intention in this chapter is to highlight the fact that the Roman Catholic church in Ghana is not operating by itself but in relationship to other Christian churches. While acknowledging from an ecumenical perspective the role and significance of historical Protestant churches *vis à vis* the Roman Catholic church, I also explore the demands and difficulties involved in contemporary efforts to be in relationship with Pentecostal/Charismatic churches as well as the independent/indigenous churches. My fundamental concern is that while the mission of Jesus calls Christians to respond to the plight of male youth, our respective divisions and differences as Christians may prevent us from achieving the communion that is necessary for authentic collaboration.

My first objective is to identify and examine the various approaches to missionary activity used by the Roman Catholic church in Ghana. My second objective is to discuss how best they can be improved upon with regard to contributing to the full humanization and evangelization of male youth in Ghana.

Chapter Two —"Beards on Fire": The Plight of African Male Youth as a Missiological Challenge to the Roman Church in Africa: A Ghanaian Analysis

In this chapter, I will begin with some social analysis of contemporary realities affecting male youth. When one considers Africa, it is estimated that about 50% of its population is below the age of 18. A greater percentage is between the ages of 18-25. Consequently, Africa is seen as the most "youthful" continent in the world.[17] However, in many countries in Africa, young people are left out of participation in the economic, political and social affairs. They are often not consulted when even programs concerning them are being fashioned out. Young people are vulnerable to poverty, disease and death. Only a handful has access to education that can prepare them adequately to enter the job market. I am of the view that due to the high poverty level, many youths in Africa have to fend for themselves and their families. This has resulted in child-labor in many countries. The same reason accounts for the youth, especially male youth, to fall prey to opportunists on the continent who see themselves as freedom fighters. They are recruited as teenage-soldiers to engage in conflicts and wars as depicted in the movie *Blood Diamonds*. The youth are often associated with crime. According to the Police Service in

---

[17] Social Science Research Council, "Africa" http://www.ssrc.org/programs/africa/2003fellows (accessed November 22, 2007).

Ghana, about 70% of all crime cases in Ghana are committed by the youth.[18] In talking about Africa today, one cannot refuse to mention the pandemic of the HIV/AIDS. It is the most affected area in the world. The estimate is about 23 million people.[19] In 2001, The United Nations General Assembly Special Session on HIV/AIDS noted, "Poverty, underdevelopment and illiteracy are among the principal contributing factors to the spread of HIV/AIDS."[20] These are some of the challenges that the Roman Catholic church has to deal with in its missionary activity. I am sure that with right attitude and approach these problems are not insurmountable. Here, I am thinking of John Paul II as a model. He really believed in young people and had confidence in them. He never stopped showing how he loved them. He loved to be in their company and listened to what they had to say. He really gave young people a voice. In *Ecclesia in Africa* he said, "It is thus necessary to help young people to overcome the obstacles thwarting their development: illiteracy, idleness, hunger, drugs. In order to meet these challenges, young people themselves should be called upon to become the evangelizers of their peers. No one can do this better than they."[21] I am of the opinion that what the African male youth needs is not sympathy. As Nagia Mohammed Essayed, the African Union's Commissioner for Human Resources, Science and Technology said "African youth are a special resource that requires special attention. They are formidably creative resource that can be harnessed for Africa's socio-economic development."[22] I cannot agree more with this. I believe that what the African male youth needs is empowerment. The Roman Catholic church in Ghana and Africa must do this in partnership with all stakeholders and other religious groups.

Chapter Three —"I am because we are and since we are, therefore, I am":
Maturity and Male Identity Formation: Recovering an African Moral

---

[18] Ghana Home Page, "IGP to launch Youth Crime Watch Programme" http://www.ghanaweb.com/GhanaHomePage/NewsArchive/artikel.php?ID=116817 (accessed November 20, 2007).

[19]Social Science Research Council, "Africa" http://www.ssrc.org/programs/africa/2003fellows (accessed November 22, 2007).

[20] Youth Coalition, "Ghana" http://www.youthaidcoalition.org/docs/Ghana.pdf (accessed November 20, 2007)

[21] John Paul II, *Ecclesia in Africa* (Vatican City: Libreria Editrice Vaticana, 1995), no. 93.

[22] Joseph Juma, "Which Way for Youth Empowerment?" February 14-21, 2007, http://www.africanexecutive.com/modules/mgazine/articles.php?article=2102 (accessed February 18, 2007).

Vision for 'Persons-in-Relation': Insights from Kwame Gyekye, John Macmurray and Augustine

In this chapter, I will point out that male youth is not just an individual. He is part of a community. As John Mbiti notes, "I am because we are and since we are, therefore, I am". The African male youth must, therefore, see himself always as part of a community. Here, three people will be considered namely: Kwame Gyekye, John Macmurray and Augustine, representing African culture, the modern children and Christian life respectively.

Kwame Gyekye is a Ghanaian philosopher. He emphasizes the relationship that exists between the individual and the community. For him, African social ethic is not a matter of either communalism or individualism. Rather, it is both. Communalism is reinforced by individualism and vice-versa.

Mbiti's assertion resonates well with what John Macmurray, a Scottish philosopher says about the human person as far as relationship is concerned. According to him, "The idea of an isolated agent is self-contradictory. Any agent is necessarily in relation to the other. Apart from this essential relation he does not exist."[23] For Macmurray, "I exit as an individual only in a personal relation to the other individual."[24] I will look at his books *The Self as Agent* and *Persons in Relation*. In this way, I think that the Ghanaian and the African male youth must realize that whatever he does has an effect on others and the community in general. Consequently, egoism and self-centeredness are always to be eschewed. They are counter-cultural. They are un-Ghanaian.

Later in the chapter, I draw upon some insights from Augustine. In his dispute with the Donatists, he pointed out that unity and communion must be maintained at all times. One cannot separate oneself from the community because of the holiness or un-holiness of some members. For Augustine, such an attitude is uncharitable. It is un-Christian. It is against the teachings and the example of Jesus who came not to call the righteous but sinners. (Mt.9: 13)

Chapter Four —Communion and Solidarity with Male Youth: A Missiological Imperative for the Roman Catholic Church in Ghana

It is often said that in unity lies strength. Before his ascension into heaven, Jesus prayed for his disciples so that they may be one just as he and the Father are one. (Jn. 17: 20-21) Unity in the Church was very important to the early

---

[23] John Macmurray, *Persons in Relation* (New York: Humanity Books, 1999), 24
[24] Ibid., 28

disciples. (1 Cor. 1:10-17)   It continued in the history of the Church. One of the champions of unity and communion in the Church is Cyprian. This is strongly advocated in his book, *The Lapsed: The Unity of The Catholic Church.* Even during the Reformation, people like John Calvin were very particular about the unity of the Church.[25] We read in the bible that Jesus asked Peter to feed his sheep and the lambs. (Jn. 21: 1-19)

In this chapter, I will discuss the Church as a communion. I will look at the place of male youth in the activities of the Church. I will point out that while in some dioceses in Ghana the youth are playing very active roles, the same cannot be said of other dioceses in Ghana and in the sub-region.

As I indicated earlier on, there are myriads of problems confronting male youth. They can go a long way to enslave them. In such a situation, they become a burden and a problem to themselves, their families and the community at large. The Roman Catholic Church cannot fail to address them. As Jean-Marc Ela, a Camerounian theologian, points out in his book, *My Faith as an African*, "in our world today, we must not let ourselves be locked up in a religious universe whose three dimensions are sin, sacraments and grace."[26] He goes on to say that colonization and neo-colonization in any form must be challenged. The poor and the impoverished lives of the people must be dealt with.[27]

Chapter Five —Theological Imagination in the Service of Male Youth: Foundational Insights from Traditional African Philosophy and Biblical Narratives: A Virtue-Based Catechesis for Young African Men

We read in the bible that from time immemorial, God has spoken to us in many and fragmentary ways through the prophets. However, in the last days, God has spoken to us through a Son. (Heb. 1: 1-2) I am of the opinion that as the Roman Catholic Church in Africa engages in its missionary activity, it must avoid any form of Christomonism. The Spirit of God is also at work. As Nathan D. Mitchell points out, "culture is the basic *site* where the Spirit's presence and activity are known, named and celebrated in word and

---

[25] John Calvin, *Institutes of The Christian Religion* (Louisville, KY: Westminster John Knox Press, 1950, Vol. 2).

[26] Jean-Marc Ela, 149

[27] Ibid.

sacrament."[28] In this chapter I will be pointing out the presence of the Spirit of God among the people before the advent of the Christian religion. The presence of the Spirit of God is depicted in the arts, artifacts, proverbs, wisdom sayings and songs of the people. Weaving together insights from African Traditional Religion, foundational Christian beliefs, virtue-based Christian ethics, African philosophical thought, young male figures from biblical narratives, and socio-pastoral imperatives, I hope to set forth a framework for dealing with the cultural formation and religious development of male youth in ways that are authentically African and Christian, socially-oriented and pastorally engaged.

My purpose in this chapter is to emphasize that if the Roman Catholic church makes use of the rich and time-tested culture of the people, it will go a long way to make Catholicism well incarnated and inculturated among male youth in Ghana[29] and in the sub-region. This, I believe, will help male youth to grow into full maturity and to become respectable and responsible citizens and Christians.

---

[28] Nathan D. Mitchell, *Meeting Mystery: Liturgy, Worship, Sacraments* (Maryknoll, New York: Orbis, 2006), 4

[29] I must emphasize at the onset that most of the examples in the book will be from the Akan ethnic group who inhabit the southern part of Ghana.

CHAPTER ONE

Missionary Dynamics of the Church in Ghana: Historical Background and Contemporary Context: A Roman Catholic Perspective with Emphasis on Ministry to Male Youth

Go therefore and make disciples of all nations, baptizing them in the name of the Father and of the Son and of the Holy Spirit, and teaching them to obey everything that I have commanded you. And remember, I am with you always, to the end of the age.
Matt. 28: 9-20

The bible tells us that Jesus was sent by the Father. He was not sent to judge or condemn the world, rather, he was sent so that through him the world might be saved. This was done out of love since it is the nature of God to love. (cf. Jn. 3:16-18) The Good News of Jesus Christ is not restricted to any particular group of people. It is for the whole of humanity. Christian witnesses have participated in God's mission from the time of the apostles, proclaiming the message of salvation. It was this same missionary impulse that led Portuguese missionaries to bring the Gospel message to the people of Ghana in the fifteenth century.

An Overview of Ghana and its People

Ghana is in West Africa. It is bordered on the north by Burkina Faso, on the east by Togo and on the west by La Cote D'Ivoire, all French-speaking countries. On the south is the Atlantic Ocean.

Ghana has a total area of 239,460 sq. km. The country is divided into 10 administrative regions and is made up of 169 districts. According to 2004 estimates, the population is about 22 million with an annual growth rate of 2.1%. Life expectancy is put at 57.2%. The rate of literacy is estimated at 57.9%.[1] Ghana is inhabited predominantly by black Africans. Europeans and other non-African ethno-racial groups account for only about 1.5% of the

---

[1] The World Bank Group, "Ghana Data Profile" http://devdata.worldbank.org/external/CPProfile.asp?CCODE=gha&PTYPE=CP (accessed April 22, 2007).

population. Ghana is a heterogeneous country made up of numerous ethnic groups. The major ones are Akans (44%); Moshi-Dagombas (16%); Ewes (13%), Gas (8%) and others. There are about 79 languages spoken in Ghana.[2] English is the official language. However, Akan, Moshi-Dagomba, Ewe and Ga are major national languages. The various dialects spoken in Ghana are shown in Map 1..[3]

The Religions of Ghana

There are three major religions practiced in Ghana, namely, Africa Traditional Religion, Christianity and Islam. As attested to by John Mbiti, a Kenyan theologian and historian, Ghanaians like other Africans, "are notoriously religious and each people has its own religious systems with a set of beliefs and practices."[4] They "do not know how to exist without religion."[5] This religious attitude of Ghanaians is confirmed by A. E. Ellis, a British commander during the colonial period when Ghana was under British rule. An agnostic, Ellis described the people of the Gold Coast in 1880 with these words, "Religion is not with them as with civilized people, a matter outside one's daily life and which is closely inter-woven with all their habits, customs and models of thoughts."[6] Ellis meant this to be a derogatory remark, though objectively considered it can be viewed positively inasmuch as it shows that for the Ghanaian and for that matter the African, life is one. It is all inviolable. It is all interconnected.

---

[2] Info please, "Ghana" http://www.infoplease.com/ipa/A0107584.html (accessed January 4, 2007).

[3] Raymond G. Gordon, Jr. ed. *Ethnologue: Language of the World*, 15th Edition, (Dallas, Tex: SIL International, 2005), http://www.ethnologue.com/show_map.asp?name=Ghana&seq=10 (accessed August 2, 2007).

[4] John Mbiti, *African Religions and Philosophy* (New York: Praeger Publishers, 1969), 1.

[5] Ibid., 2. Peter Sarpong has the same idea when he said, "For Africa, the role of traditional religion in determining the *modus vivendi* has been vital. African cultures are known for their religious orientation. In fact, African cultures are religious cultures. It is not possible to *study* African culture in isolation from religion. Religion permeates the ideal African culture from cradle to grave."—*Can Christianity dialogue with African Traditional Religion?* http://www.afrikaworld.net/afrel/sarpong.html (accessed February 18, 2008).

[6] Quoted in Hans W. Debrunner, *A History of Christianity in Ghana* (Accra: Waterville Publishing House, 1967), 2.

Map 1: Dialects Spoken in Ghana by Region

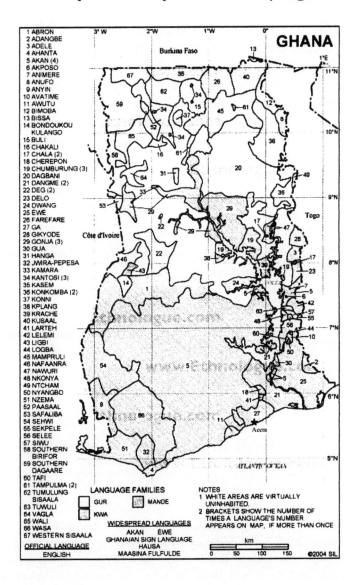

1 ABRON
2 ADANGBE
3 ADELE
4 AHANTA
5 AKAN (4)
6 AKPOSO
7 ANIMERE
8 ANUFO
9 ANYIN
10 AVATIME
11 AWUTU
12 BIMOBA
13 BISSA
14 BONDOUKOU
   KULANGO
15 BULI
16 CHAKALI
17 CHALA (2)
18 CHEREPON
19 CHUMBURUNG (3)
20 DAGBANI
21 DANGME (2)
22 DEG (2)
23 DELO
24 DWANG
25 ÉWÉ
26 FAREFARE
27 GA
28 GIKYODE
29 GONJA (3)
30 GUA
31 HANGA
32 JWIRA-PEPESA
33 KAMARA
34 KANTOSI (3)
35 KASEM
36 KONKOMBA (2)
37 KONNI
38 KPLANG
39 KRACHE
40 KUSAAL
41 LARTEH
42 LELEMI
43 LIGBI
44 LOGBA
45 MAMPRULI
46 NAFAANRA
47 NAWURI
48 NKONYA
49 NTCHAM
50 NYANGBO
51 NZEMA
52 PAASAAL
53 SAFALIBA
54 SEHWI
55 SEKPELE
56 SELEE
57 SIWU
58 SOUTHERN
   BIRIFOR
59 SOUTHERN
   DAGAARE
60 TAFI
61 TAMPULMA (2)
62 TUMULUNG
   SISAALA
63 TUWULI
64 VAGLA
65 WALI
66 WASA
67 WESTERN SISAALA

OFFICIAL LANGUAGE
   ENGLISH

LANGUAGE FAMILIES

GUR
MANDE
KWA

WIDESPREAD LANGUAGES
AKAN   ÉWÉ
GHANAIAN SIGN LANGUAGE
HAUSA
MAASINA FULFULDE

NOTES
1 WHITE AREAS ARE VIRTUALLY
  UNINHABITED.
2 BRACKETS SHOW THE NUMBER OF
  TIMES A LANGUAGE'S NUMBER
  APPEARS ON MAP, IF MORE THAN ONCE

km
0   50   100   150   ©2004 SIL

GHANA
Burkina Faso
Côte d'Ivoire
Togo
Accra
ATLANTIC OCEAN

The History of Ghana

Historically, Ghana was home to many kingdoms which extended throughout West Africa during pre-colonial times. As a crown colony, it included the Ashanti Protectorate, the Northern territories, and Trans-Volta Togoland.[7] The ancient Ghana Empire lasted until the thirteenth century. Ghana was formerly called the Gold Coast, a name given to the country in 1471 by the Portuguese sailors when they first set foot on the land and discovered gold. They started to trade in minerals with the inhabitants. The abundance of gold and its easy accessibility soon attracted other Europeans. Among them were the English, the Dutch, the Swedes, the Danes and the French. There ensued a struggle among the European nations to control the gold trade in the Gold Coast. In 1820, the British overcame the other nations and the Gold Coast became a British colony. Following 130 years of British rule, Ghana gained independence on March 6th 1957, electing Kwame Nkrumah as its first president. The name "Ghana" was chosen at independence.[8]

Ghana Today

After a series of military interventions since independence, Ghana is now under a democratically elected government, having changed successfully from one civilian government to another in 2000.

Ghana is predominantly an agricultural country with about 60%-70% of the population engaging in subsistence farming. Its major sources of foreign exchange are cocoa, gold and timber.[9] According to the World Bank, Ghana is ranked as the fastest reforming nation in Africa and the ninth in the world,

---

[7] Wikipedia, "Ghana" http://en.wikipedia.org/wiki/Ghana (accessed January 4, 2007).

[8] Ghana was the first country south of the Sahara to attain political independence. On attainment of independence, Kwame Nkrumah felt that the independence of Ghana was meaningless unless it was linked with the total liberation of Africa. He was of the view that the black people were capable of managing their own affairs. Together with other people like Marcus Garvey (1887-1940), (http://www.kasnet.com/heroesofjamaica/mg/g6/g6.htm accessed August 4, 2007), they formed the Pan-African Movement. It was a liberation movement. He became the first president. He helped to train many African leaders to fight against colonialism in order to attain independence. Today, majority of African nations owe their independence to the Pan- African Movement.

[9] Wikipedia, "Ghana" http://en.wikipedia.org/wiki/Ghana (accessed January 4, 2007).

given B+ in terms of sovereign credit rating.[10]   The Global Peace Index considers Ghana as the second most peaceful nation in Africa after Tunisia and the fortieth most peaceful nation in the world.[11]

Education is considered a great asset to the development of any nation. For this reason, the governments of Ghana have always placed great emphasis on education.   The country has six state-funded universities.   Other private universities have been established by religious bodies such as the Methodists, Presbyterians, Roman Catholics, Seventh Day Adventists, Pentecostals and the members of the International Central Gospel church.   With the setting up of the Ghana Education Trust Fund (GETFUND), a lot of investments are being made in education.   Apart from improvements to the infrastructure development of educational institutions, the GETFUND helps to train personnel to resource the state institutions.   Ghana now has instituted a Free Compulsory Universal Basic Education (FCUBE).   As the name depicts, pupils in the basic schools do not pay any school fees.   It is also compulsory for all Ghanaian children of school-going age (6years) to be in school until they finish Junior High School.   The FCUBE is for children in government-assisted schools.   To encourage pupils to go school, school children in uniform do not pay any fare when they ride on government buses.   In addition to these, schools serve lunch for pupils in some selected districts during the school year as a pilot program.[12]

Antecedent of Christianity in West Africa

Frequently, Africa is given bad publicity in the international media.   Negative things like abject poverty, disease and civil war are highlighted.   The question is: Can anything good come from Africa? (cf. Jn. 1: 46)   This question extends to Christianity.   As Lamin Sanneh points out there is the tendency to separate the ancient North African Church and accede it to the European Church because

---

[10] S. K. B, Asante, "Ghana has made progress in spite of economic challenges" http://www.myjoyonline.com/archives/news/read.asp?contentid=467   (accessed   January   4, 2007).

[11] Vision of Humanity, "Global Peace Index Ranking"
  http://www.visionofhumanity.com/rankings (accessed August 3, 2007).

[12] This feeding program is to be extended to all districts. These programs have boosted in-take in the basic schools.   In some places, the percentage of new enrollment is about 30%. This has resulted in the demand for more classrooms, furniture and teaching materials.

Africa is always seen to be inferior.[13] He goes on to say that in the same way, the Ethiopian Orthodox Church is most of the time taken away and made a subset of Judaeo-Christian religion as if Ethiopia is not part of Black Africa. For Sanneh, "such academic categories are deeply divisive and distort profoundly the historical process of the unfolding story of Christianity from the time of the apostles."[14]

Christianity in West Africa cannot be properly understood when severed from the history of apostolic times. It was the desire to see one Prester John, a Christian king in Ethiopia[15] that motivated the early Christian missionaries from Portugal to set sail along West Africa. They wanted to know from him the extent of the Muslim conquest after the fall of the ancient Church in North Africa. Secondly, they had heard that he had much gold in his land. With money, the king of Portugal could be enriched to undertake crusades against the Muslim conquests who had taken over the whole of North Africa.

It is recounted in the bible that when Herod was looking to kill the infant Jesus, Africa played host to the Holy Family as Joseph and Mary sought refuge in Egypt.[16] (cf. Mt. 2:13-15) In addition to that when Jesus was being led to be crucified, Luke's gospel tells us that one Simon of Cyrene was forced to carry the cross after Jesus since they wanted him to suffer an ignominious death on the cross. (cf. Lk. 22: 26) Cyrene can be found in present day Libya. Furthermore, Africa's connection with the early Christianity can be seen in the story between Philip and the Ethiopian eunuch who was wont to go to Jerusalem for worship. (Acts 8:26-40) This Ethiopian eunuch was not an ordinary person. He was an important and influential person. He was a court official at the queen's office. Secondly, he was the one in charge of her treasury. It can be presumed that after his baptism by Philip he returned home and spread the faith. In speaking about Christianity in Africa today and its relationship with the ancient church of North Africa, John Paul II noted,

---

[13] Lamin Sanneh, *West African Christianity: The Religious Impact* (London: Hurst and Co. Publishers, Ltd. 1983), 243. See also David Tuesday Adamo, *Africa and Africans in the New Testament* (Lanham, Maryland: University Press of America, Inc. 2006).

[14] Ibid.

[15] For more on Prester John see Wikipedia, "Prester John" http://www.en.wikipedia.org/wiki/Preseter_John (accessed August 9, 2007).

[16] Eternal Word Television Network, "The New Evangelization—Africa" http://www.ewtn.com/new_evangelization/africa/history/continent.htm (accessed August 6, 2007).

In recalling the ancient glories of Christian Africa, we wish to express our profound respect for the churches with which we are not in full communion: the Greek church of the Patriarch of Alexandria, the Coptic church of Egypt and the church of Ethiopia, which share with the Catholic church a common origin and the doctrinal and spiritual heritage of the great Fathers and Saints, not only of their land, but of all the early church.[17]

The African Church and the Early Christianity

According to tradition John Mark visited Egypt and founded a church there.[18] Thomas is alleged to have visited Egypt and carried out some apostolic work while he was on his way to India.[19] In talking about Christianity in Africa, one cannot loose sight of the Catechetical School of Alexandria and the significant contributions of African theologians like Origen, Athanasius, Cyprian and Augustine. These are the legacies of the ancient North African Church to Christendom.[20] Unfortunately, the African Church in the early centuries could not extend its influence to other parts of the continent.[21] The reasons are multi-faceted, in part related to nature or part to human construction. The vast Sahara desert and the thick equatorial forest in the Central Africa created an impenetrable barrier to the south. It made traveling both difficult and hazardous. Internal disagreements and conflicts in the ancient North African church dissipated a lot of energies. For example, Athanasius was a bishop for about forty six years (328-373. C. E). He was sent into exile five times and spent seventeen years of his bishopric in exile.[22] There were many conflicts in the ancient Church in North Africa in the early centuries. These internal disputes were typical cases of a house divided against itself. As Jesus points out such a house cannot stand. (Lk. 11:17) Weakened internally, the Church could not withstand the Muslim invasion in the eighth and ninth centuries.

---

[17] John Paul II, *Ecclesia in Africa* (Vatican City: Libreria Editrice Vaticana, 1995), 33

[18]   St.   Antonius   Coptic   Orthodox   Church,   "The   Coptic   Church" http://www.antonius.org/articles/009.php (accessed August 6, 2007).

[19] Lamin Sanneh, *West Africa Christianity*, 4.

[20] John Paul II, *Ecclesia in Africa*, 31-32.

[21] For more on the Church in Africa and the Early Christianity see, Keith Augustus Burton, *The Bible and African Christianity: The Blessing of Africa* (Downers Groove, IL: InterVarity Press, 2007). [21] See also, David Tuesday Adamo, *Africa and the Africans in the Old Testament* (San Francisco: International Scholars Publications, 1997); Alfred Dunston, *The Black man in the Old Testament and its World*, (Trenton, NJ: Africa World Press, 1992); Elizabeth Isichei, *A History of Christianity in Africa* (Grand Rapids: Lawrenceville, NJ: Africa World Press, 1995).

[22] Khaled Anatolios, *Athanasius: The Early Church Fathers* (New York: Routledge, 2004), 33.

Despite the Muslim conquests there were pockets of Christians practicing their faith in spite of opposition from Muslim leaders. In the fifteen century, as noted earlier on, there was an attempt by Christian missionaries to know the extent of the Muslim invasion in order to know how to counter it. This desire led to the establishment of Christianity in West Africa.[23]

The History of the Roman Catholic Church in Ghana

The establishment of the Roman Catholic Church in Ghana has a long history. The Church was not established at once. Indeed, various attempts were made before the Church took hold. It went through several stages before rooting itself in the soil of Ghana.

First Phase

The first stage of Roman Catholicism in Ghana was not something that was well planned. Portuguese merchants and sailors were on their way to India to trade in spices. They had to make their way by the Atlantic Ocean due to the fact that the earlier and shorter route through the Mediterranean Sea had fallen to the Muslims making the route unsafe. They had to look for an alternative. The only option was by way of the Atlantic Ocean. According to historian, Ralph M. Wiltgen, the need for fresh water compelled the Portuguese merchants and sailors to come to the shores of Ghana.[24] When they reached the shore they noticed that gold was easily accessible and in abundance. They named the land the "Gold Coast". They began to trade with the inhabitants, exchanging cloth and gun power for gold.[25] The Portuguese found the gold trade very lucrative. Consequently, they established permanent settlements. They built castles and forts along the shores on the Gold Coast. In time, other Europeans including the Danes, the Dutch, the English and the French were also attracted to the Gold Coast. All of them endeavored to control the gold trade. It is important to note that the Portuguese merchants and sailors traveled in the company of chaplains. The chaplains like the merchants and sailors

---

[23] Norbert D. K. Okoledah, *Problems and Prospects of the Search for a Catholic Spiritual Tradition in the Ghanaian Catholic Pastoral Ministry* (Muster, Germany: Lit Verlag, 2006), 34.

[24] Ralph M. Wiltgen, *Gold Coast Mission History 1471–1880* (Techny ILL: Divine Word Publications, 1956), 2. See also Helene M. Pfann, *History of The Catholic Church in Ghana* (Cape Coast, Ghana: Catholic Mission Press, 1965), 5.

[25] Ibid.

became caught up in the gold trade. They did not make any serious attempts at evangelization even though few inhabitants were baptized after many years.

The one who is credited to have played a major part in the expansion of Christianity south of the Sahara was Prince Henry the Navigator,[26] the third son of King John I of Portugal. Unfortunately, his dreams were not realized before he died. Henry had heard of Prester John, king of Ethiopia and a very devout Christian. He also heard that there were many people who had fallen under the influence of Islam. Furthermore, Prince Henry learned that the land had much gold, the possession of which would enrich greatly the king of Portugal and his people. Secondly, it would help to finance the crusade to reclaim Africa from Muslim control.[27]

In 1557, the French and the English formed an alliance in the Gold Coast to drive the Portuguese out of the Gold Coast in order to control the gold trade. They were not successful. When the Dutch arrived 1593, they too had their eyes on the defeat of the Portuguese strongholds. In 1642, they were able to drive away the Portuguese after capturing Axim the last Portuguese settlement. When the Portuguese left the shores of the Gold Coast, there were Roman Catholics at Elmina and other towns along the coast. However, the Dutch Reformed Church did not permit them to hold public services. Consequently, Roman Catholicism went into a period of decline in the Gold Coast.

Second Phase

The Portuguese did not give up in their commitment to gaining a foothold in the Gold Coast. In part, this was because they had been given a mandate by the pope in the fifteenth century, not only to defend the Catholic faith but also they were to help in its expansion.[28] For example, the Portuguese Knights, known as the Order of the Knights of Christ committed themselves to fight against the Muslims.[29]   In 1554, the king of Portugal, John III instituted an educational

---

[26] Wikipedia, "Henry the Navigator" http://en.wikipedia.org/wiki/Henry_the_Navigator (accessed August 9, 2007).

[27] Wiltgen, *Gold Coast Mission History 147–1880*, 3.

[28] It was Pope Alexander VI who divided the world into two vast missionary territories between Portugal and Spain in 1493. They were to help in funding the new mission territories. For more information, see Wiltgen, *Gold Coast Mission History 147–1880*, 11.

[29] First, it was Popes Eugene IV and later Callistus III in 1461 who gave the Knights of Christ the spiritual jurisdiction over all churches in the West and even as far as India. In 1471, Pope Sixtus

program for the missions. The plan linked education with evangelization. This way, it was thought that the evangelization of those in the mission countries would be effective and successful. To help to take over the educational institutions in the mission countries and to stem the tide of scandalous attitude of the clergy in Elmina,[30] the Jesuits were approached to see if they could go the Gold Coast. According to Lamin Sanneh, for some reason, the Jesuits could not respond positively to the request.[31] Wiltgen notes that the letter was addressed to Fr. Juan de Polanco, S. J. then secretary to St. Ignatius at the Gesu in Rome where the Society of Jesus had its Generalate. Wiltgen reports that the archives of the Jesuits are silent as to the response given by St. Ignatius of Loyola. Consequently, the reason for the refusal may never be known for certain, only by way conjecture. Wiltgen wonders, "Was it the sickening climate that made him hesitate? Or was it because his missionaries were having so much trouble in Portuguese Congo? Or was it rather because all his available personnel had to be sent to the new expanding Abbyssinian and Brazilian missions? We can only guess."[32] The Portuguese Augustinians were contacted. They took the challenge readily.

Portuguese Augustinians (1572–1576)

The Augustinians arrived in the Gold Coast in 1572. They were serious about their missionary work. They taught the people especially children how to read, write, sing and pray. The medium of instructions was Portuguese. They did not stay only in Elmina. They moved about and were able to establish churches in nearby towns like Komenda and Efutu. In the course of their work some misunderstanding arose between the missionaries and the inhabitants. Some of the inhabitants felt that the missionaries were poaching their believers in the traditional religion to their church. The church buildings were burnt down and the missionaries left.[33]

IV renewed this mandate, Wiltgen, *Gold Coast Mission History 1471-1880*, 8. See also Okoledah, *Problems and Prospects of the Search for a Catholic Pastoral Ministry*, 34.

[30] Wiltgen, *Gold Coast Mission History 1471–1880*, 18.

[31] Sanneh, *West African Christianity*, 26.

[32] Wiltgen, *Gold Coast Mission History 1471–1880*, 19.

[33] Okoledah, *Problems and Prospects of the Search for a Catholic Pastoral Ministry*, 34.

French Capuchins (1633–1639)

The French Capuchins arrived in 1633 when the King of Portugal approached them. They also made an attempt to establish Roman Catholicism in the Gold Coast. They readily won the confidence of the inhabitants and their missionary activity was progressing well. However, in 1639, a fierce conflict arose between the inhabitants and the European traders. It was extended to the Capuchins who had to flee for their lives. This affected the future of Catholicism in the Gold Coast. It could not take deep root.

Analysis of the Two Phases

A critical analysis of these two phases to establish Roman Catholicism in the Gold Coast reveals the problems inherent in both approaches. First, most of the early missionaries stayed too long on the coast. The coast was full of mosquitoes which were a bane to the early missionaries. Consequently, most of them died soon after arrival. The West Coast of Africa had the reputation of being the white man's grave.[34] Later missionaries like the Anglicans, the Methodists and the Presbyterians learned from their predecessors' mistakes. They moved into the hinterland where the environment was cool and conducive for their stay, enabling them to spread the gospel. As a result, they were able to establish their respective churches in their first attempts.

A second reason for the failure of earlier Roman Catholic phases of missionary activity was that the early missionaries did not separate themselves from the European merchants and sailors.[35] They were seen as being in alliance with them. As it is commonly said in Ghana, "the ship that brought the bible was the same ship that brought the gun powder."[36] For this reason, any misunderstanding between the inhabitants and the merchants and sailors was extended by association to the missionaries. This is because the missionaries were seen as partners of the merchants and the sailors.[37]

The third reason is the pastoral approach adopted by the early missionaries. Their efforts did not include and involve the indigenous people. They operated alone. As it is pointed out later on, the first Anglican missionaries in the Gold

---

[34] Wiltgen, *Gold Coast Mission History*, 122.

[35] This is captured by Aylward Shorter with the title of his book, *Cross and Flag in Africa: The "White Fathers" during the Colonial Scramble (1892–1914)* (Maryknoll, NY: Orbis Books, 2006).

[36] J. M. Bane, *Catholic Pioneers in West Africa* (Dublin: Cahill and Co. Ltd. 1956), 174.

[37] See I. Tuffour, "Relations between Christian Missions, Europeans Administrators and Traders", in *The History of Christianity*, ed. O. A. Kalu, (Hong Kong: 1980).

Coast involved the people immediately and things worked out very well for them. Among other reasons, these are few that explain the problems inherent in the previous phases to establish Roman Catholicism in the Gold Coast.

In conclusion, the approach of the early Roman Catholic missionaries was theologically and pastorally problematic. The missionary does not bring God to any people. God is not physically challenged to be carried or helped around the world. God is omnipotent and omnipresent. God is everywhere. We read in the Bible that it is the intention of God to save all. (1 Tm. 2: 4-5) Furthermore, it is said "Long ago God spoke to our ancestors in many and various ways by the prophets, but in these last days he has spoken to us by a Son, whom he appointed heir of all things, through whom he also created the world." (Hebrew 1:1-2) In the opinion of Nathan D. Mitchell, "Culture is the basic *site* where the Spirit's presence and activity are known, named, and celebrated in word and sacrament."[38] It follows, therefore, that God makes Godself present and available to all people everywhere and at any time. What missionaries need is to look for the presence of God wherever they go and point out to the people the God who is present in their midst. This is the approach which Paul used in his ministry in Athens,

> Athenians, I see how extremely religious you are in every way. For, as I went through the city and looked carefully at the objects of your worship, I found among them at the altar with the inscription, 'To an unknown god'. What therefore you worship as unknown, this I proclaim to you. The God who made the world and everything in it, he who is Lord of heaven and earth, does not live in shrines made by human hands, nor is he served by human hands, as though he needed anything, since he himself gives all mortal life and breath and all things. From one ancestor he made all nations to inhabit the whole earth, and he allotted the times of their existence and the boundaries of the places where they would live, so that they would search for God and perhaps grope for him and find him—though indeed he is not far from each one of us. For 'In him we live and move and have our being'. (Acts 17: 22-28)

Unfortunately, this was not the approach that the early Roman Catholic missionaries to the Gold Coast used. They condemned the cultural and religious practices of the people as pagan. They considered the people as idol worshippers who did not know God. They were, therefore, intent upon teaching the people how to know and serve God as if for the first time. However, as Hans Debrunner, a European writing about the history of

---

[38] Nathan D. Mitchell, *Meeting Mystery: Liturgy, Worship, Sacraments* (Maryknoll, New York: Orbis Books, 2006), 4.

Christianity in Ghana testifies, "Christ was there before the arrival of missionaries. He was there in the boisterous and lively atmosphere of that country, the peculiar atmosphere so different from that of some other African countries, animated as it is by an immense zest for life. Prayer for life and the desire for life are at the heart and soul of 'pagan' tribal religions of Ghana."[39]

There is no doubt that Christianity has entered into many cultures throughout its history. Though it has been heavily cloaked with Roman and European cultural influences, it has been always important to distinguish between what is essentially Christian and what is Roman or European culture. No culture is more important than others. No culture should be imposed on others. In evangelization, what God has done for humanity in Jesus Christ is what must be preached at all times. People cannot forgo their cultures before becoming Christians inasmuch as they cannot do away with their God-given and time-tested cultural and religious practices which make them who they are as Christians. This would be contrary to the decisions of the Council of Jerusalem. (cf. Acts 15:1-35) This was something that the early Roman Catholic missionaries failed to recognize and understand. They could not see anything good nor could they discern the presence of God among the people of the Gold Coast. However, as Brain Hearne humbly acknowledges, "We can discern the seeds of the Word within African culture; we can see how in many ways the mysterious work from the beginning of time has found expression in the many beautiful values that we as missionaries have to learn from African situation—a value of harmony in the community, of solidarity, and of relationship."[40] In brief, these are some of the realities which accounted for the failure of the initial attempts of European Roman Catholic missionaries in the Gold Coast.

Third Phase

Despite the previous failures, vision to establish Roman Catholicism in the Gold Coast was never abandoned. Ralph M. Wiltgen notes that two lay people are credited as having worked for the establishment of the Roman Catholic

---

[39] Debrunner, *A History of Christianity in Ghana*, 2.
[40] Brian Hearne, "The Church in Africa", *A New Missionary Era*, ed. Padraig Flanagan (Maryknoll, NY: Orbis Book, 1982), 47.

Church in the Gold Coast in its third attempt in the nineteenth century. They were Sir James Marshall and Pierre Bonnat.[41]

Sir James Marshall (1829–1889)

Sir James Marshall was a convert to Catholicism. Marshall was once a soldier who was wounded and lost an arm. He had wanted to become a priest.[42] Later on in his life, he became the chief justice in the Gold Coast in 1880, after his transfer from Nigeria. At that time the West Coast of Africa was under the jurisdiction of the Holy Ghost Fathers. They were stationed in Sierra Leone and Nigeria. However, they had no resident priest in the Gold Coast. Being an influential person in the Gold Coast, Sir James Marshall wrote to the superiors of the Holy Ghost Fathers in Rome. In the letter, he was emphatic that a mission ought to be established in the Gold Coast since it was an ideal place for Roman Catholicism.[43]

Pierre Bonnat (1833–1922)

Pierre Bonnat was a French Catholic. He was well-known to the Protestant Basel missionaries in the Gold Coast. He was a merchant who traded mostly in gold.[44] During 1860's there were many wars in the Gold Coast prominent among them were the Asante wars with the British. Asantes refused to be under the British Protectorate.[45] During one of the wars in 1869 some missionaries together with Pierre Bonnat were captured. They were sent to Kumasi which is in the middle of the country. He spent four years in captivity. When he was released, he went to Sierra Leone and visited the Holy Ghost Fathers. He convinced them to open a mission station in Kumasi.

---

[41]Wiltgen, *Gold Coast Mission History 147–1880*, 127–133. See also Archdiocese of Cape Coast, "Catholic Archdiocese of Cape Coast" http://www.archcapeghana.org/page.php?id (accessed April 20, 2007).

[42]   Stephen   Leslie,   *Marshall,   Sir   James   (1829–1889)*,   238-239, http://books.google.com/books?id=yUJAAAAIAAJ&pg=PA&238&dpg=PA238&dq=sir+mars hall&source=web&ots=wW (accessed August 3, 2007).

[43]Wiltgen, *Gold Coast Mission History 1471–1880*, 127-133.

[44] Alluvial Exploration and Mining, "Gold—the Exploration and Mining History—Part 1" http://www.minelinks.com/alluvial/gold1.html (accessed August 3, 2007).

[45]   Globe   Oneness   Commitment,   "Ashanti   Confederacy" http://www.experiencefestival.com/a/Ashanti_confederacy_-_History/id/481053   (August   3, 2007).

Furthermore, when he was in France, Bonnat made an appeal to the Society of African Missions (SMA) to establish churches in Kumasi and Salaga. In his opinion, they were ideal places for Roman Catholicism. The two cities were well-organized and populated.[46] In 1879, after persistent appeals from different quarters, Propaganda Fidei sent Fr. Louis Charles Gommenginger, a Holy Ghost Father, to go and survey the place. He came to Cape Coast on May 8, 1878 and arrived in Kumasi on May 16, 1878.[47]

Fr. Augustine Plangue (1826–1907)

As these two lay men were working for the establishment of the Roman Catholic church in the Gold Coast, their efforts were supported by Fr. Augustine Plangue. He was a founding member of the Society of African Missions (SMA). Later on, he became the superior. In 1870, he appealed to Propaganda Fidei to allow the SMA to take responsibility of the Gold Coast in addition to Benin since the congregation needed a sanatorium.[48] Initially, the proposal was not accepted since the Gold Coast was under the jurisdiction of the Holy Ghost Fathers. He never gave up since he felt that it was an ideal place and that no missionary (congregation) had a station there. His persistence paid off. On September 27, 1879 Propaganda Fidei finally made the Gold Coast an Apostolic Prefecture and entrusted to the SMA.[49]

The Society of African Missions in the Gold Coast

The SMA was founded on December 8th, 1856. It was founded by Monsignor Melchoir de Marion Bresilllac in France.[50] It had two main goals:

---

[46] Wiltgen, *Gold Coast Mission History 1471–1880*, 132.

[47] Ibid., 136.

[48] Society of African Missions (SMA), "SMA Missions in Ghana" http://www.smafathers.org/smahtml/history.html (accessed August 2, 2007). See also Wiltgen, *Gold Coast Mission History 1471–1880*, 128. The SMA Fathers wanted to have a place on the West Coast of Africa where they could go and recuperate especially when they fell sick due to their missionary work.

[49] Wiltgen, *Gold Coast Mission History, 1471–1880*, 140. See also J. Van Brakel, *The First 25 Years of SMA Missionary Presence in the Gold Coast: 1880–1905*, (Drunkkeskellechef Guelle, Nymegen, 1992).

[50]Society of African Missions (SMA), "SMA Missions in Ghana" http://www.smafathers.org/smahtml/history.html (accessed August 2, 2007). See also Society of African Missions (SMA), "SMA—History—The Irish Province" http://www.sma.ie/index.php?article-sma_history (accessed August 3, 2007).

1. To adapt the church to the customs of the African people

2. To educate the native clergy to take charge of the church and to be
    supported by a strong lay apostolate.[51]

On May 18th, 1880, two French SMA Priests, August Moreau and Eugene
Murat came to the Gold Coast. From that point on, it is possible to speak of a
plan for Roman Catholic missionary activity in the Gold Coast. No sooner had
they set foot on the land than both were down with malaria. Unfortunately, Fr.
Murat could not survive. He died 3 months after their arrival. The SMA,
however, were not down-hearted. They sent another person to take his place.
Missionary activity was carried on. After the Christmas Eve mass, they had
their first baptism which was a year old boy.[52]

Society of the Divine Word (SVD) in the Gold Coast

There is no doubt that the third phase to establish Roman Catholicism in the
Gold Coast was sustained by the SMA. However, it is important to note that
their efforts were supported by other religious congregations such as the Society
of the Divine Word (SVD).[53] Initially, they were operating in Lome, Togo, a
country on the eastern border of Ghana. They began their missionary endeavor
on the Gold Coast in 1904 and established many churches in the Volta and
Greater Accra regions. The spread of Roman Catholicism on the eastern
corridors of the country can be attributed to the SVD.[54]

Society of Missionaries of Our Lady of Africa (White Fathers)[55]

Another congregation was the French White Fathers who were stationed in
Ouagadougou, Burkina Faso which is the northern neighbor of Ghana. They
wanted to enter and work in the Gold Coast. The Northern part of the Gold

---

[51] Ibid. See also Pashington Obeng, *Asante Catholicism: Religious and Cultural Reproduction Among the Akan of Ghana* (New York: E. J. Brill Seiden, 1996), 103.
[52] Wiltgen, *Gold Coast Mission History 1471–1880*, 153. The baptism was done by Fr. Boutry, a visiting priest. Fr Moreau acted as the godfather. Fr. Murat had died by then. See also Archdiocese of Cape Coast, "Catholic Archdiocese of Cape Coast" http://www.archcapeghana.org/pate.php?id=33 (accessed April 20, 2007).
[53] Divine Word Missionaries, "Ghana Province" http://www.divineword.org (accessed August 2, 2007).
[54] Ibid.
[55] Aylward Shorter, *Cross and Flag in Africa*, 19.

Coast was at that time under the British Protectorate. The government favored Islam and did not want Roman Catholicism. It is possible that since the British governors were predominantly Anglicans, they were not eager to have Roman Catholicism to come and compete with Anglicanism. Many attempts were made to thwart their efforts. The White Fathers persisted and did not give up. In the final analysis, they were told that they could enter the Northern Protectorate under certain conditions:

1. They were to establish churches only in the district capitals where they could be monitored.

2. They were not to establish a church where there were Muslims.

3. They were to set up schools side by side with the churches they established.

4. The medium for instruction was to be English.

The White Fathers accepted these conditions. They entered the Gold Coast in 1906 to begin their missionary activity. They started in Navrongo and spread out to other stations in the Northern part of the Gold Coast.[56] This historical overview of the origins of Roman Catholicism in Ghana illustrates a number of points. A critical look at the third phase shows that the missionary activity was thought through more strategically in terms of planning. Secondly, it was geared solely for the purpose of evangelization. Unlike the previous phases, it was not linked with any other activities like trading or mining. The missionaries were unattached politically and economically and the inhabitants of the Gold Coast saw them as such. They were dedicated to God's mission. They were accepted and found worthy of trust by the people.

The pastoral approach of the missionaries, in the third attempt, accounts also for the success of Roman Catholicism in the Gold Coast. The SMA and the White Fathers were founded as congregations solely for mission in Africa. There was a concerted effort and a defined focus. As the goals of the SMA point out, they were, first and foremost, to adapt the church to the customs of

---

[56] Missionaries of Africa, "The Church in North Ghana" http://www.mafrwestafrica.net/content/view/97/81/lang,en/ (accessed August 3, 2007). See also Ghana News Agency, "Catholic Church Winds up Centenary Celebration", http://www.ghanaweb.com/GhanaHomePage/religion/artikel.php?ID=123003 (accessed April 27, 2007).

the African people. In order to do so they were instructed not to privilege European culture and to learn the cultures of the African people. This enabled them to understand where the Africans were coming from. In this way, they endeavored to put in check any form of superiority complex and to recognize the Africans as fellow companions on the journey of faith. Thus the missionaries were readily accepted. As Pashington Obeng points out, "unlike most of the European traders, some missionaries learned the customs, languages, and the religions of the Gold Coast. That new willingness to learn about local people enabled the missionaries to at least partly understand the local culture and thus to discover points of contact and disagreement between the religion and that of the local culture."[57]

The second pastoral approach that helped in the establishment of Roman Catholicism in the Gold Coast was the involvement of the local people. The second goal in the founding of the SMA was the formation of local clergy to take charge of the Church and the training of laity to support them. This, the SMA carried out with commitment. They established minor and major seminaries for the formation of priests. For all the years that the SMA operated in the Gold Coast, they did not allow any Ghanaian to join the congregation. However, in later years they have allowed Ghanaians to join them. All aspirants to the priesthood were to be incardinated into a diocese under a diocesan bishop. This has helped dioceses in Ghana to have many priests with some even being sent as missionaries or international priests to work in other countries like the United States, Botswana, Canada, Nigeria, South Africa and Zambia to name but a few. It is only recently that the SMA have amended their Constitution to admit Ghanaians as members due to the shortage of priests they are experiencing now.[58]

It is worth mentioning that when the SMA arrived, some elements of Roman Catholicism prevailed in the Gold Coast which were remnants of earlier attempts of evangelization. Examples are the "Santa Mariafo"[59] and the "Santanafo".[60] The "Santa Mariafo" were a group of men and women who every Friday were seen wearing white robes, holding rosary beads and praying before the statue of the Blessed Virgin Mary. The "Santanafo" were devotees

---

[57] Pashington Obeng, *Asante Catholicism*, 113.

[58] Society of African Missions (SMA), "SMA missions in Ghana" http://www.smafathers.org/smahtml/history (accessed August 2, 2007).

[59] Wiltgen, *Gold Coast Mission History 1471–1880*, 142.

[60] Ibid., 144.

of St. Anthony. These expressions of European popular piety were embraced by the Ghanaian people. They harmonized well with religious piety in African Traditional Religion (ATR) where visits to shrines to consult the gods were frequent and most of the times devotees were dressed in white. Most of time believers in ATR went to the shrines in white. Secondly, the use of beads is common in Ghana. They are worn around the neck, the wrist, the ankle and the waist.

Another point in the success story of the third phase of the establishment of Roman Catholicism in the Gold Coast was the multi-faceted approach of the different missionary congregations. While the SMA were working in the South, members of the SVD were active in the Eastern part of the country. At the same time the White Fathers were engaged in evangelization in the North. This concerted effort in missionary activity allowed the activities of various congregations to compliment each other rather than compete. It was like a new building being constructed with steel-binders, carpenters, masons, plumbers, electricians and painters, all working together from different angles.

The history of Roman Catholicism in the Gold Coast would not be complete without an acknowledgement of the roles played by missionaries of other Christian bodies in earlier periods. Pashington Obeng captures this beautifully when he says, "The pioneer work of Protestant missionaries in translating grammar books, making alliances with local chiefs and people, the establishment of schools and church agricultural projects aided the eventual success of Catholic missionary efforts which were resumed in the 1880's."[61]

The Current Situation of the Roman Catholic Church in Ghana

After about one hundred and thirty years, Roman Catholicism has taken root in Ghana. The Church can be found in the four corners of the country. It exists in all the ten administrative regions of Ghana. Out of a population of about 22 million, Roman Catholics account for about 20%. The map of the Roman Catholic Church in Ghana has four ecclesiastical provinces made up of four archdioceses, fifteen dioceses and an Apostolic Prefecture. It has produced two cardinals and all the local ordinaries are Ghanaians. About 90% of priests and religious sisters and brothers engaged in the missionary activity of the Church are indigenous people.

---

[61] Obeng, *Asante Catholicism*, 103.

The Akans say, *tete wo bi ka, tete wo bi kyere, enti hwe na sua*—the past has something to say, it has something to teach, so learn from it. The Roman Catholic church in Ghana cannot neglect its past if it wants to continue to grow and expand. It must always pay attention to the attitude and approach adopted by the SMA. It must seek ways to adapt the Church to the culture of the people in situations where Christianity and the culture are compatible. Otherwise, Christianity will remain a foreign religion and its appropriation will be nothing more than skin-deep.

From May 31–August 2, 1969 Paul VI visited Kampala, Uganda. Among other things he said to the bishops, "you may, and you must, have an African Christianity."[62] Similar sentiments were expressed by John Paul II during his pastoral visit to Zaire (now Democratic Republic of Congo) from May 2–5, 1985. He challenged the Zairean bishops and said to them, "Africanization is your task."[63] He went on to say, "A break between the gospel and the culture would be dramatic."[64] The Roman Catholic church in Ghana is very committed to the process of inculturation. It seeks to find ways to make the Christian message more meaningful in the Ghanaian context. This is to avoid a situation where the Ghanaian Catholic becomes a cultural mulatto, not knowing his/her Ghanaian culture and at the same time not being too familiar with what they are trying to imitate. As the first Synod of Wa[65] acknowledges, "so many years after Christianity has been implanted in our Diocese, we still have many of our Christians having one foot in traditional religion and the other in Christianity. In various areas of their lives, they feel torn between their culture and Christianity… In all these cases, people do not feel psychologically secure."[66] Similar sentiments were expressed by Archbishop Albert K. Obiefuma of Eastern Nigeria when he said

---

[62]   Paul   VI,   "Journey   to   Uganda   July   31-   August   2,   1969" http://www.vatican.va/holy_father/paul_vi/travels/sub-index_uganda.htm (accessed August 5, 2007). See also Jean-Marc Ela, *My Faith as an African*, xiii.

[63]   John   Paul   II,   "African   Travels" http://www.vatican.va/holy_father/john_paul_ii/travels/sub_index1980/tra_africa.htm (accessed August 5, 2007). See also Jean-Marc Ela, *My Faith as an African*, 145.

[64] Ibid.

[65] Wa is one of the Roman Catholic dioceses in Ghana. It is the capital of Upper West Region.

[66] Cited in Anthony Y. Naaeke, *Kaleidoscope Catechesis: Missionary Catechesis in Africa Particularly in the Diocese of Wa in Ghana* (New York: Peter Lang Publishing, 2006), 25.

Christianity has made an impact on our people…. But times without number, the remark reaches us that our Christians are worshipping 'idols', false gods. They swear on idols. They erect shrines in their homes, in their compounds. They hide fetishes in their shades in the market place and in their workshops. Catechists, seminarians on apostolic work in the towns and villages are stunned at the degree of idol worship and superstitious practices that still exist among a people that are mostly baptized Catholics. At every retreat, Catholics bring out from their homes fetishes and charms of all kinds, idol worship, superstitious practices, fear of witchcraft, charms, and all sorts of vain observances are realities among our Catholics. We cannot simply deny they obtain.[67]

This phenomenon of some Roman Catholics being torn between their culture and Christianity is not something that is peculiar to West Africa. It repeats itself in many places on the continent. As Archbishop Buti TIhagale of Bloemfontein (South Africa) notes,

It is not clear whether the locus of power has indeed shifted from the ancestors to God or to Jesus Christ or the Trinity for that matter. Ancestors are still not seen as mere parents who are deceased. Condemnation of ancestor veneration by the church has simply driven it underground. Traditional healers who claim to receive their revelations from the ancestors still ply their trade with a measure of success. Commands or instructions from the ancestors continue to be communicated through dreams… the indigenous people continue to be a "cure seeking" people. They seek protection from evil spirits that populate their cosmos… Rituals that are performed with the African social world continue to be understood as efficacious.[68]

The dichotomy between culture and Christianity that seems present in the lives of some Roman Catholics in Ghana is due to an earlier catechesis which considered the African culture as being embedded in fetishism. How could the Ghanaian abandon his/her culture (personhood) in order to become a Christian? Was that the approach of the early disciples? The message of the Council of Jerusalem (cf. Acts 15: 1-35) was that the Gentile converts did not have to become Jewish (undergo circumcision) before becoming Christians. The important thing that needed to be done was to discover how the Gospel could be inculturated in the Ghanaian context. As Pedro Arrupe points out, inculturation is "The incarnation of Christian life and the Christian message in a particular cultural context, in such a way that this experience not only finds experience through elements proper to the culture in question, but becomes a

---

[67] Ibid., 26.
[68] Ibid.

principle that animates, directs and unifies the culture, transforming and remaking it so as to bring about 'a new creation'."[69]

An example of a place where inculturation has been carried out earnestly in Ghana is the Archdiocese of Kumasi under the leadership of the former diocesan bishop, Peter Sarpong. Pashington Obeng enumerates his experiences of inculturation by way of three examples: Sunday liturgy at Holy Rosary Parish in Suame,[70] the celebration of a marriage at St. Peter's Cathedral,[71] and a diocesan Corpus Christi celebration at the diocesan level.[72] In these celebrations Asante cultural practices are fused into the Christian liturgy. They make the celebrations more meaningful for the people and they are well attended.

One aspect of inculturation that has helped the Roman Catholic church in Ghana today is the holistic approach adopted in efforts to deal with needs and hopes of the Ghanaian Catholic. The African and by extension the Ghanaian lives in a spirit-filled world. There is a strong believe in spirits and the spirit-world. The Ghanaian believes that there are good as well as evil spirits. The good spirits are always there to protect us. On the other hand, evil spirits often associated with witchcraft are there to harm and destroy others. Bad omens, diseases, and deaths, especially sudden deaths and the death of young ones, are most of the time attributed to the machinations of evil spirits. Some people believe that their enemies can cast an evil eye and destroy them by means of curses. There is, therefore, an immediate need, both real and perceived, for protection against evil forces. There were times that priests, both expatriates and indigenous, did not take this belief system seriously. They thoughtlessly dismissed people who came to them regarding evil spirits. The priests interpreted these issues as psychological problems. As a result many people came to the priests initially but then ended up going to *Juju-men*[73] for protection.

---

[69] Pedro Arrupe, "Letter to the Whole Society on Incarnation" in *Studies in the International Apostolate of Jesuits*, 7 (June 1978), 9.

[70] Obeng, *Asante Catholicism*, 133.

[71] Ibid., 170.

[72] Ibid., 180.

[73] They are magicians to whom many people in traditional African society go to seek protection against evil forces like witches, wizards and the devil in order to have a good life. Other people may go to them to with the intention of seeking their help to harm others. For more on Juju-men see Peter K. Sarpong, *Peoples Differ: An Approach to Inculturation in Evangelization* (Accra, Ghana: Sub-Saharan Publishers, 2002), 101-102. See also his *Some Notes on West African Traditional Religion: Advanced Level* (Unpublished, December, 1990), 57-58.

In times of sickness or inexplicable deaths in the family, they went to the "Spiritual" or the Pentecostal churches. They were ready to listen and help them. The majority of people seeking such assistance were the young. The Roman Catholic church was, therefore, losing its youthful population. However, in recent years, the Roman Catholic church has changed its attitude towards such practices. Pashington Obeng recounts one such healing service at the St. Peter's Cathedral in the archdiocese of Kumasi. He says that the priest in charge of the service offers an opening prayer. After that he blesses water and salt. The congregation offers prayerful songs invoking the presence of God. Amidst singing, drumming and dancing, the congregation moves in an orderly manner to the sanctuary and kneels around the altar. The priest sprinkles holy water on them. After that he lays his hands on them one by one without uttering any word.[74]

Healing service has become an integral part of Roman Catholic church's ministry in Ghana today, in some measure due to the Roman Catholic Charismatic Renewal Movement.[75] It came up very strongly during the first synod of the Kumasi diocese in 1984. Lay participants questioned the hesitations of the Roman Catholic church's hierarchy as far as healing services were concerned. They pointed out that in the bible Jesus took a holistic approach in his dealing with people. He did not only preach and feed them but he also healed them of their infirmities both spiritual and physical. There are many instances when Jesus casts out evil spirits. (Mk. 1: 29-39) What did the Roman Catholic church in Ghana have to say to that? They asked for an interpretation of what Paul meant when he wrote to the Christian community at Ephesus:

> Finally, be strong in the Lord and in the strength of his power. Put on the whole armor of God, so that you may be able to stand against the wiles of the devil. For our struggle is not against the enemies, of blood and flesh, but against rulers, against authorities, against the cosmic powers of this present darkness, against the spiritual forces of evil in the heavenly places. Therefore, take up the whole armor of God, so that you may be able to withstand on the evil day, and having done everything to stand firm. Stand therefore, and fasten the belt of truth around your waist, and put on the breastplate of righteousness. (Eph. 6: 10-14)

---

[74] Ibid., 153.

[75] This is an International Renewal Movement started by some professors and students of Duquesne University in America in the 1967 during a retreat. It was a new way to revive their faith in the Catholic church. Since then it has spread to other Roman Catholic churches all over the world.

The First Synod of Kumasi Diocese in 1984 was forced to make a decision. In the Acts and Declarations after the Synod, healing services were to be part and parcel of the Roman Catholic church's ministry throughout the diocese. This has been followed to the letter. An example is what Pashington Obeng gave earlier on about what he witnessed at the St. Peter's Cathedral.

Today, many priests and many leaders in the Charismatic Renewal Movement are involved in healing ministry and exorcism in the Roman Catholic Church in Ghana. This has limited the numbers of youth and others from being attracted to these other churches, specifically because of their healing services. Furthermore, pastoral care and counseling have been intensified in seminaries and houses of formation. This was an eye-opener to the Roman Catholic church due to the influence of the Pentecostal and Charismatic churches. Secondly, the laity also influenced the church very much in this direction. It is now a common practice in many parishes to witness healing services being held on Fridays. These services are well-attended and supported. This innovation has made the Roman Catholic church more engaged with the Ghanaian people, especially the youth.

Inculturation is always done at the local level. It is best done when careful attention is given to the people. It is best practiced when the whole community at the grassroots is involved. It cannot be the singular work of experts at the top. In spite of the Roman Catholic church's attempts to inculturate the Gospel, there are some youth, especially young men who are not satisfied with what is going on. They remain disaffected and alienated from the church. This poses an important challenge to the Roman Catholic church in Ghana as it envisions its future.

In facing the disaffection and alienation of youth, the Roman Catholic church in Ghana must work interdependently with other Christian churches. In the next section, I endeavor to explore and explain some of the reason why this is the case.

Other Christian Churches

As noted earlier the success story of the third phase of Roman Catholicism cannot be separated from the pioneer work of the Protestant churches. It was through their efforts that Christianity took root in the Gold Coast. The Protestant bodies were the Anglicans, the Presbyterians and the Methodists:

Anglicans

After the first two phases of Roman Catholicism failed to establish Christianity, it was Anglicanism that made its first appearance in the Gold Coast. One Rev. Thomas Thompson, an Anglican priest, volunteered and came to the Gold Coast in 1751.[76] It was under the auspices of the Society of Propagation of the Gospel (SPG) that he adopted a pragmatic approach in order to incarnate Christianity in the Gold Coast. This involved the training of the indigenous people to be involved in the missionary work. He sent three young men to Europe for studies. Unfortunately, two died. Only one Philip Quicoe survived and was ordained into the priesthood. He returned to the Gold Coast. Through his efforts, Anglicanism spread in the Gold Coast.[77]

Presbyterians

In 1828, the Basel mission entered the Gold Coast.[78] The first four missionaries who were sent to the Gold Coast died on arrival.[79] This did not stop the Basel mission from giving up on the Gold Coast. Three more missionaries arrived. Among these was Rev. Andreas Riis. Unfortunately, two of these three also died. This left Rev. Andreas Riis alone. He moved to the eastern part of the country where it was cooler and the environment was free from mosquitoes which had negative effects on many Europeans who settled along the coast. It was realized that the people from Europe could not withstand the hard conditions of West Africa. The Basel mission sent two more missionaries. This time, they were sent from Jamaica and Antiqua. This served two purposes. First, it was thought that being blacks, they could better withstand the harsh conditions on the west coast of Africa. Secondly, it was

[76] Anglicans online, "The Church of the Province of West Africa" http://www.anglicansonline.org/resources/history.htm#africa (accessed August 3, 2007). See also Anglican Diocese of Accra, "History of Parishes" http://www.anglicandioceseofaccra.com/index.php?option=com_content&task=viewed&id=5&Itemid=&34 (accessed August 3, 2007).

[77] Dictionary of Africa Christian Biography, "Quaque Philip, 1741-1816, Anglican, Ghana" http://www.dacb.org/stories/ghana/quaque3_philip.html (accessed August 3, 2007). See also Sanneh, *West African Christianity*, 112.

[78] Presbyterian Church of Ghana, "History of Presbyterian Church of Ghana" http://www.pc-ghana/.org (accessed August 4, 2007).

[79] Presbyterian Church of Ghana, "History of Presbyterian Church of Ghana" http://www.pc-ghana/detail/htm#beginning (accessed August 4, 2007). See also Wiltgen, *Gold Coast Mission History*, 109.

believed that black missionaries would demonstrate to the indigenous people that Christianity was not a religion for only white people. The strategy worked. They made their way into the interior of the country and founded many faith communities. Pashington Obeng points out that the Basel mission in the Gold Coast was successful. Some reasons for the Basel mission's success include: "The translation into vernacular (four gospels) for the local people, missionaries leaving the coastal areas for the inland places with healthier climates, the establishment of schools and vocational institutes, as well as agriculture. That they also founded their own trading company helped them determine and monitor the merchandise which flowed from the coast to the hinterland where mission stations were being opened."[80]

Methodists

The Methodist Church came to the Gold Coast in 1835.[81] Unfortunately, Joseph Dunwell, the first Methodist to be sent died five months later. Arriving in 1835, Thomas Birch Freeman, the son of an African father and an English mother, is credited as being the one who championed Methodism in the Gold Coast.[82] Lamin Sanneh describes him as "indefatigable pioneer who was not afraid to push ahead and confront new problems. His energy for work was matched only by his vision, and the limits he set to both exceeded the normal."[83] One approach that helped the Methodists as well as various other Christian denominations in their missionary work was the setting up of schools.[84] In the opinion of Lamin Sanneh, "the period from about 1850 to the end of the century witnessed tremendous development in education, at least in terms of social attitudes."[85] The setting up of the schools helped in opening up the horizon of the indigenous people. They were able to communicate well with the European missionaries and helped in the propagation of the Gospel in the Gold Coast.

---

[80] Pashington Obeng, *Asante Catholicism*, 100.
[81] Wikipedia, "Methodist Church, Ghana" http://www.wikipedia.org/wiki/Methodist_Church_Ghana (accessed August 3, 2007). See also *Wiltgen, Gold Coast Mission History*, 112.
[82] Bartels, F. L., *The Roots of Ghana Methodism* (Cambridge: Cambridge University Press, 1965).
[83] Sanneh, *West African Christianity*, 120.
[84] Methodist Church Ghana, "Projects—Education" http://www.methodistchurch-gh.org/projects.htm (accessed August 3, 2007).
[85] Sanneh, *West African Christianity*, 146.

Analysis of Protestant Efforts

The success of the Protestant missionaries to establish Christianity in the Gold Coast is worth telling. They were able to succeed in their first endeavor unlike the Roman Catholics because they adopted more pragmatic approaches. Scripture tells us when Jesus began his public ministry, he called the people, first to be with him and secondly, to be sent out to preach and heal. An example is the story of two disciples of John the Baptist who came to Jesus after the Baptist pointed him out as the Lamb of God. (cf. Jn. 1: 35-42) In this particular case as in many cases, it was after the disciples had been with Jesus and spent some time with him that they were sent. This was the approach the early Protestant missionaries adopted. They first made some contacts with the indigenous people and formed some of them through education for discipleship. Those educated and formed for discipleship became partners in the missionary activity of the Church.

The early Protestant missionaries recognized the social position of the chiefs in the communities and accorded them respect. Chiefs occupy important positions in the Ghanaian society. They are highly respected. They are considered to represent the ancestors who are revered in the Ghanaian society. They entered into alliances with the chiefs. Thus they enjoyed the favors of the chiefs. This enabled them to go about their work of evangelization without hindrance from any quarters.

The Protestant missionaries were ready to learn the culture, customs, language and norms of the indigenous people of the Gold Coast. This helped them to learn from the people and to understand them. Secondly, they were able to fraternalize and socialize with the people. They were, therefore, accepted and welcomed wherever they went. This approach by the early Protestant missionaries has continued until contemporary times.[86]

Another approach of the early Protestant missionaries was the setting up of schools. Education went hand-in-hand with evangelization. Schools contributed

---

[86] Today, in many Roman Catholic Archdioceses and Dioceses in Ghana, non-indigenous priests and religious are not allowed to engage in the missionary activity of the Church until they have gone through a three-month orientation program. In the course of this program, they learn the customs, language, norms and other aspects of the culture of the people they are going to work with. In addition to that they cannot be appointed substantive parish priests or pastors if they cannot speak the language after two years. This has helped evangelization among the people of Ghana. Non-indigenous priests and religious communicate well with the people and they are able to propagate the Christian faith better.

to the ways in which people appreciated the Christian message. Education helped to improve the living conditions of the people. Today in Ghana, the churches continue to partner with the government in providing educational infrastructures to train the needed caliber of people to manage the affairs of the country. The mission schools are among the best in the country.[87]

In addition to these previously discussed approaches of the early Protestant missionaries, attention must be drawn to their single-mindedness of purpose. They did not come to the Gold Coast with any ulterior motive, their main purpose was evangelization. They remained focused and spent all their energies on this goal. There was no divided attention. This enabled them to succeed as evangelizers. Their approaches tremendously influenced Roman Catholic missionaries in their third phase of missionary activity in Gold Coast.

The story of the Christianity in Ghana cannot be completely told without reference to "Spiritual" and Pentecostal or Charismatic churches. They are now very common in the country.

The African Indigenous Churches (AIC)

Apart from Roman Catholics, Anglicans, Lutherans, Methodists and Presbyterians there are countless Charismatic churches in Ghana. They are churches and sects normally initiated by Africans. As noted by Rufus Ositelu Okikilaolu Olubiyi, "the acronym AIC may stand for a number of things:

1.   African Independent Churches

2.   African Instituted Churches

3.   African Initiated Churches

4.   African Initiatives in Christianity

5.   African Indigenous Churches

6.   Some refer to them as African Christian Initiatives.[88]

---

[87] Ghana News Agency, "Education", www.ghanaweb.com/GhanaHomePage/NewsArchive/artikel.php?ID=140481 (accessed March 9, 2008).

[88] Rufus O. O. Ositelu, *African Instituted Churches: Diversities, Growth, Gifts, Spirituality, and Ecumenical Understanding of African Initiated Churches* (Piscataway, NJ: Transaction Publishers, 2002), 39.

In *Prophetism in Ghana*, G. C. Baeta recounts how the first AIC in Ghana, namely, "The Church of the Twelve Apostles (*Nackabah*)" and *Musama Disco Christo Church* (Army of the Cross of Christ Church, MDCC) came into being."[89] The origin of AIC can be attributed to William Wade Harris (1860–1929).[90] He was from Liberia. He was imprisoned in 1910. His charge was that he was instigating a revolt against the government of Liberia. According to his own account certain events happened to him while he was in prison which changed his life. He said that he used to have some trances in the prison. In the trances he used to have visits from Moses, Elijah, Angel Gabriel and Jesus. They used to speak to him alone. In fact he said that it was the Angel Gabriel who called him to become a prophet. As a prophet he went about preaching the Word of God in the West African sub-region. In his preaching he called people to a life of repentance, renewal and reconciliation with God. His message touched many lives and many people were attracted to him. He did not establish a church himself. Rather, he encouraged people to go to their individual churches. They were to be committed and dedicated Christians and wait for the coming of Christ. According to Kwame Bediako, he was reported to have converted about 12,000 people to Christianity during the two years of his preaching.[91] Prophet Harris arrived in the Gold Coast in 1914. One of his early converts was Madam Grace Tani. She was initially a priestess of the Tano River. When she converted, she followed the Prophet. When the Prophet departed from the Gold Coast, Grace Tani began to assemble new converts. She named the community of believers "The Twelve Apostles Church". She was assisted by John Nackabah. He was literate unlike Grace Tani. Grace never relinquished power to John Nackabah even though the latter was well-known since he was able to reach out to many people through his literacy.

Musama Disco Christo Church was founded by Joseph William Egyanka Appiah. He was born in 1893. He was later called Prophet Jemisemiham Jehu-Appiah or Akaboha I. He was a teacher and a member of the Methodist

---

[89] G. C. Baeta, *Prophetism In Ghana: A Study of "Some" Spiritual Churches* (London: SCM Press, 1962), 9.

[90] For more on William Wade Harris see David A. Shank, "God Made His Soul a Soul of Fire", http://www.dacb.org/stories/liberia/legacy_harris.html (accessed August 4, 2007).

[91] Kwame Bediako, *Christianity in Africa: The Renewal of a Non-Western Religion* (Maryknoll, New York: Orbis Books, 1995), 92.

Church. He was accused of preaching occultism and expelled finally from the Methodist Church in 1923.[92]

In the opinion of Baeta, the AIC seceded from the mission Church not for political reasons. It was a period when there were strong liberation movements agitating for political independence in the Gold Coast. He believes that no anti-Western or European feeling played a role in the establishment of the AIC. These AIC were eclectic. They still borrowed from the West or Europe.[93] This assertion is confirmed by Ositelu when he said "many of the AIC grew out of a response of the failure of missionaries to relate Christianity to the traditional African view of the world. Often the missionaries condemned the traditional African way of life. They wanted to transform Africans into "Black Europeans", that is they laid more emphasis on the European culture than the Gospel truth of the Bible."[94] According to Brigid Sackey, "In the early 1990's Ghana experienced an overwhelming proliferation of AIC's, particularly those of the Charismatic paradigm."[95] In many instances, these AIC are considered as protest movements. They are geared mainly against the model of the Church brought to Africa.[96]

Characteristics of AIC

African Independent churches continue to spring up in Ghana every now and then. These AIC have common characteristics. Brigid Sackey did a 20 year study on the AIC in Ghana which were headed by women. The study has some interesting insights. Brigid reports that

1.   Women constitute about 80% or 90% of the members of AIC. She said, "Women attend these churches primarily due to health, family,

[92] Kofi A. Opoku, "Changes within Christianity: The Case of the Musama Disco Christo Church", in *The History of Christianity*, ed O. A. Kalu (Hong Kong: Sing Cheung Printing Co. Ltd., 1980).

[93] Baeta, *Prophetism in Ghana*, 128.

[94] Ositelu, *African Instituted Churches*, 47.

[95] Brigid Sackey, *New Directions in Gender and Religion: The Changing Status of Women in Africa Independent Churches* (New York: Lexington Books, 2006), 163.

[96] John S. Pobee and Gabriel Ositelu II, *African Initiatives in Christianity: The Growth, Gifts and Diversities of Indigenous African Churches: A Challenge to the Ecumenical Movement* (Geneva: WCC Publications 1998), 42.

financial, or other social problems."[97] Her conclusion is that women can be said to be the foundation, sustenance and stability of AIC.

2. In AIC religion and development have not been put together. Religion is the sole prerogative of the founders and members.[98]

3. "Separation and proliferation in the AIC are closely linked; the churches are eclectic in their appropriation of African and Christian beliefs and practices."[99]

4. All the women in her study were formerly Methodists. This confirmed her observation of the relationship between Protestantism and the formation of AIC.

She demonstrated that there were more people from Protestant churches who began AIC when compared to those from the Roman Catholic Church.[100] Her observation was confirmed by what Ositelu also observed. He said, "most of indigenous churches originate from the Protestant, Anglican, and Lutheran Church background, with very few of them originating from the Roman Catholic and the Orthodox Church."[101]

When it comes to the mode of worship, Brigid notes again some common ways of doing things.

a. Emphasis on the Holy Spirit of God as the source of charisms.

b. Healing, deliverance, prophesying, speaking in tongues, foretelling the future.

c. Preaching prosperity, solving socio-economic problems of people.[102]

These common ways of worship are similar to the lists presented by John Pobee and Ositelu II. When they studied the AIC, they found some common ways contributing to their *modus operandi*:

---

[97] Brigid Sackey, *New Directions in Gender and Religion*, 4, 167, 201.

[98] Ibid., 5.

[99] Ibid., 29.

[100] Ibid., 107.

[101] Ositelu, *African Instituted Churches*, 33.

[102] Sackey, *New Directions in Gender and Religion*, 34.

1.   Consciousness of the experience of the Holy Spirit

2.   Penchant for healing and exorcism

3.   Insistence on personal testimony.[103]

Analysis of AIC

As noted by Brigid Sackey, separation and proliferation are characteristics of the AIC. Another element is what has come to be known in Ghana as "Prosperity Religion". It is mostly about the acquisition of material goods and deliverance from perceived enemies. The question is where is the cross of Christ in all this? Christianity without the cross is meaningless. The symbol of Christianity is the cross. The cross points to us the extent that God will go to save humanity, "And just as Moses lifted up the serpent in the wilderness, so must the Son of man be lifted up, that whoever believes in him may have eternal life. For God so loved the world that he gave his only Son, so that everyone who believes in him may not perish but may have eternal life." (Jn. 3: 14-15) There is no doubt that the cross is a shameful death. However, for Christians, it has become a sign of God's love and hope. It demonstrates the love of God. It shows the extent that God would go to save humanity. Secondly, it gives humanity the hope that suffering in this world will not be in vain. Death will not have the final say. After death, there is a resurrection.

The AIC in Ghana cannot neglect the cross of Christ in their ministry. Neither can it be an appendix. It is to be the core of the Christian message. By refusing to acknowledge this, AIC are not being authentic and faithful to the Christian message. Secondly, they are sending a wrong and a misleading signal to people most especially the young men in Ghana. Life is not easy. There are no roses without thorns. Life is full of ups and downs. It is like a series of mountains. You climb and descend. As the Akans say, *obra ye bona*—life is war. As the Genesis account reveals, since the fall of Adam and Eve, suffering and death have become part and parcel of our lives as human beings. The young men in Ghana must be told without mincing words that the world is full of

---

[103] Pobee and Gabriel Ositelu II, *African Initiatives in Christianity*, 41. For more on the Charismatic churches and Deliverance see, Allan Anderson, "Demons and deliverance in African Pentecostalism", in *Angels and Demons: Perspectives and Practice in Diverse Religious Traditions*, eds. Peter G. Riddell and Beverly Smith Riddell (Nottingham: Inter-Varsity Press, 2007), 42-62. See also, Nigel Scotland, "The Charismatic Devil: Demonology in Charismatic Christianity", in *Angels and Demons: Perspectives in Diverse Religious Traditions*, 84–105.

challenges, hardships and sufferings. Hardships and sufferings may come their way. What they need to cultivate is self-discipline so that with the grace of God, they can carry their crosses like Jesus and so enter into glory. The Theology of the Cross, therefore, cannot be avoided when preaching to male youth. As noted by Daniel J. Harrington, "There is no better summary of that gospel than "Christ has died; Christ has risen; Christ will come again". When a church loses focus and makes other ideals or projects more important than proclaiming the gospel, it loses its identity and its reason for existing."[104] Paul puts it nicely when he said, "For the message about the cross is foolishness to those who are perishing, but to us who are being saved it is the power of God." (1 Cor. 1: 18)

A third point on the AIC in Ghana is the separation between religion and development. The AIC seem to be less concerned about human development and social justice than 'religion'. As Jean-Marc Ela says about religion, "given the situation today, must we let ourselves be locked up in a religious universe whose three dimensions are sin, the sacraments and grace?"[105] Jesus adopted a holistic approach in dealing with people during his earthly ministry. The same approach must be adopted by the churches in whose mission is the proclamation of the gospel. As Jurgen Moltmann notes, "Mission embraces all activities that liberate the human person from his/her slavery in the presence of the coming God, slavery which extends from economic necessity to God forsakenness."[106]

So far, the chapter has been a discussion of the beginnings and activities of the various Christian denominations in Ghana. It considered how the various Christian denominations operate as individual churches. The next section looks at how they come together and work in communion.

The Roman Catholic Church and the Christian Council of Ghana

In view of the ecumenical movement today, any discussion on the Church as communion will not be complete without reference to the other Christian denominations operating in Ghana. In faithfulness to the spirit of the Second Vatican Council, the Roman Catholic church in Ghana does not act alone. Often, it seeks consultation and cooperation with the Christian Council of

---

[104] Daniel J. Harrington, *The Church According to The New Testament: What The Wisdom and Witness of Early Christianity Teach Us Today* (Franklin: Wisconsin, Sheed and Ward, 2001), 157.

[105] Jean-Marc Ela, *My Faith as an African*, 149.

[106] Jurgen Moltmann, *The Church in the Power of the Spirit* (New York: Harper and Row, 1977), 10.

Ghana. The Christian Council of Ghana is made up of all the mission churches like the Anglican, Lutheran, Methodist, Presbyterian and Pentecostal and Charismatic churches. The communion between the Roman Catholic church and the Christian Council of Ghana is best seen during national crises. On a number of occasions when the political temperature of the country was at its highest point, the churches came together to wither the storm. For example, in 1978, the Roman Catholic Secretariat together with the Christian Council of Ghana met with the then Head of State and Chairman of the Supreme Military Council of Ghana. Ghana at that time was under a military regime. They submitted a memorandum. It was basically "an attempt to ensure that our search for a new form of government would be conducted in an atmosphere of peace and concord."[107]

In 1989, the Roman Catholic church and the Christian Council of Ghana came together again in the spirit of communion and challenged a law of the ruling government of the day. It was during the rule of the Provisional National Defense Council (PNDC). It was a military regime. The law in question was PNDC 221. It was entitled, "Religious Bodies (Registration) Law 1989. The law stated that "Every religious body in Ghana shall be registered under the law and religious body in existence in Ghana shall, after three months from the commencement of the law, *operate as such unless it is registered under this law*. The Roman Catholic church and the Christian Council of Ghana felt that the law was not just. So, they could not obey it. They wrote:

> The Law is *a serious violation of the fundamental human rights of freedom of Worship*. This is because it seeks to make registration with the state *a condition for being allowed to worship God*. In our opinion, it also contradicts PNDC Law 42 section 1(b) which state: "Respect *for fundamental human rights* and for the dignity of human persons are to be cultivated among all sections of the society and established as part of *the basis of social justice*.[108]

They went on to say,

> The Law is so vaguely written in some of its detail that it leaves plenty of room for dangerous and arbitrary interpretation. Worst of all, *by the stroke of a pen* the Chairman of the National Commission for Culture *can order the seizure and disposal of our Church*

---

[107] *Ghana Bishops' Speak: A Collection of Communiqués, Memoranda and Pastoral Letters of the Ghana Catholic Bishops' Conference* (Accra, Ghana: National Catholic Secretariat), 20.
[108] Ibid., 155.

properties and assets. His decision is final. We do not have the right to appeal to a court against the decision…

Dear sons and daughters in Christ Jesus, PNDC Law 221 threatens our very existence as Christians and our freedom to worship God, when, where and how we feel called by our God to do so. The Law is not in the true interest of our dear country, churches and, for that matter, of all religious worshippers in the country.[109]

As a result of the coalition efforts of the Roman Catholic church and the Christian Council of Ghana, the Law was never implemented.

It is not only in times of national crisis that the communion that exists among the churches is demonstrated. There are many other avenues through which the communion is shown. The Roman Catholic church and other Christian churches like the Anglicans, the Methodists and the Presbyterians have a common lectionary for Sunday services and worship. Furthermore, every year the churches come together to celebrate Octave of Christian Unity from January 18–25[110] and Christian Home Week in June.[111] During these celebrations, the local assembly of churches moves from one church to the other for common prayer and seminars. In addition to these, there are occasional non-denominational services for special events for all churches in some communities. To show-case the communion between the Roman Catholic church and the Anglican church, every year in Tepa, Ghana, there is a joint Palm Sunday procession through the principal street of the town. At the end of the procession, each church goes in for its own Sunday worship. Communion is best seen in how the members of the different churches live together in peace and harmony. There is no doubt that the communion between the Roman Catholic church in Ghana and the Christian Council of Ghana has contributed immensely to the peaceful atmosphere in Ghana.[112]

---

[109] Ibid.

[110] This is a week dedicated to prayer for Christian Unity. It is working towards the fulfillment of the prayer of Jesus to his Father that all his disciples "May be one." (cf. Jn. 17: 1-26) Christians know that disunity among them is a scandal to the world. So after many years of acrimony every year during that period Christians all over the world pray and work towards that unity.

[111] It was instituted by Roman Catholic Bishops' Conference and the Christian Council of Ghana. It is to promote ecumenism in Ghana. For the celebration of the week Local churches in various communities meet and carry out different programs. They may include prayer sessions, talks, clean-up exercises, visits to hospitals and prisons.

[112] It cannot go without a comment that the recent Vatican document, Benedict XVI,
"The True Church of Christ", http://www.vatican.va/roman_curia/congregations/ cfaith/documents/rc_con_cfaith-doc_20070629_responsa_quaestiones (accessed August 5, 2007)

It must be noted that it is not only in Ghana that the plight of male youth has come up. All over the world it has been a concern and ways are being found to address it. Various world bodies are responding to the plight of male youth.

An Assessment of Recent Documents dealing with the Plight of Male Youth

In this section, some documents of The United Nations Organization and The African Union which deal with the plight of male youth are discussed.

United Nations (UN) Initiatives and Documents

According to the UN, young people account for half of the population in many of the world's poorest countries and regions, particularly Africa.[113] In spite of this, they are not consulted as a social entity whenever strategies for poverty reduction are being fashioned out. The world body thinks that "new development programmes are necessary to minimize the growing youth crisis often ignored by policymakers, in the world's poorest countries." It goes on to say, "Education and training, especially in agriculture, is particularly key, and rural youth are impeded by a lack of access as well as low-quality schooling."[114]

It is estimated that about 60% of the population in West Africa is made up of youth below the age of 20. 50% of this number is either unemployed or underemployed.[115] Mats Karlson, the former World Bank (WB) Country Director of Ghana, has noted that some countries in the West Africa, like Ghana, have managed to have some level of sustainable macro-economic

---

has made some people to question the sincerity of the Roman Catholic church on ecumenism. It has dampened the spirit of ecumenism. It has upset some members of the Protestant and Orthodox churches. Commenting on the document, Pope Shenouda III, leader of the about 10 million Coptic Christians in Egypt said, "This man (Pope Benedict XVI) makes enemies every time. In his statements a few months back, he lost all the Muslims. And now this time, he lost a lot of Christian denominations because he has begun to err against Christians themselves", Pope Shenouda III, "Catholic Pride in 'One True Church' makes Enemies" http://www.Christianpost.com/article/20070717/28483_Catholic_Pride_in_in_%5C'One_True _Church%5_Makes_Enemies (accessed August 5, 2007).

[113] UN News Centre, "Young people must not continue to be neglected" February 18, 2007 http://www.un.org/appa/news/story.asp?NewsID=21588&Cr=ifad&Cr1=develoment (accessed February 19, 2007

[114] Ibid.

[115] Ghana News Agency, "Macro Economic Stability has not created jobs for youth", 2/19/2007, http://www.myjoyonline.com/archives/business/200702/1743.asp (accessed February 19, 2007).

stability. However, he thinks that that is not enough. The reason is simple. It has not led to the creation of jobs for the youth. In his opinion, "what is left for Ghana to do is to begin to embark on action programme that would lead to movement of Small and Medium Scale Enterprises (SMES) from the informal to the formal sector in order for there to be more permanent jobs for the youth."[116]

In the same vein, Kandell Kolleh Yumkella, the Director-General of United Nations International Development Organization (UNIDO) has noted the endemic nature of poverty in Africa. He believes that it is because African states have for a long time been trying to manage poverty instead of concentrating on poverty alleviation. He is convinced that "we cannot keep applauding ourselves for having successful programme implementation in our various countries if those programmes do not provide jobs for our youth."[117]

Availability of jobs for the youth is very crucial to nation building. It is related to conflict prevention and management. Idle youths are easily frustrated. They become easy targets for recruitment by opportunists to wage civil wars. It is in this light that the United Nations Development Programme (UNDP) office in Ghana voted US $800, 000 "to build the capacities of various local institutions and groups to play effective roles in conflict prevention and management in the country."[118] According to Daouda Toure, UNDP Resident Representative in Ghana, job creation for the youth is very crucial not only to the development of the nation but also to conflict prevention. He goes on to say, "it is also very important to deal with conflict with a regional approach as there is a possibility of spill-over from neighbouring countries."[119]

Documents of the African Union

The International Labour Organization (ILO) report of 2006, gives a grim picture of youth employment in Africa. It points out that while the youth labor

---

[116] Ibid.

[117] Ibid. It must be noted that corruption and embezzlement of public funds in many African countries has also contributed to non-availability of jobs for the youth. A greater portion of loans and grants given by donor countries, agencies and multilateral institutions meant to provide jobs and create wealth in order to alleviate poverty end up in people's private accounts in foreign banks.

[118] Ghana News Agency, "US $800,000 for Conflict Prevention in Ghana", 1/22/2007, http://www.ghanaweb.com/GhanaHomePage/NewsArchive/artikel.php?ID=119685 (accessed February 23, 2007).

[119] Ibid.

force in the sub-region Africa grew by 29.8%, youth unemployment grew only by 34.2% in the region in the last ten years.[120]   According to Juan Somavia, the Director-General of ILO, the African situation is the worst in the world. He notes that it is the only region in the world where the total number of young workers lives on less than US $1 per day. This has gone on for years. Unfortunately, it has been on the increase. In 1995, the figure was 36 million. It rose to 45 million in 2005. He goes on to say, "nearly six out of ten working youths in the sub-region of Africa still live in extreme poverty and only one in ten earns enough to lift themselves and their families above the US $2 per day poverty level." The report concludes, "Without adequate access to the labour market allowing a good start in professional life, young people are less likely to make the right choices to improve their employment perspectives and those of their future descendants. This perpetuates the cycle of insufficient education, low-productivity employment and working poverty."[121]

The plight of male youth in Africa is very tragic. The unavailability of jobs has forced many of them into desperate situations.[122] As the Akans say, *wo tena faako, wo tena woadee so*—If you sit and stay idle in one place, you sit on your fortune.   Again it is said, *se anomaa antu a, obua da*—If the bird does not fly, it starves. In recent times, the tendency among male youth has been to migrate to other countries notably Europe. The situation has become so alarming that European Union ministers have taken the issue up.   They have been considering how to control the tide of Africans trying to migrate to Europe using Spain as a route. In 2006, it was estimated that 24,000 Africans landed on the shores of Spain trying to enter into Spain.[123] Unfortunately, many lose their lives in their desperate attempts. "Bodies are swept offshore on the southern shores of Spain almost on weekly basis. Most of the time, Africans who make it after crossing the Mediterranean Sea have no travel documents, and rarely talk

---

[120] Global employment trends for youth, "ILO Report Bewails Youth Unemployment and "Working Poverty", (Geneva: October 2006), http://www.africanexecutive.com/modules/ magazine/articles.php?article=1030&magazine (accessed February 18, 2007).

[121] Ibid.

[122] African Union, "World Refuge Day"
http://www.africa-union.org/root/ua/Conferences/2007/juin/PA/20%/20juin/Meeting.htm (accessed August 11, 2007).

[123] James Shikwati, "African Migration: Should We Stem the Tide?" 14–21 February, 2007, http://www.africanexecutive.com/modules/magazine/article.php?article=979&magazine=90 (accessed February 18, 2007).

about their countries of origin."[124]   They deliberately refuse to mention their countries of origin so that they cannot be repatriated to any country.

Summary

Chapter One has been a discussion on the historical background of the Roman Catholic church and other Christian churches in Ghana. It talked about the various phases the Roman Catholic church went through before Roman Catholicism was established in Ghana. This was after the Protestant churches had been able to plant Christianity in the Gold Coast. It also considered the current situation of the Church in Ghana. The various approaches that Christian missionaries used to propagate the gospel message of Jesus Christ were discussed. In addition to these, documents of world bodies such as the United Nations and the African Union which deal with the crisis of male youth in Ghana and Africa were examined.

The next chapter addresses the problems which young men in Africa have to grapple with in their lives.

---

[124] Ibid.

CHAPTER TWO

"Beards on Fire":
The Plight of African Male Youth:
A Missiological Challenge to the Roman
Catholic Church in Africa—
A Ghanaian Analysis

I came that they may have life, and have it abundantly.

Jn. 10:10b

In Christian anthropology, every human person is considered to have been created in the image and likeness of God.[1] (cf. Gen. 1:26) According to the author of Genesis, the Lord God formed humans from the dust of the ground and breathed into their nostrils the breath of life; and humans became living beings. (Gen. 2:7) This biblical narrative harmonizes well with the Akan concept of the relationship between the human person and the Supreme Being. The Akans say, *yennsan kokromotire ho mmo po*—One does not by-pass the thumb to make a knot. This teaches that one cannot do without the Supreme Being as far as human existence goes. The Supreme Being features prominently in the birth, the adult life, marriage and the death of the human person in the traditional societies of Africa. Human life is meaningless without the Supreme Being.

Rites of Passage

In many cultures the human person is considered to be a precious gift. Different cultures throughout the world look with expectation and make adequate preparations to receive new-born infants into their families and into

---

[1] Augustine believed that the human person was created purposely to be in relationship with God. Consequently, the human person cannot attain rest (happiness) on his or her own. Happiness depends on relationship with God the creator, *Confessions,* trans. Henry Chadwick (Oxford: University Press, 1991), Book 1: 1. Similar sentiment was expressed by Pope Benedict XVI when he said, "a world without God has no future", Joseph Ratzinger and Marcello Pera, *Without Roots: The West, Relativism, Christianity and Islam*, trans. Michael More (New York: Basic Books, 2006), 80.

the world. During one's life time, from cradle to grave, people go through rites of passages. In some cultures these rites of passage are critical to identity and social cohesion.[2]

In Ghana, many ethnic groups celebrate rites of passage across the life span. Prominence, however, is given to child-naming ceremonies and final funeral rites. Among the Akans, a new-born baby is not considered a member of the family until *abadintoo*—a naming ceremony is performed. Before that the child is called simply by the day on which he/she was born.[3]

Naming Ceremony

A special day is set aside for the proper naming ceremony. On the appointed day, the paternal aunt of the infant performs the ceremony. To begin with, a libation is poured by the head of the family or a representative. The naming ceremony consists of the aunt placing the infant on her lap. She pronounces the name to be given to the infant. The new-born infants are usually named after an ancestor or a living person of good repute. Then the aunt dips her finger into water and drops it on the tongue of the infant. She speaks to the

---

[2] Rites of Passage as noted by Arnold van Gennep constitute three phases: rite of separation; rite of transition and incorporation rite, *The Rites of Passage*, trans. Monika B. Vizedom and Gabrielle L. Caffee, (Chicago: The University of Chicago Press), 10.

[3] A new-born infant may be called:

Day	Male	Female
Sunday	Kwasi	Akosua
Monday	Kwadwo	Adwoa
Tuesday	Kwabena	Abena
Wednesday	Kwaku	Akua
Thursday	Yaw	Yaa
Friday	Kofi	Afua
Saturday	Kwame	Amma

Kwame Gyekye notes that One's day of birth, *krada*, is held to be a factor in determining one's personal characteristics and aspects of one's behavior. People born on Monday are said to be suppliant, humble, calm (*okoto*); those born on Tuesday are said to be compassionate (*ogyam*); those born on Wednesday are said to be champions of the cause of others (*ntoni, atobi*); those born on Thursday are said to be courageous, aggressive, warlike (*preko*); those born on Friday are said to be wanderers (*okyin*), that is bent on exploring, discovering; those born on Saturday are said to be great (*atoapem*) and problem solvers (*oteanankaduro*; literally "he who knows the antidote for the serpent); and finally, those born on Sunday are said to be protectors (bodua; literally, tail of the animal), Kwame Gyekye, *An Essay on African Philosophical Thought: The Akan Conceptual Scheme*, Revised Edition (Philadelphia: Temple University Press, 1995), 172.

infant by mentioning the newly-given name of the infant and says, *se wohunu nsuo a, ka se nsuo*—If you see water, say it is water. After that she dips a finger into an alcoholic beverage and again drops it on the tongue of the infant. For a second time, she mentions the newly-given name and says, *se wohunu nsa a, ka se nsa*—If you see a drink, say it is a drink. This is to teach the newly-named infant the moral lessons of honesty and truthfulness. It is to guide the infant throughout the critical formative years until he or she reaches puberty.

Puberty Rite

As children grow and develop the passage from childhood to adolescence gives a change in social status for boys and girls in many cultures in Ghana. Puberty rites are performed mainly among the Krobos of the Eastern Region and the Asantes of the Ashanti Region in Ghana. These particular ceremonies mark the entry of the young women into adulthood. In Ghana, it is only a small number of groups, mostly in the North that have initiation rites marking the entrance of young men into adulthood. Most of these are done quietly and are not given as much prominence as the rites of passage for young women. The reason is explained by David Osei-Adu in the following way:

> In the Akan culture women represent the beauty, purity and dignity of the society and are guarded against corruption by our traditional laws and regulations. The most lasting impressions about life and the character of children are built during early and formative years which they spend mostly with their mothers. So the Akans believe that they need properly trained mothers with good morals to bring up good children. It is therefore little wonder that the initiation of women into adulthood is given more prominence in the Akan society than that of men.[4]

This assertion resonates well with what Sam Keen says about parenting,

> Woman, as a mother, continues to have enormous power over our adult lives because her most important lessons are taught wordlessly. She shapes us before we understand language, and therefore her influence is hidden from our adult consciousness. Her instructions remain within us like posthypnotic suggestion. Imagine that long ago your mother wrote and inserted the software disk that preprogrammed your life. She etched a script for your life, inserted a philosophy-of-life program, on the blank pages of your

---

[4] David Osei-Adu, "Puberty Rites", http://www.ghanaweb.com/GhanaHomePage/tribes/puberty-rites.php (accessed January 3, 2007).

Mission, Communion and Relationship

mind. This set of instructions remains in the archaic layers of your psyche and continues to shape your perceptions and feelings well into adulthood.[5]

Boys and girls in Ghana are educated socially to complement and cooperate with each other for the cultivation of peace and tranquility in the country. Each is formed to fulfill certain roles in the community. Traditionally, young men are ushered into adulthood by being given a cutlass. This is symbol of hard work. The male youth is instructed to be a hard worker and be responsible person in caring for his family. Young women are given a basket and a broom which symbolize the importance of maintaining a household. However, it is important to note that these gendered roles are not set in stone. Young men also are trained to carry out household chores like cooking, washing dishes and sweeping. In the same way, young women are taught to be active outside of the household since they may be called upon some day to provide for their families financially. This may happen if the husband looses his job or dies. In such cases, the woman as a single parent will have to raise her children by herself. The Akans say, *se wosum boodee dua a, na woasum kwadu nsoso dua*—If you protect the plantain tree, you also must protect the banana tree. All children must be helped to live their lives as true human beings; neither boys nor girls can be left behind.

Rite of Marriage

Once a person goes through the puberty rite, the next important stage is marriage. Prominence is given to marriage in Ghana and many African societies since through it the family lineage is continued. It is not simply a ceremony between the marrying-couples. Rather, marriage brings two families (clans) together. In many places, it is a whole community affair. Careful scrutinies take place before family-heads approve of marriages. It is the expectation that marriages will result in the bearing of children. For this reason, childless couples, most especially the women, are subjected to ridicule and insult by some family members. In some cases, this can lead to the dissolution of the marriage in traditional societies.

---

[5] Sam Keen, *Fire in the Belly: On Being A Man*, (New York: Bantam Books, 1991), 19.

Funeral Rites

The final rite of passage which also is given prominence in traditional society is the celebration of funeral rites of deceased members of the clan or tribe. Such rites are believed to enable the deceased 'to travel safely' to the land of the ancestors. This rite has become so elaborate and expensive that many religious leaders and chiefs have called for the opulence shown at such celebrations to be scaled back.

Dislocation in Society

In Ghana today, while many cultures still perform rituals to celebrate births and deaths, initiation into adulthood is less frequently talked about, let alone celebrated. This loss of traditional customs has left a great vacuum in the life of many youths leading to the disorientation and disorganization of many. As Sam Keen points out,

> In many ways rites of passage, cruel as they were, were socially and psychologically economical. They gave both men and women secure identities and a comfortable knowledge of the roles they were to play. Men didn't have to wonder: Am I a man? How do I achieve manhood? The male rite of initiation had a virtue of being a social event. At a specific time a boy underwent a series of ceremonies after which he was pronounced a man. Overnight his identification and social status changed.[6]

Today in Ghana, many of male youth are not culturally ushered into adulthood. Their social position is, therefore, not clearly defined. They are no longer boys and they do not yet see themselves as men inasmuch as adults do not consider these young men to be their equals. Many young men are left hanging in a balance having to fend for themselves. As a consequence, their future is endangered. If they happen to fall into a bad company, they may be ruined for life. Since in some communities, their positions in the society are not secured, these young men are easily manipulated as depicted in the movie *Blood Diamond*.

Even in situations where a young man does not fall into bad company, his social position is rarely recognized. Young men are rarely consulted when programs designed to help them are being planned in their communities. As the UN News Center points out, "Young people account for half the population in many of the world's poorest countries, particularly in Africa, yet

---

[6] Ibid., 32.

they have been neglected as a social category in poverty reduction schemes."[7] This is one of the plights in which the majority of young men in Africa find themselves. Their position in the society is not defined and their youthful exuberance is not well tapped. As a consequence, they are unable to make a positive contribution and end up on the slippery slopes of underdevelopment and self-destruction as characterized by illiteracy, streetism, unemployment, emigration, drug abuse, crime, imitation of foreign and sexual promiscuity and disease.

Illiteracy

It is often said that the greatest asset of any nation is its people. For any nation to develop and progress, its people need to be properly educated especially in this technological age. Any nation that neglects to invest in the education of its citizens cannot compete or survive. Such a nation will be left behind and its citizens will wallow in abject poverty. It is for this reason that successive governments in Ghana have put a high value on education since the country's independence. Despite this fact, the statistics on literacy in Ghana are not encouraging.   According to the 2004 report released by the World Bank, the literacy rate of citizens in Ghana who are 15 years of age and above in Ghana was 57.9%.   In the same report, it was noted that the completion rate for primary school was 65.4%. Furthermore, it was reported that enrollment for secondary education was 41.8%, while that of tertiary education was only 3.1%.[8] Based on the findings of this report, about 34.6% of the population does not complete primary school. Of those who manage to graduate, about 58.2% do not complete secondary education. This means that a very large percentage of the youth are not able to enter a job market that requires competency and proficiency in higher education. One cannot but wonder about the future of Ghana's young people given these statistics.

As a predominantly agricultural country, the majority of Ghana's population lives in the rural areas. The cutlass and hoe method of farming cannot continue. The country can no longer rely on rain-fed agriculture. Given the demands of the 21st century, there is a need to modernize farm technologies

---

[7] UN News Centre, "Young people must not continue to be neglected", http://www.un.org/apps/news/story.asp?NewsID=21588&Cr=ifad&Cr=development (accessed February 18, 2007).

[8] The World Bank Group, "Ghana Data Profile", http://devdata.worldbank.org/external/CPProfile.asp?CCODE=gha&PTYPE=CP (accessed April 21, 2007).

in Ghana. Machines like tractors and ploughs are needed to increase productivity. Dams are needed to irrigate large farms in order to produce enough food to feed the population. If the country is self-sufficient in food production, it will be in a position to export the surplus food to other needy countries thereby raising more foreign exchange for the development of other sectors of the economy. However, if the literacy rate of Ghana does not improve, this scenario of national progress will never become a reality. The negative consequences of the high illiteracy rate of the country are reflected in the lives of countless young men. Due to the fact that they are uneducated, they cannot secure meaningful work or well-paying jobs. Many resort to menial jobs that do not provide enough income for a decent standard of living. Young men who enter into the agricultural sector continue the old way of farming. Since they do not employ improved methods of farming, their turnovers continue to dwindle. Many are not able to care for themselves and their families. As a consequence, as prices of goods and services in the country continue to rise they cannot afford to adequately educate their children and the cycle of poverty is perpetuated. Farming becomes less attractive to young men and as a result of this fact they migrate from rural areas to the urban areas in search of jobs for which they are ill-prepared and envisioned opportunities that do not exist. This leads to the phenomenon of streetism with all its negative consequences for individuals and society at large.

Streetism

It is the phenomenon whereby young men and often young women from the rural areas leave their homes and migrate to the cities and big towns. This kind of migration was unheard of in Ghana years ago.[9] According to the Ghana Department of Social Welfare and some local Non-Governmental Organizations (NGOS), recent statistics indicate that "there are about 21,000 children living and working in Accra's[10] streets without a parent to protect

---

[9] For more information on streetism in Ghana see The Statesman, "Streetism and Ghana's Future," October 11, 2006, http://www.thestatesmanonline.com/pages/editorial_detail-php?newsid=63&section=0 (accessed August 19, 2007).

[10] Accra is the capital of the Greater Accra Region and also the capital of Ghana with a population of about three million people.

them."[11] Taking the country as a whole, the figure is estimated to be about 50,000[12] with many of them located in Kumasi.[13]

In addition to factors such as poor education, a survey conducted by Catholic Action for Street Children (CAS) an NGO based in Accra, "more than 80 percent of under-sixteen working on the streets in Ghana left home because of family problems, such as neglect or parents separation."[14] The survey went on to enumerate other causes such as "the collapse of rural livelihoods as traditional industries like fishing going into decline, lack of jobs, poor schools outside the cities, and forced marriage."[15] The survey concludes that "the breakdown of traditional African family structures, wherein it used to be normal for children to be sent to cities to live with distant relatives, is another factor that has contributed to growing numbers of street children throughout West Africa."[16]

A story is told of one Joshua Anderson, a thirteen year old boy who lives on the streets in Accra. According to him, he left home because his mother would not let him keep on going to school. Rather, the mother wanted him to go to the market with her. As a result, one night he left home and came to Accra. He thought that someone might support him in his education. Instead, what he does now is work. "He lugs boxes and cases, often taller than he is, in one of the city's bus stations. In exchange he gets a handful of coins. At night, he sleeps on a cardboard mat in front of a meat shop."[17]

In talking about the new phenomenon of streetism in Ghana, one cannot lose sight of the issue of absent and irresponsible fathers. It takes a very long time for a young person to grow into adulthood. For this reason, the raising of children is a challenging and often difficult task. The Akans say, *se baanu so a, emmia*—When two people carry a load it is less heavy. One person endeavoring

---

[11] UN Integrated Regional Information Networks, "What Hope for Thousands of Street Children?"

http://www.ghanaweb.com/GhanaHomePage/NewsArchive/artikel.php?ID=120454 (accessed March 8, 2007).

[12] Ibid.

[13] Kumasi is the capital of Ashanti Region and the second city after Accra. Its population is about two million people.

[14] UN Integrated Regional Information Networks, "What Hope for Thousands of Street Children?"

[15] Ibid.

[16] Ibid.

[17] Ibid.

to raise a child is a herculean task and most of the time it is young women who are left alone to assume this responsibility. Some men who impregnate women refuse to admit their responsibility. They do not marry the women and they neglect to provide child welfare support as time goes on. In some cases, the fathers run away and leave the women with their babies to fend for themselves. Since young women have few resources from which to cater for their children, older ones often run away from home and become victims of streetism and so the cycle of poverty goes on. According to the survey findings of CAS, the phenomenon of streetism is further complicated by the fact that older boys often beat the younger ones. At times they take their money and belongings. Worst still, they engage in acts of rape and other forms of sexual abuse.

Unemployment

As pointed out in the first chapter, Ghana has been enjoying favorable ratings by international bodies in recent times. However, as the former World Bank (WB) Country Director in Ghana, Mats Karlson pointed out the "sustainable macro-economic stability attained by Ghana was not enough since it had not yet led to job creation for the youth."[18] For him, "job creation was the only meeting point for the economic and social dimensions of any development agenda." He went on to say, "if all the good macro-economic indicators do not lead to job creation we cannot talk of development."[19] He suggested that "what is left for Ghana to do is to begin to embark on action programmes that would lead to movement of Small and Medium Scale Enterprises (SMEs) from the informal to the formal sector in order for there to be more permanent jobs for the youth."[20]

According to the Ghana's former Minister of Manpower, Youth and Employment, Alhaji Boniface Abubakar Saddique, it is estimated that the figure of unemployment in the country is about 2 million. Out of this figure, 78,000 representing 26% of the population are between the ages of 18-25.[21] The

---

[18] Ghana News Agency, "Macro economic stability has not created jobs for youth", http://www.myjoyonline.com/archieves/business/2007021/1743.asp (accessed February 19, 2007).

[19] Ibid.

[20] Ibid.

[21] Daily Graphic, "Two million unemployed in Ghana", http://www.ghanaweb.com/GhanaHomePage/NewsArchive/artikel.php?ID=116290 (accessed May 12, 2000).

unemployment situation has worsened in recent years due to the energy crisis. According to the National Labour Department, "thousands of Ghanaian workers have lost their jobs since the current energy crisis which began in August 2006.[22]   The document goes on to say, "the statistics show that from September 2006 to the first quarter of this year, March 31, 2007, a total of 33 companies filed for bankruptcy. As a result 2,333 workers lost their jobs.[23] It gives the breakdown of statistics, noting that "In the last quarter of last year—September to December 2006, 21 companies filed for insolvency with 1,798 workers asked to go home. For the first quarter of this year, January to March 31, 2007, 12 applications for redundancy were recorded with some 535 workers losing heir jobs."[24] The unemployment situation for young men in Ghana is desperate. Following the thought of John Paul II,[25] unemployment negates the existence of young men as human beings. It does not help them to raise and maintain their families. Furthermore, it does not help them to make a contribution to the development and progress of their country and humanity. In the end, they become susceptible to all kinds negative influences. It is in this light that the National President of the Planned Parenthood Association of Ghana (PPAG), Frances Owusu- Daaku, has expressed concern about unemployment among the youth, noting how the situation has made them increasingly more vulnerable.[26] Furthermore, as a lecturer at the Department of Clinical and Social Pharmacy at the Kwame Nkrumah University of Science and Technology, she notes that "unemployment among the youth causes idleness, frustration that at times make them resort to illegal activities which affect their lives."[27] Unemployment worsens the poverty level of male youth in Ghana.

The African Situation

As one surveys the continent of Africa, it is clear that the situation is no better in many places. For example, in Liberia, it is said that "80% of the total

---

[22]   Public   Agenda,   "Energy   crisis   renders   over   2,300   workers   jobless", http://www.myjoyonline.com/archives/business/200705/4526.asp (accessed May 14, 2007).
[23] Ibid.
[24] Ibid.
[25] John Paul II, "Laborem Exercens" (Vatican City: Libreria Editrice Vaticana, 1981), http://www.vatican.va/holy_father/john_paul_ii/encyclicals/documents/hf_jp-ii_enc14091981_laborem-exercens_en.html (accessed April 30, 2007).
[26]   Ghana   News   Agency,   "PPAG   Concerned   about   unemployment", http://www.ghanaweb.com/GhanaHomePage?NewsArchive/artikel.php?ID=119281   (accessed February 16, 2007).
[27] Ibid.

population of 3.2 million people live below poverty line. Life expectancy is low and adult literacy is only 38%."[28] The many years of civil war destroyed much of the country's infrastructure. Many investors left the country for their own safety. This has left many of the youth unemployed.

Commenting on the situation in Kenya, the Minister for Labor and Human Resource Development, Newton Kulundu, points out that "over 60% of Kenyans are people below 30 years of age, 32 percent of the entire population in the critical age bracket of 15 to 30 years… Many are unable to find gainful employment."[29] In his opinion, "the single most important challenge for the ministry and nation is to inculcate the right character and relevant skills into the youth and come up with strategies that will harness their energies into purposeful and productive development activities."[30]

Emigration

Among the Akans, it is said that *anoma antu a, obua da*—If a bird does not fly, it starves. Again it is said that *yenntena faako nnye animguase. Se baabi annye wo a, baabi begye wo*—One does not stay in one place to be disgraced. If one place despises you, another place may accept you. All things being equal, people tend to remain close to family and friends. However, when situations become difficult or unbearable, people start to consider alternatives. One option is to move to another place in order to see if one may prosper there. This approach has been the choice of the many youths in the rural areas of Ghana and most especially those from the northern part of the country. Since they are beset with unemployment in their areas, the tendency is for them to pack their bags and move to the cities and the big towns in search of work opportunities. Finding nothing, they roam about vulnerable to the phenomenon of streetism.

In the opinion of the former World Bank Country Director of Ghana, Mats Karlson, "Ghana's urban migration is still high, and requires an urgent effort to address the phenomenon."[31] He pointed out that "the problem of urban migration and its associated risks are high… the end result of the expeditions to

---

[28] Economic Community of West Africa States, "Liberia" http://www.ecowas.info/liberia.htm (accessed January 12, 2007).
[29] Newton   Kulundu,   "Education   Must   Satisfy   Market   Demands", http://www.africanexecutive.com/modules/magazine/articles.php?article=1023&magazine (accessed February 18, 2007).
[30] Ibid.
[31]   Daily   Express,   "Ghana's   urban   poverty   too   high", http://www.myjoyonline.com/archives/news/200703/2539.asp (accessed March 15, 2007).

the city is the creation of slums in the big cities. These areas have become the bedrock of poverty because they lack very important social amenities, good shelter and education."[32] He concluded by saying, "While it appears that Ghana is making strides in eradicating poverty in general, it is loosing the fight against poverty in the cities where a lot people live."[33]

It must be noted that it is not only rural-urban migration that has bedeviled Ghana. Highly qualified professionals, trained at the expense of the tax-payers money leave the shores of the country to work in places like North America, Europe and the Middle East for better remuneration. It is estimated that it costs the nation about $80,000 to train one medical doctor from primary school to the university.[34] According to statistics, about 2,800 doctors left Ghana between 1969 and 2000.[35] Records indicate that between 1999 and 2004, 448 doctors, or 54% of those trained in the period left to work abroad.[36] The number of nurses who have left the country since 1996 is 11,000 in addition to a large number of pharmacists, laboratory technicians and other health professionals.[37] According to the former Head of the Ghana Health Service, Professor Agyeman Badu-Akosa, "the trend for young doctors and nurses to seek high salaries and better working conditions mainly in the West is killing the healthcare sector in Ghana... It is the single most significant impact on healthcare delivery in this country."[38]

Youth emigration from Ghana to foreign countries has increased significantly in recent years. The phenomenon compelled the President, John Agyekum-Kuffour, on the occasion of the 50th anniversary of Ghana's independence to make a passionate appeal to the nation's youth, "to resolve to stay at home using your energies and your enthusiasm to serve Africa."[39]

---

[32] Ibid.

[33] Ibid.

[34] Daily Graphic, "Doctors urged to stay at home", http://www.myjoyonline.com/archives/heath/200704/3012.asp (accessed April 2, 2007).

[35] Ibid.

[36] AFP, "Brian drain killing healthcare sector", http://www.ghanaweb.com/GhanahomePage/NewsArchives/artikel.php?ID=121028 (accessed March 18, 2007).

[37] Daily Graphic, "Doctors urged to stay at home"

[38] AFP, "Brain drain killing healthcare sector"

[39] Ibid.

The African Situation

Emigration of youth to foreign countries in search of jobs and better remuneration is not peculiar to Ghana alone. In Chapter One, it was noted that thousands of young people risk their lives each year in order to cross over The Mediterranean Sea into Europe. Writing on migration, Raphael Lara points out that "the drama of migration is becoming more pronounced. Approximately three thousand people have died in the last six-months on the route from Africa to the Canary Islands. The number of victims of clandestine immigration is increasing at a horrifying rate."[40] He indicates that according to the Red Cross Report of May 2006, at the start of the year, "The Atlantic waters separating West African coast from the Canaries had swallowed 1,500 people."[41]

The desire of many African youths to travel to Europe and America has consumed their lives. They will do anything and everything to take a chance. For this reason, some unscrupulous people have duped many of them. Not long ago the International Organization for Migration (IOM) reported that 34 boys who had been duped by a bogus football agent were rescued. He had promised the boys contracts with European soccer clubs. The boys were all passionate soccer players. They were members of a club in one of the poorest districts of Abidjan, Cote d'Ivoire. Their parents had paid between $200-$600 each. For three months the parents did not see their sons thinking that they had been taken to Europe. Instead, they were held in an abandoned house in Mali, a neighbouring country where they were given little food and living in terrible conditions. According the IOM spokeswoman, Jemini Pandya, "this kind of scam which exploits the hopes and dreams of young people is becoming more common."[42]

Drug Abuse

Another problem besetting the young men of Ghana is the use of alcohol and narcotics. Even though it has not reached an epidemic level, it is on the ascendancy. Some of the male youths are becoming drug addicts. In his book, *Addiction and Grace: Love and Spirituality in the Healing of Addicts*, Gerald G. May points out that

---

[40] Raphael Lara, "Migration from Africa to Spain", *Concilium*, Vol. 5, eds. Andres Torres Queiruga, Luiz Carlos Susin and Jon Sobrino (London: SCM Press, 2006), 131.

[41] Ibid., 132.

[42] BBC News, "Football trafficker cons Ivorians", http://news.bbc.co.uk/2/hi/africa/6500539.stm (accessed March 27, 2007).

Addictions exist wherever persons are internally compelled to give energy to things that are not their true desire… Addiction is a state of compulsion, obsession, or preoccupation that enslaves a person's will and desire. Addiction sidetracks and eclipses the energy of our deepest, truest desire for love and goodness. We succumb because the energy of our desire becomes attached, nailed, to specific behaviors, objects, or people.[43]

In his opinion,

our addictions are our own worst enemies. They enslave us with chains that are of our own making and yet that, paradoxically, are virtually beyond our control. Addiction also makes idolators of us all, because it forces us to worship these objects of attachment, thereby preventing us from truly, freely loving God and one another. Addiction breeds willfulness within us, yet again paradoxically, it erodes our free will and eats away at our dignity.[44]

The most common addiction in Ghana is alcohol. However, the use of hard drugs like marijuana, cocaine and heroin are on the increase. It is well-known that drug abuse disturbs the proper functioning of the brain. In addition, it interrupts the normal functions of the heart, kidney, lungs and the pancreas.[45] Regardless of these facts, the use of drugs continues to increase.

In March 2007, the U. S. Bureau of International Narcotics and Law Enforcement Affairs released a report on narcotics in Ghana. The report said "Ghana has become a major trans-shipment point for illegal drugs, particularly cocaine from South America as well as heroin from Southeast and Southwest Asia."[46] It was noted in the report that "South American cocaine trafficking rings increased their foothold in Ghana, establishing well-developed distribution networks run by Nigerian and Ghanaian criminals."[47] According to the report, "trafficking had also fuelled domestic drug consumption."[48]

---

[43] Gerald G. May, *Addiction and Grace: Love and Spirituality in the Healing of Addictions* (New York: HarperCollins Publishers, 1988), 14.

[44] Ibid., 4.

[45] Ghana News Agency, "Porters warned against effects of hard drugs", http://www.myjoyonline.com/archives/news/200702/2082.asp (accessed February 28, 2007).

[46] Ghana News Agency, "Ghana's major efforts against drug abuse, but problems remain" http://www.ghanaweb.com/GhanaHomePage/NewsArchive/artikel.php?ID=121071 (accessed March 19, 2007).

[47] Ibid.

[48] Ibid.

This assertion of the U.S. Bureau of International Narcotics and Law Enforcement Affairs is confirmed by a research conducted by the Enquirer Newspaper of Ghana. According to the research, "peddling and consumption of hard illicit drugs among students in Cape Coast, the Central Regional capital is gaining alarming notoriety with kids from influential and rich families controlling the distribution and demand chain."[49] The research notes that the suppliers of the drugs mostly come from Accra and Tema. "The peddlers usually referred to by the students as Dons had recruited some students who sold on campuses and rendered daily accounts. Similar drug points had been established in homes closer to some of theses schools."[50]

The use of these hard illicit drugs has been having a telling effect on many students. Many of them have ended up in psychiatric hospitals.[51] According to the Head of Electro-Convulsive Unit of the Accra Psychiatric Hospital, "out of a total of 731 inmates admitted last year (2006), for drug-related cases, as high as 690 of them were students from the first, second and tertiary institutions."[52] He gave the break down as follows: first cycle—388; second cycle—265; third cycle—37.[53] He also indicated that 614 of the inmates at the hospital were young persons between 15 and 40; 86 inmates between 41 and 50; 29 were between the ages of 51 and 60 and only two inmates were between the ages of 61 and 70.[54] He indicated that "students and young people below the age of 40 years accounted for about 90 percent of the drug-related cases recorded last year."[55]

It must be pointed out that it is not only students who are involved in the drug menace. Those young people who have fallen into the phenomenon of streetism are also at great risk. It is for this reason that The Ghana National Commission on Children recently organized workshops for porters and truck

---

[49] The Enquirer, "Cocaine, heroine biz booming in Cape Coast schools", http://www.myjoyonline.com/archives/news/200702/1726.asp (accessed February 19, 2007).
[50] Ibid.
[51] Joseph Kow Chunney, Joanne Marie Greer and John Allen, "African Spiritual Worldview: Its Impact on Alcohol and other Drug Use by Senior Secondary School Students in Ghana", in *Research in the Social Scientific Study of Religion: A Research*. Vol. 10, eds. David O. Moberg and J. M. Greer (Greenwich, Conn: Brill, 1999).
[52] Ghana News Agency, "Students top drug abuse cases in 2006", http://www.myjoyonline.com/archives/health/200702/1830.asp (accessed February 21, 2007).
[53] Ibid.
[54] Ibid.
[55] Ibid.

pushers at Ho central market[56] on the theme: "Streetism and Child Labour: The
Effects on the Child, Family, Community and the Economy."[57]   At the
workshop, a senior community health nurse, Benedicta Seshie, advised the
porters and truck-pushers to desist from using hard drugs. She told them that
the drugs would not make them strong as they believed. Rather, such drugs
would "interfere with the proper functioning of their brains leading to
abnormal behavior."[58]   This is confirmed by the statistics at the Accra
Psychiatric Hospital where in addition to students, 41 inmates were illiterates.[59]

The drug menace facing male youth in Ghana is a microcosm of what is
happening on the African continent. This is confirmed by the annual report
issued by The International Narcotics Control Board (INCB) in 2006. The
INCB "expressed concern about the inadequate drug control mechanisms and
skilled human resources to deal with drug trafficking in Africa in the report."[60]
The INCB was of the opinion that the drug menace needed to be tackled head
on and adequately dealt with. It goes on to say, "if left unchecked, the problem
of drug trafficking in Africa might further exacerbate existing social, economic
and political problems."[61] The report pointed out that what was happening on
the African continent was worrisome. This is due to the fact that "drug
trafficking networks were taking advantage of the weak interdiction capacities in
Africa and using the region as a transit area for smuggling cocaine from South
America through Western, Central and Southern Africa."[62]

Another disturbing aspect of the drug menace is that Africa is not only a
transit quarters. "As a spill over effect of the ongoing transit trafficking in
heroin in Eastern Africa, the abuse of heroin has become a problem there."[63]
What is more worrisome in the report is "the serious difficulties facing many
African countries in providing adequate treatment and rehabilitation for persons
using cannabis, as health-care facilities often lacked the necessary resources."[64]

---

[56] Ho is the capital of the Volta Region.
[57]   Ghana   News   Agency,   "Porters   warned   against   effects   of   hard   drugs",
http://www.myjoyonline.com/archives/news/200702/2082.asp (accessed February 28, 2007).
[58] Ibid.
[59] Ghana News Agency, "Students top drug abuse in 2006".
[60]   Daily   Graphic,   "Drug   trafficking   in   Africa   disturbing",
http://www.myjoyonline.com/archives/news/200703/2124.asp (March 1, 2007).
[61] Ibid.
[62] Ibid.
[63] Ibid.
[64] Ibid.

Crime

Peace is something that majority of people cherish so that they can live their daily lives and go about their duties with some measure of security. However, when the environment is threatened by crime-waves, people become agitated and worried. Consequently, they seek immediate solutions so that unsafe situations will be restored to normalcy. As the crime rate in the country keeps on rising, many Ghanaians are looking for immediate solutions. This is attributed to the proliferation of arms in the country in recent years. According to the former Deputy Minister of Interior, Kwaku Agyeman-Manu, there are about 220,000 small firearms that are in the hands of civilians in the country. Out of this number, only about 95,000 are registered. 75,000 of them were illegally manufactured locally by blacksmiths.[65] The unfortunate situation is that these illicit weapons have fallen into wrong hands. They are used to perpetuate violent crimes. This has resulted in an increase of armed robberies in homes and on highways. Statistics from the Agona Swedru[66] Divisional Police Command of the Ghana Police Service indicate that the district recorded 45 cases of armed robbery in 2006. In the previous year, 2005, the figure was 76.[67] By way of example, the police in Sunyani[68] arrested two suspected armed robbers at a police check-point. They were going to carry out an operation somewhere. When the car was searched, the police found in the taxi they were using, one pump action gun loaded with five rounds of ammunition, one Russian made shot gun, two foreign pistols, two face masks, pliers, scissors, knives and iron bars.[69]

The country's higher institutions have not been spared by this upsurge of armed robbery in Ghana. In February 2007, "over 1,000 students at the University of Ghana, Legon staged a demonstration on campus, calling for

---

[65] Ghana News Agency, "Parliamentarians deliberate on a draft bill on small arms and light weapons", http://www.ghanaweb.com/GhanaHomePage/NewsArchive/artikel.php?ID=120986 (accessed March 18, 2007).

[66] Agona Swedru is the capital of Swedru District in the Central Region.

[67] Ghana News Agency, "Armed robbery reducing in Agona District", http://www.myjoyonline.com/archives/news/200702/1712.asp accessed (February 18, 2007).

[68] Sunyani is the regional capital of the Brong Ahafo Region.

[69] Ghana News Agency, "Sunyani police arrest suspected armed robbers", http://www.myjoyonline.com/archives/news/200705/4661.asp (May 16, 2007).

tighter security measures in the face of an escalating spate of gun violence."[70]
This is all because three gun-point robberies had taken place at the University
within a period of three weeks. In the first incident, a lecturer was attacked in
his bungalow on campus, in which his wife was shot. In the second instance, a
student was shot on the balcony of his Sarbah Hall Annex B accommodation.
In the third episode, it was said that four students were attacked and robbed by
armed robbers who wore masks while they were browsing in the Afronet
Internet Café.[71] Similar attacks have been reported in the University of Cape
Coast. In one particular incident, a group of non-resident students were
attacked. The attack lasted for three hours. When it was all over, one of the
students was hospitalized with serious cutlass wounds.[72]

In recent years, the crime wave in the country has been taken into
cyberspace. Some young people are able to dupe prospective investors through
contacts on the internet. Three male youths, Samuel Kena, 18, Nana Kofi, 19
and Bernard Nartey, alias Barrister Louis Nukunu, 20 duped a Canadian woman
of 114,000 Canadian dollars through contacts on the internet. When the case
was reported to the Police Criminal Investigation Department, they were able to
arrest the young men.[73] In May 2007, a Canadian company reported numerous
fraudulent charges on its credit cards. They were used to buy TV's, DVD's,
clothing, shoes, herbal remedies and computers. Their investigation led to the
arrest of two Ghanaian men ages 21 and 23 at the airport in Accra.[74]

It is amazing the length to which some Ghanaian youth will go to amass
wealth. The 'get-rich-quick' attitude of many youth has driven some to pursue
lives of crime and violence. As attested to by the Deputy Superintendent of
Police, Kwesi Ofori, the crime rate among the youth in Ghana is very high and

---

[70]   Statesman,   "Gun   Terror   Grips   Legon",
http://www.ghanaweb.com/GhanaHomePage/NewsArchive/artikel.php?ID=119406 (accessed
February 19, 2007).
[71] Ibid.
[72] Ibid.
[73]   GHP,   "3   Arrested   for   Cyber   Fraud",
http://www.ghanaweb.com/GhanaHomePage/NewsArchive/artikel.php?ID=123632 (accessed
May 19, 2007).
[74]   Edmonton   Journal,   "Two   arrested   in   online   scam",
http://www.ghanaweb.com/GhanaHomePage/NewsArchive/artikel.php?ID=124288 (accessed
May 19, 2007).

rising. He points out that about 70% of all crime cases in Ghana involve youth under the age of thirty.[75]

The African Situation

As pointed out in the Introduction, many African countries have experienced civil wars that raged on for many years. One can mention countries like Mozambique, Angola, The Republic of Congo, Uganda, Sudan, Liberia and Sierra Leone not forgetting the genocide that took place in Rwanda in 1994 which claimed about 880,000 lives and displaced many people who were compelled to take refuge in other countries. These wars were fuelled by the proliferation of weapons on the continent. It is estimated that there are over 600 million illicit weapons in the world. Out of this number about 30 million are found in Africa. "About eight million illicit weapons are currently circulating in West Africa."[76] It is these illicit weapons which opportunists and rebel fighters make use of and give them to teen-agers to carry out their guerrilla war-fare. As pointed out in the Introduction, in the Liberian and the Sierra Leone civil wars, the teenage soldiers were the most fearsome. They tortured, raped and killed without any mercy or remorse. Those who could not stand them fled for their lives. This created a massive refugee situation. About 40,000 Liberians sought refuge in Ghana alone during that country's civil war where they were put up in the Buduburam camp in Ghana.[77]

Imitation of Foreign Cultures

As human beings, we are born into particular contexts. Each of these contexts has its own culture and sub-culture. Through these cultures, human beings are formed and raised up. These cultures give human beings their identities. As noted by Nathan D. Mitchell,

> Culture is the sum total of all the ways human persons interacts and lives together. It includes their social contacts, contracts, conventions, and covenants; their shared language and literature; their arts and artifacts, their science and technology; their

[75] Kwame Tawiah, "IGP to launch Youth Crime Watch Programme", http://www.ghanaweb.com/GhanaHomePage?NewsArchive/artikel.php?ID=116817 (accessed January 7, 2007).
[76] Ghana News Agency, "National Commission on Small Arms Bill passed", http://www.myjoyonline.com/archives/news/200703/2785.asp (accessed March 23, 2007).
[77] Ghana News Agency, "UNFPA donates kit to Buduburam Camp", http://www.myjoyonline.com/archives/health/200705/4174 (accessed May 3, 2007).

meanings and memories, beliefs and behaviors, icons and images; and not least, their religious convictions and values transmitted in song and story, and rehearsed in ritual action.[78]

Culture is something that human beings cannot do without. To try to jettison one's culture is to lose one's identity as a person. This is a problem that is confronting many youths in Ghana. Many youths in Ghana have the tendency to look down on their own Ghanaian culture as they privilege foreign ones. In the opinion of the Coordinator of the National Volunteer Service, George Gado, "colonialism has resulted in psychological misdirection of the youth."[79] He thinks, "The problem, which had made the youth to prefer foreign culture and goods to local ones, was the greatest challenge facing them."[80] He concludes that "the youth are fast losing their local identity and have imbued foreign ideas."[81]

The same sentiments were expressed by the Eastern Regional Director of the Centre for National Culture, Kingley Obeng, when he observed that "Ghana is still suffering from mental slavery."[82] For him "while political freedom has been won, that of mental slavery continues to assail the people."[83] He is very surprised "at the voluptuous appetite for foreign products including second-hand panties while very few people patronize local fabrics manufactured to promote national identity."[84] According to Obeng, "many Ghanaians have become depersonalized and dominated by foreign values."[85]

Turning his attention to the youth he said, "They have developed a false perception which did not see anything attractive about Ghanaian cultural products."[86] Needless to say, this is a tragic situation.

[78] Nathan D. Mitchell, *Meeting Mystery*, 3.

[79] Ghana News Agency, "Youth Suffering from Psychological misdirection", http://www.myjoyonline.com/archives/news/200704/3332.asp (accessed April 11, 2007).

[80] Ibid.

[81] Ibid.

[82] Ghana News Agency, "Ghana suffers from mental slavery", http://www.myjoyonline.com/archives/news/200705/4740.asp (accessed May 18, 2007).

[83] Ibid.

[84] Ibid.

[85] Ibid.

[86] Ibid.

The African Situation

Earlier on there was a discussion on migration of African youths to other countries especially Europe and America. It was pointed out that unemployment forces many young people to migrate from their countries of origin. However, one cannot dispute the fact that for some of them, it is both the tendency to disdain their own culture and their desire for foreign goods that compel them to attempt to go to the developed countries. For such youths, they would do anything and everything to realize their dreams. Most of them do so through illegal means. It is estimated that in 2006, about 30,000 immigrants were caught trying to reach the Canary Islands. Unfortunately, many died in the process.[87] Acquisition of foreign culture can be seen as one of plights besetting male youth in Africa.

Sexual and Reproductive Health—HIV/AIDS

The crisis of male youth in Ghana and in Africa cannot be discussed completely without reference to their sexual and reproductive health. This is due to the well-known high rate of HIV/AIDS infections in Africa. Statistics indicate that young people between the ages of 0-24 account for about 52% of the total population of Ghana.[88]

With regard to sexual activity among young people in Ghana it is estimated that 4 in 10 Ghanaian women and 2 in 10 men aged between the ages of15-19 have had sexual intercourse. By the age 20, 83% of women and 56% of men had had sex. The medium age of first intercourse is 17.4 for women and 19.5 for men.[89]

According to the figures from the Alan Guttmacher Institute of New York, "92% of 12-14 years olds in Ghana have never had sex, never had a boyfriend or girlfriend, and never experienced kissing or fondling." It also says that 29% of 15-19 year old female and 15% of such males have had sex."[90]

---

[87] BBC News, "Spain sends African migrants home", http://news.bbc.co.uk/2/hi/europe/6674295.stm (accessed May 20, 2007).

[88] "National Youth Shadow Report: Progress Made on the UNGASS Declaration of Commitment on HIV/AIDS: Ghana", http://www.youthaidscoalition.org/docs/Ghana.pdf (accessed May 21, 2007).

[89] Ibid.

[90] Alan Guttmacher, "Adolescents in Ghana", http://www.guttmacher.org/pubs/2006/06/01/fb_ghana_adolescents.pdf (accessed May 21, 2007).

On the use of contraceptives, the Institute pointed out that "nearly half of the unmarried sexually active young women and more than one-third of all sexually active young men currently use no contraceptive methods; 4 in 10 of these young women and half of these young men use the male condom."[91] Among those who are married "only 16% of married young women use the condom; 60% use no contraceptive method."[92]

On HIV/AIDS, The World Bank Group puts the infection rate of Ghana in its 2005 report at 2.3%.[93]   The Director-General of Ghana AIDS Commission, Professor Awuku Sakyi-Amoah, has attributed the rapid spread of HIV/AIDS to "the upsurge of moral indiscipline and promiscuity among the populace, especially the youth."[94]   Other contributory factors he pointed out include the proliferation of pornographic materials on the internet and in the media, as well as negative and harmful cultural practices such as female genital mutilation and non-circumcision of males among some ethnic groups.[95]   He discloses that "the largest number of HIV/AIDS cases were recorded among women aged between 20 and 44 years and men between the ages of 30 and 44."[96]

The African Situation

The HIV/AIDS pandemic is devastating in many African countries.[97]   Figures from some countries are most discouraging.   The infection rates of some countries are as follows: Burundi—5.4%; Kenya—10.2%; Zambia—15.6% and Botswana—34.9%.[98]   In Swaziland it is reported that 1 in 3 adults is invested

---

[91] Ibid.

[92] Ibid.

[93]   The   World   Bank   Group,   "Ghana   Data   Profile", http://devdata.worldbank.org/external/CPProfile.asp?CCODE=gha&PTYPE=CP   (accessed April 12, 2007).

[94]   Ghana   News   Agency,   "AIDS   Commission   frowns   on   Stigmatization", http://www.myjoyonline.com/archives/health/200704/3617.asp (accessed April 18, 2007).

[95] Ibid. See also Craig Timberg, "Circumcision offered to Africans: Part of Bush's Anti—AIDS Push" in *The Boston Globe*, Vol. 272, No. 51, August 20, 2007.

[96] Ibid.

[97] Lisa Sowle Cahill, "Bioethics, AIDS, Theology and Social Change", in *Reflecting Theologically on AIDS: A Global Challenge*, ed. Robin Gill (London: SCM Press, 2007).   See also James Keenan's "AIDS and a Casuistry of Accommodation" in the same book.

[98]   Gatonye   Gathura,   "HIV/AIDS   Statistics: Misleading?" http://www.africanexecutive.com/modules/magazine/articles.php?article=796&magazine=78

with HIV.[99] According to statistics, in 1992 the rate of infection in Uganda was 18.3%. In some centres it was 30%.[100] The situation is worse in South Africa. It is estimated that about 1,000 AIDS death occur daily.[101] No one can dispute the fact that "in the past two decades, the HIV/AIDS pandemic has constituted a crisis of virtually unprecedented proportions confronting younger generations of Africans. Africa is the most affected area in the world, with more than 23 million people estimated to be infected with HIV or to have full-blown AIDS."[102]

These are some of the major issues confronting young men in Ghana in particular and on the African continent in general. The situation in Ghana may not seem so bad when compared to other countries. As indicated in the Introduction, *se wohunu se egya erehye wo yonko abodwese a, na wo asa nsuo asi wodee ho*—When you see that your neighbor's beard is on fire, you must provide water as a stand-by in case yours also catches fire. This being said, my argument is that the plight of male youth in Ghana must be confronted and dealt with before it generates into the devastating reality confronting other countries on the continent. Since the church is a sacrament of Christ, it must be a major partner in providing means to deal with the plight of male youth so that they can live their lives as true human beings created in the image and likeness of God. The next section of this chapter looks at the Church's response to the plight of male youth in Ghana.

Roman Catholic Church's Response

We read from the scriptures that Jesus came into the world out of love for humanity. (cf. Jn. 3: 16) He came so that human beings may have life and have it abundantly. (cf. Jn. 10: 10b) As a sacrament of Christ, the church's mission

---

(accessed February 18, 2007). For more on the situation in Kenya see Eunice Kamaara, *Gender, Youth Sexuality,* and *HIV/AIDS: A Kenyan Experience* (Eldoret, Kenya: AMECEA Gaba Publications, 2005).

[99] Timberg Craig, "Circumcision offered to Africans: Part of Bush's Anti—AIDS Push", *The Boston Globe,* Vol. 272, No. 51, August 20, 2007.

[100] Uganda Aids Commission, "The HIV/AIDS Epidemic", http://www.aidsuganda.org (accessed August 18, 2007).

[101] Averting HIV & AIDS, "South Africa—HIV & AIDS Statistics", http://www.avert/aidssouthafrica.htm (accessed August 18, 2007). See also UNAIDS, "South Africa", http://www.unaids.org/en/HIV_data/epi2006/default.asp (accessed August 18, 2007).

[102] Social Science Research Council, "Africa", http://www.ssrc.org/programs/africa/ 2003fellows.page (accessed February 18, 2007).

cannot be uncoupled from the mission of Christ. For this reason, the church has a responsibility to proclaim both Jesus' message of eternal salvation as well as earthly liberation from all cultural, economic, political and social shackles which enslave the human person. The church must be committed to delivering people from the forces of evil that dehumanizes the children of God.[103]

Social Position

In Chapter One, I discussed why the two initial attempts to establish Roman Catholicism in Ghana did not yield fruits. I also noted how the third attempt succeeded due to the more adequate and appropriate methods used by later missionaries. They studied and adopted the culture of the people. They recognized the prominent roles that the young men played in their communities. For that reason, they recruited some of the young ones and trained them to help them in the work of evangelization. Since then the youth have occupied a prominent place in the life of the Roman Catholic Church in Ghana. Various archdioceses and dioceses have endeavored to advance the youth apostolate. They have established youth offices and appointed youth chaplains. To the extent that such efforts have been successful, the youth in the Roman Catholic church have not been sidelined and neglected. They are recognized as integral parts of the church.[104] Their contributions in the work of evangelization are greatly appreciated in the Roman Catholic church in Ghana. Still, given the contemporary challenges and unprecedented threats to the well-being of young men, the Church must be proactive and visionary as it looks to the future. More on this is said in the Chapter Four which is on Communion and Solidarity with Male Youth: A Missiological Imperative for the Roman Catholic Church in Ghana.

Education

The Roman Catholic church has always adopted a holistic approach towards its missionary activity in Ghana. Right from the beginning of the establishment of

---

[103] Roland Martinson, "Engaging the Quest: Encountering Youth and God in Their Longing" in *The Princeton Lectures on Youth, Church, and Culture 2004: Longing for God: Youth and The Quest for a Passionate Church*, eds. Kenda Creasy Dean et alii. (Princeton, NJ: Princeton Theological Seminary, 2004), 32–38.

[104] Reginald Blount, "Journeying with Youth toward Living Waters" in *The Princeton Lectures on Youth, Church and Culture 2005: Longing for God: Youth and The Quest for a Passionate Church*, eds. Kenda Creasy Dean et al. (Princeton, NJ: Princeton Theological Seminary, 2005), 11-16.

Roman Catholicism in Ghana, the early missionaries paid great attention to education.   Consequently, they founded schools side by side with the establishment of the churches. The aim was to educate and train people who would act as catechists in the work of evangelization.   In addition, they established seminaries to form the local clergy to propagate the gospel among their own people. Today, the Roman Catholic church in Ghana can boast of "about 20 per cent of public schools at the basic school level; 10 out of the 21 public Girls Secondary Schools; 40 percent of the 22 public Boys Secondary Schools; 58 Vocational and Technical institutes and a University."[105]

The aims and approaches of the Roman Catholic church have not been lost sight of by majority of the people of Ghana. The Administrator of Ghana Education Trust Fund (GETFUND), Fosuaba Akwasi Mensah-Banahene, once pointed out "the important role the first missionaries, the Catholic church and priests continue to play in the socio-economic development of the nation."[106]

Speaking at the 60th anniversary of St. John Bosco Training College, the former Vice President of Ghana, Alhaji Aliu Mahama among other things said to the students, "but for the Catholic church most of you sitting here from this part of the country might not have received formal education."[107] In the same vein, speaking at the 77th Speech and Prize Giving-Day of St. Augustine College, the then Minister of Public Sector Reform, Paa Kwesi Nduom, paid tribute to Catholic education in Ghana which laid much emphasis on the core values of life including discipline, hard work, selflessness, fear of God and caring for one's neighbor with the view to achieving success and prosperity.[108] He noted that "through the 50 years of independence, Catholic education has made an important contribution to all aspects of the national life and that Catholic educational institutions have established a great tradition not just as institution of learning but also homes for the shaping of values."[109]   He congratulated the Roman Catholic church "for the wonderful work that it has

[105] Ghana News Agency, "Unbridled materialism hampers efforts at nation-building", http://www.myjoyonline.com/news/read.asp?contentid=464 (accessed January 4, 2007). See also Ghana News Agency, "Education", http://www.myjoyonline.com/education/200803/14473.asp (accessed March 17, 2008).
[106] Ibid.
[107] Ghana News Agency, "We need patriotic teachers", http://www.myjoyonline.com/archives/news/200705/4780.asp (accessed May 20, 2007).
[108] Ghana News Agency, "Ghana needs successful people to be prosperous", http://www.myjoyonline.com/archives/education/200703/2633.asp (accessed March 19, 2007).
[109] Ibid.

been doing for several decades in educating the youth throughout the country."[110]

In April 2007, the Roman Catholic church in the Northern part of the country celebrated its centenary celebration. The guest speaker was the former President of Ghana, John Agyekum-Kuffour. In his speech, the president also paid tribute to the Roman Catholic church. He pointed out the church's immense contribution to the socio-economic development of the Upper West, Upper East, and Northern regions (Northern Ghana) and the nation as a whole. He acknowledged the fact that in the course of its 100 years of missionary activities in Northern Ghana, "The church had spread the gospel and contributed to the improvement of health and education, provided water, engaged in income generation activities and conflict prevention and peace-building."[111] On education, the president said that "the impact of the church in educational development was particularly evident everywhere in Northern Ghana."[112] In spite of the recognition and the various commendations that the Roman Catholic church in Ghana has received as far as its educational developments are concerned, it cannot rest on its laurels. More needs to be done to continue to educate and holistically form people especially young men to be able to face the many challenges that may come their way.[113] Secondly, they need to be educated and formed adequately to be well-equipped to enter into the job-market in this information and communication technologically advanced world.

Employment

God is seen as a worker who worked for six days and rested on the seventh day. (cf. Gen. 1:1–2:1-7) In the same way, Jesus is seen a carpenter's son who did manual labor. Paul, in his second letter to the Christian community at Thessalonica pointed out, "for even when we were with you, we gave you this

---

[110] Ibid. See also, Ghana News Agency, "BECE Students can now re-sit exams to better grades", http://www.ghanaweb.com/GhanaHomePage/NewsArchive/artikel.php?ID=140481 (accessed March 9, 2008).

[111] Ghana News Agency, "Catholic Church winds up Centenary Celebration", http://www.ghanaweb.com/GhanaHomePage/religion/artikel.php?ID=123003 (accessed April 27, 2007).

[112] Ibid.

[113] Peter Christian Olsen, *Youth at Risk: Ministry to The Least, The Lost and The Last* (Cleveland, Ohio: The Pilgrim Press, 2003), 86-103.

command: anyone unwilling to work should, not eat. For we hear that some of you are living in idleness, mere busybodies, not doing any work. Now such persons we command and exhort in the Lord Jesus Christ to do their work quietly and to earn their own living." (2 Thess. 3:10-12) The Roman Catholic church has always taught that there is dignity in human labor. People must, therefore, eschew idleness and work in order to provide for themselves and their families. The Roman Catholic church in Ghana does not just speak against the high unemployment level in the country; it seeks ways of providing employment opportunities to some people. The number of educational institutions that the Roman Catholic church in Ghana has set up has contributed to the literacy rate of the country and enabled people to acquire the necessary qualifications to enter the job-market. Also, it is important not to lose sight of the fact that these educational institutions have offered employment to many people who otherwise would have been unemployed. Here, apart from the teaching staff, the non-teaching staff is considered. These laborers include the dedicated men and women who work in the kitchen, the grounds and security. The Roman Catholic church in Ghana has set up not only educational institutions. It also has established health facilities. It has 106 health facilities. This includes 32 hospitals. It is on record that it was the Roman Catholic church in Ghana which first started the Health Insurance Scheme before the government became involved.[114] These health facilities are sited mostly in the rural areas. They do not only offer proper medical care to the rural population but also generate employment opportunities for many people.

The Archdiocese of Kumasi as an Example

Apart from the establishment of educational and health facilities, the Roman Catholic church in Ghana has entered into other ventures which go a long way to offer and guarantee employment to people especially, the youth. The Roman Catholic archdioceses and dioceses in Ghana have many individual projects which invariably offer employment to people. An example is the Archdiocese of Kumasi.

The Kumasi Archdiocese has among other things: a Pastoral Center, a Center for Spiritual Renewal, two guest-houses, a pharmacy, a mechanical workshop, a printing press, a bookstore and a multi-purpose store. In addition,

---

[114] Ghana News Agency, "Unbridled materialism hampers efforts at nation building", http://www.myjoyonline.com/news/reads.asp?contentid=464 (accessed January 4, 2007).

parishes in the archdiocese have their own business ventures. These include computer laboratories and stores. Some parishes, along with religious groups in the parishes, run transport services. All these projects set up in the archdiocese and the parishes have opened job opportunities to many people with particular reference to young men who otherwise would be without work or underemployed.

Credit Union

Apart from setting up the various institutions which offer employment to many people, the Roman Catholic church in Ghana is well aware of the fact that it is limited in what it can do. Simply put, it cannot offer employment to everybody. What it can offer, however, is some financial assistance to others to set up their own businesses. This is done through the setting up of credit unions in the dioceses and in the parishes. Through the credit unions, people are helped financially to set up their own small and medium scale enterprises. In this way, many people become self-employed. They are able to earn some income to care for themselves and their families.

This is the example of one archdiocese in Ghana. When one considers the other 18 archdioceses and dioceses together, it should be that the Roman Catholic church in Ghana employs a considerable percentage of the labor force and prepares many individuals for positions of leadership and governance in the private and public sector.

Response to Streetism

Streetism has increased in Ghana in recent years.[115] A large number of children and youth roam about in the streets of the cities and the big towns. Many of them are from the Northern part of the country. The youth on the streets do not receive any formal education. Furthermore, their survival on the streets often puts them at risk threatening both their health and well-being. They have poor diets and no personal hygiene. In many cases they have to struggle to earn

---

[115] Streetism must be distinguished from Thug Life in America. While the latter involves gangsterism and violent crimes with the intention of controlling certain neighborhoods in black communities in America and Canada, the former is mainly economic. The street children in Ghana want to care for themselves due to poverty at home. They engage in menial jobs in urban areas to make a living. For more on the phenomenon on Thug Life see, Kenneth J. Johnson, "Five Theses on the Globalization of Thug Life and 21st Century Missions", in *Antioch Agenda: Essays on the Restorative Church in honor of Orlando E. Costas*, 201-222.

money for food. Even the little they receive is often stolen. They are subjected to all kinds of street violence, including rape and assault.[116]

Catholic Action for Street Children

The Roman Catholic church in Ghana is not oblivious to the phenomenon of streetism. The plight of the youth living in the streets stirs the conscience of the church.[117] Consequently, a Non-Governmental Organization (NGO) to address the needs of the youth who live in the streets has been formed. It is called the Catholic Action for Street Children (CAS). The organization sends out field workers who comb the streets looking for youth, especially in the capital city of Accra. They know where the youth work and sleep. They endeavor to gain the confidence and trust of these youths. They invite them to the organization's day care center, called House of Refuge. On any given day, CAS caters for about 80 street children. At the House of Refuge, the street children are able to take baths and wash their clothes. For many of the street children, the House of Refuge is a home away from home which offers an opportunity to rest and play games.[118]

According to the Director of CAS, Jos van Dinther, children who show interest in leaving the streets are sent to Hopeland Training Center and sponsored by CAS. This is a separate facility which is located outside Accra. There, the children are tutored individually. They do intensive study which prepares them for admission to vocational schools or high schools. Once they finish their training or studies they are given money to start a business or helped to find a job. Jos van Dinther points out that through this process CAS has been able to improve the lives of about 1,500 former street children.[119]

In an effort to address the phenomenon of streetism in Ghana, research was done by CAS to identify causes of this social problem. It was found out that many of the children living in the streets were from broken families. Often they were brought up by single parents—usually their mothers. When their

---

[116] UN Integrated Regional Information Networks, "What Hope for Thousands of Street Children?"

http://www.ghanaweb.com/GhanaHomePage/NewsArchive/artikel.php?ID=120457 (accessed March 8, 2007).

[117] Peter Stow and Mike Fearon, *Youth in the City: The Church's Response to Challenge of Youth Work* (London: Hodder and Stoughton Limited, 1987).

[118] UN Integrated Information Networks, "What Hope for Thousands of Street Children?"

[119] Ibid.

mothers could no longer care for them, the children leave home to find ways of supporting themselves in urban areas.   One of the causes of streetism was traced to absent or irresponsible fathers.   Mindful of this fact, the Roman Catholic bishops in Ghana have intensified their efforts in advancing catechesis that focuses upon the family in the world today.

Formation of Christian Fathers' Association—(CFA)

The Christian Fathers Association is a new organization that has been growing in many parishes in the Roman Catholic church in Ghana.   It is a complement to the longstanding Christian Mothers' Association (CMA) which has impacted positively the missionary activities of the church in many parts of Ghana.   The CMA is found in almost all the parishes of the Roman Catholic dioceses in Ghana.   Also it has a national office at the Secretariat of the Bishops' of Ghana. It is hoped that the Christian Fathers' Association will function in ways similar to the Christian Mothers' Association.   Once it firmly takes root in all the parishes of the Roman Catholic church in Ghana, its members can serve as mentors and role models for male youth in Ghana.   This can help to raise and form male youth to be responsible husbands and fathers when they marry and take good care of their children.   This, hopefully, will help to reduce streetism to the minimum if not completely eliminated.

Drug Abuse and Crime

The Roman Catholic church in Ghana is very much aware of the tragic ill-effects of narcotics on male youth in Ghana.   The church leaders know how addictions can destroy the future of these children.   It is aware of the consequences of the drug menace on the youth themselves, their families and the society at large.   The church is aware of the fact that the usage of narcotics is linked to increase in the crime wave in the country.[120]   For this reason, the Roman Catholic church takes proactive measures so that male youth do not fall into drugs before being rescued and rehabilitated.   It has established programs like Laity Week, Youth Week and Bible Week.   During these weeks, it organizes lectures, seminars, symposia, workshops and other programs for its people. During these periods, people are invited from within and without the church to

---

[120]   United   Nations   Information   Centre,   "UNICS   reach   out   to   Youth", http://www.unic.org/index.php?option=com_content&task=view&id=45&Itemid=73 (accessed August 18, 2007).

share their expertise on pertinent issues confronting the members, especially the youth. In this way, many of the youth are made aware of the dangers of the use of narcotics. They are shown the mode of operations of drug barons and how not to fall prey to them.

Roman Catholic Chaplaincies in Schools

To make its presence felt among the youth in the schools, the bishops of Ghana have assigned full time priest-chaplains in all the countries' higher educational institutions. In this way, catechetical instruction and other Roman Catholic religious activities are carried out for students and staff. In addition, the bishops have established chaplaincies in all the public universities.[121] First and foremost, these chaplains minister to the Roman Catholic church's population. They also minister to those who may find the church's activities beneficial to their lives.[122]

Chaplaincies for Non-Catholic Schools

Since the Roman Catholic church in Ghana puts a greater value on the youth and does not want to leave young Catholics studying in public or private schools unaccompanied and unguided, it has established chaplaincies for non-Catholic institutions in the various dioceses.[123] Once again, these chaplaincies minister to Catholics who are in non-Catholic institutions. Chaplains organize weekly services and other religious programs such as days of recollection and retreats for them. Their ministry includes catechetical instructions as well as the preparation of students for the reception of the sacraments.[124]

---

[121] There are at the moment six public universities in Ghana and they all have Roman Catholic chaplaincies. The chaplains are also professors at the universities and they are paid by the government.

[122] David F. White, *Practicing Discernment with Youth: A Transformative Youth Ministry Approach* (Cleveland, Ohio: The Pilgrim Press, 2005), 36–40.

[123] Chaplaincies for Non-Catholic Institutions have been part of diocesan structures in Ghana. The chaplains are not attached to any parish and do not have any parish responsibilities. Their primary responsibility is to minister to Catholics in non-Catholic secondary, vocational and technical schools. As a diocesan structure, they draw their budgets from the dioceses.

[124] For more information on Chaplaincies for Non-Catholic Institutions see Archdiocese of Cape Coast, "Chaplaincy for Non-Catholic Institutions" http://www.archcapeghana.org/page.php?ID=16 (accessed August 21, 2007).

Prison Ministry

An image that Jesus used to describe himself during his ministry on earth is that of a shepherd. He described himself as a good shepherd. (cf. Jn. 10:1-30) As a good shepherd, he not only leads the sheep to greener pastures, (Ps. 23) but also goes in search of the lost sheep. (cf. Lk. 15:1-7) As a sacrament of Christ, the Roman Catholic church in Ghana cannot neglect the lost members who have wandered away from the large community. The church's ministers must search them out. As a church that is responsible for reaching out to those who have committed crimes and are in prison, a fully trained priest-prison chaplain works with the Prison Service of Ghana.

One person among the hierarchy of the Roman Catholic church in Ghana who has championed the cause of prison inmates in Ghana is Archbishop Peter Sarpong. When he became the bishop of Kumasi in1970, he made prison ministry a major concern of his Episcopal ministry. For the past thirty-six years, every year on December 26th, he pays a pastoral visit to the Kumasi Main Prison where he shares the word of God with the inmates and the prison officials. On December 26, 2007 during one of his yearly visits, Archbishop Sarpong appealed to the government to grant amnesty to some prisoners in the country as the country was preparing to celebrate its 50th anniversary of independence.[125] In the opinion of Archbishop Sarpong, "such a gesture would not only decongest the nation's overcrowded prisons but would also reconcile the nation as well as heal the wounds of affected families."[126] Speaking to the inmates, he called on them, "not to see themselves as outcasts, who have come to the end of the road but to use the period to take stock of their lives, forgive themselves and plan towards life after serving their jail terms."[127]

It is worth mentioning that as part of the 50th anniversary celebrations, the former President of Ghana, John Agyekum-Kuffour granted amnesty to 1,200 prisoners on humanitarian grounds.[128] These were made up of 150 first time offenders who had served half or more of their sentences; 11 who were seriously sick and incapacitated and therefore pose no threat to the larger society; 3 who were over 70 years of age and weak and 2 nursing mothers who

---

[125] Ghana News Agency, "Grant mass amnesty to prisoners at Ghana's 50th anniversary", http://www.myjoyonline.com/archives/news/200612/384.asp (accessed May 12, 2007).

[126] Ibid.

[127] Ibid.

[128] Ghana News Agency, "1,200 Prisoners receive "Jubilee" Presidential Pardon", http://www.myjoyonline.com/archives/news/200703/2229.asp (accessed May 12, 2007).

had had a change of character. In addition, 36 prisoners who were on death-row had their sentences commuted to life in prison and 3 others who had life sentences had their sentences changed to a definite term of 20 years in prison.[129]

To the extent that the Roman Catholic church in Ghana has played a pivotal role in the development of the country during the 20th century, its contribution to the larger society has been appreciated by many Ghanaians. The former Northern Regional Minister, Alhaji Mustapha Ali Idris, commended the Roman Catholic church in Ghana "for its interventions especially, in the areas of education, health, agriculture and the provision of portable water."[130] He paid tribute to the church and other religious organizations for their role in containing the conflict situation in the Dagbon area[131] and said, "when the history of the difficult situation comes to be written, your names would be printed in letters of gold."[132]

Missionary Dynamics of Empowerment—The Case of Archdiocese of Cape Coast

The Archdiocese of Cape Coast can be used as an example of what the Roman Catholic church in Ghana is doing to empower all people to live their lives as true human beings. The Archdiocese covers the entire region of the Central Region of Ghana. It is the fourth poorest region among the ten regions in Ghana after the Upper West, Upper East, and Northern Regions. It has a population of 1,593,823 according to the 2000 census. Seventy percent of the inhabitants of the region live in the rural areas. The region has low income,

---

[129] Ibid.

[130] Ghana News Agency, "Religious Bodies must lead crusade against crime, indiscipline", http://www.myjoyonline.com/archives/news/200702/1766.asp (accessed February 20, 2007).

[131] Dagbon area is paramountcy in the Northern Region of Ghana. Two tribes or gates, Abudus and Andanis are found mostly in Tamale and Yendi in the Northern Region. Both gates are legible to the throne of the paramountcy. There has been a long chieftaincy dispute between the two gates. In 2002, the conflict resulted in the murder of Yakubu Andani II, the paramount chief and 40 other people. Since then the area has been under a peace-keeping force made up of soldiers and the police. For more on the Dagbon crisis see, http://www.ghanaweb.com/GhanaHomePage//features/artikle.php?ID=74619 , (accessed August 18, 2007). See also Dzodzi Tsikata and Wayo Seini, "Identities, Inequalities and Conflicts in Ghana", Accra: November 2004, http://www.crise.ox.ac.uk/pubs/workingpaper5.pdf. , (accessed August 18, 2007).

[132] Ibid.

high incidence of unemployment, low educational opportunities and health conditions.[133]

The Cape Coast archdiocese is the first and oldest ecclesial circumscription (Vicariate, Diocese and Archdiocese) in Ghana. It is headed by Peter Cardinal Appiah-Turkson. The Catholic population in the archdiocese is about 300,000 which is about one-fifth of the population of the region. The others are Protestant (Mainline and Evangelicals), Independent churches, Muslims and followers of ATR.[134]

As a sacrament of the Christ, the Archdiocese of Cape Coast has made the mission of Jesus Christ its own. When he came into this world, Jesus said, "The Spirit of the Lord is upon me, because he has anointed me to bring good news to the poor. He sent me to proclaim release to the captives and recovery of sight to the blind, to let the oppressed go free, to proclaim the year of the Lord's favor." (Lk. 4: 18-19) The Cape Coast Archdiocese is very intentional about its missionary activities. It adopts a holistic approach to its mission of evangelization. It brings good news to the poor. It seeks to empower its people in ways that contribute to them having a more descent living as true human beings. In accordance with this aim, the archdiocese recently launched a 5-Year Development Plan (2007-2012).[135]

---

[133] Archdiocese of Cape Coast, "Programmes and Activities of the Archdiocese of Cape Coast", http://www.archcapeghana.org/page.php?id=1 (accessed May 30, 2007).

[134] Ibid.

[135]Archdiocese   of   Cape   Coast,   "CAFDIL   Project", http://www.archcapeghana.org/page.php?id=29   (accessed May 30, 2007). The Development Plan has 4 components:

Pastoral Development

The aim is to deepen its teaching in addressing theological and scriptural needs of its faithful. This is to combat the misinformation of its members by other people which hinders the growth of the faith.

Health Development

This is to address 3 major issues: (a) HIV/AIDS (b) Maternal Health (c) Health Insurance Scheme.

Development Structures

This will involve: (a) Construction of a new Cathedral (b) Construction of church buildings for communities.

Development of Socio-Economic Activities

The aim is to improve living standards in the archdiocese. This will be done through: (a) Vocation Education and Training (b) Poverty Reduction and Income-Generation Projects.

To help to accelerate the socio-economic training activities of the region, the Cape Coast Archdiocese has set up a Socio-Economic Department (SED). The vision of SED is "to promote the well being of the poor and disadvantaged groups within the Central Region of Ghana through community empowerment, entrepreneurship, development and investments."[136] To guarantee that the vision of SED does not just remain on paper, the Archdiocese has set targets to be achieved by the year 2011. These targets include:

- 1,000 viable socio-economic projects, with at least 3 in every parish or rectory (41 parishes / rectories in all).

- 2,500 youths trained in leadership skills, with at least 10 representatives from each of the parish / rectory each year.

- 500 people trained in skills of entrepreneurship.

- 2,500 enterprises created (at least one enterprise by each trained person).

- 5,000 new jobs created (at least 2 jobs by each enterprise).

- at least 30 well-established credit unions in parishes / rectories.[137]

In addition to all the works that the Cape Coast Archdiocese is doing to empower the inhabitants of the Central Region through the establishment of educational institutions and health facilities, it has made the youth of the archdiocese its special focus. It has established a Youth Office as well as Non-Catholic chaplaincy. Their responsibilities include:

- Celebrating mass for students

- Administering the sacraments

- Teaching Catholic faith, doctrine and ethics

- Providing Counseling Services

---

136 Archdiocese of Cape Coast, "Socio-Economic Development Office", http://www.archcapeghana.org/page.php?id=13 (accessed May 30, 2007).
137 Ibid.

- Organizing programs to educate students on HIV/AIDS, Drug Abuse, Career Counseling, Personal Hygiene and Responsible Behavior.[138]

The Cardinal's Foundation for Distance Learning (CAFDIL)

Education has a central place in the pastoral activities of Peter Cardinal Appiah Turkson, the Archbishop of the Cape Coast Archdiocese. Every year since 1994, he has organized vacation programs for the senior high school students in the Central Region during the month of August. This is usually followed up with "Career Counseling Workshops" for senior school students.

In pursuance of his educational policies, Peter Cardinal Appiah-Turkson has established the Cardinal's Foundation for Distance Learning. It is administered by a 12-member board of trustees. The reasons for the establishment of the Foundation are two-fold:

- "The manifest but regrettable gap in the quality and standard of education between urban and rural youth in Ghana, with the latter as the most disadvantaged.

- The general lack of knowledge and education in the rural communities."[139]

The objectives that the Foundation seeks to achieve are:

- "To help eliminate illiteracy, and to contribute to the establishment of a stable democratic society (governance) through the provision of and access to education and knowledge.

- To collaborate with Government in providing deprived and disadvantaged communities with a suitable learning process.

- To educate the largest possible audience in rural communities in the areas of healthcare, disease control, nutrition, civic and moral values.

- To accelerate the accessibility of quality education to the disadvantaged rural children, youth and adult learners.

---

[138] Archdiocese of Cape Coast, "Chaplaincy for Non-Catholic Institutions", http://www.archcapeghana.org/page.php?id=16 (accessed May 30, 2007).

[139] Archdiocese of Cape Coast, "CAFDIL Project", http://www.archcapeghana.org/page.php?id=72 (accessed June 3, 2007).

- To participate in the implementation of **Millennium Development Goal 2: Achieving Universal Primary Education in Ghana**."[140]

According to the planners of the program, the Project will be carried out in 2 principal modes: a reception only mode and an interactive mode.

> In the **'reception only mode'** of transmission, lessons and education materials will be produced on DVD and distributed to the learning centres for replay under the guidance of local learning facilitators. Supplementary materials will be broadcast from the central transmitting point in Cape Coast, and received as television signals in learning centres. For this mode, a centre will be equipped with a television set, a DVD player, decoder and an antenna for receiving transmission signals. In the **'interactive mode'** of transmission, the learning centres will be provided with equipment to enable them interact with teachers and pupils in other learning centres during lessons.[141]

Lessons for this distance learning, according to the planners, will be based on the Ghana Education Service (GES) syllabus and curriculum. Subjects which will be covered include: Mathematics, Science Education, English Language, Local Language (Fante/Twi), History/Geography of Ghana (Social Studies).[142]

The Archdiocese of Cape Coast programs are laudable initiatives. They can go a long way to raise the literacy level in the region, offer employment to the youth in particular, create wealth and reduce poverty. This can raise the standard of living of the people.

Though historically speaking the Roman Catholic church in Ghana has done much to foster the well-being of Ghanaians, it must respond to new challenges posed by a rapidly changing world and the destabilizing forces of economics, culture, politics and globalization. Key to this response is a missionary commitment to form and equip young men in Ghana with the necessary skills and moral character to shun bad example and become witnesses and ambassadors of Jesus Christ to others in the sub-region.

Since the Roman Catholic church in Ghana is not operating in isolation, it is important to acknowledge the contributions to the welfare of male youth made by other Christian denominations. Mindful of the ways in which they too contribute to the citizenry of the country and in the spirit of the ecumenical character of the Second Vatican Council, the Roman Catholic church must

---

[140] Ibid.
[141] Ibid.
[142] Ibid.

work hand in hand with other Christian denominations to deal with the crisis of male youth in Ghana. With a concerted effort, more can be achieved and the crisis of male youth transformed into possibility and realized potential.

The Responses of Other Christian Denominations

Social Position

In Chapter One, it was pointed out that when the European Protestant missionaries first came to the Gold Coast, they trained some of the youth to assist them in the work of evangelization. This approach has continued in many churches to the present-day. Attending to the needs of the youth in their churches, the Boys' and Girls' Brigades of the Methodist Church, have brought young people together and formed them for leadership. Imbued with cultural and Christian values, The Methodist church has helped them to mature as young adults and avoid delinquency. Secondly, it has helped them to become good and responsible citizens of the country and authentic Christians. Consequently, the youth of The Methodist church see themselves as an integral part of the church, they do not feel on the margins and they contribute what they can to the growth and development of the church.[143]

Education

Right from the beginning of Protestantism in the Gold Coast, education was linked with evangelization. Early on there was a firm conviction that education of the inhabitants would contribute to the work of evangelization. Therefore, the early Protestant missionaries set up schools alongside the establishment of Christian communities. They set up schools to educate boys and girls separately, an approach that continues to the present-day. At the present time, the best schools include those run by the Methodist and Presbyterian missions. Two noteworthy schools include the Wesley Girls High School and Mfantsipim in Cape Coast. The former, always comes out at top of all the secondary schools in Ghana as demonstrated by the findings of the West African Examination Council which releases the annual results for the end of the year

---

[143] Methodist Church–Ghana, "Projects", http://www.methodistchurch-gh.org/projects.htm (accessed August 21, 2007).

examinations.[144] These mission schools are noted not only for their academic excellence but also for their discipline.[145]

Due to overcrowding in the public universities, the Methodist[146] and the Presbyterian[147] churches have already established their own universities to counteract lack of discipline and under-achievement. Mention also must be made of the Pentecost and the International Central Gospel churches. They also have entered into higher education by setting up the Pentecost University[148] and the Central University College[149] respectively. The Seventh Day Adventists also have established Valley View University.[150] These mission universities offer a variety of programs including information and communication technology as well as medical sciences. They offer quality and holistic education to the youth of Ghana thereby enabling them to enter into the job-market while at the same time inculcating into them Christian principles, values and practices.

Employment

Apart from owning and sponsoring educational institutions, some Protestant churches own other facilities as well. The Methodist church of Ghana, for example, has Donewell National Insurance Company.[151] Some of these churches have clinics and hospitals. Others have stores. Still others run transport services. Besides making these churches self-supporting in terms of finance, they offer Christian service to the citizens of the country. Most importantly, they offer employment to many people especially the youth. Without these jobs, the unemployment rate of Ghana would have been higher

[144] Ibid.

[145] Presbyterian Church of Ghana, "Values", http://www.pc-ghana.org (accessed August 21, 2007).

[146] Methodist University College of Ghana, "Welcome Message", http://www.mucg.edu.gh (accessed August 21, 2007).

[147] Presbyterian Church of Ghana, "University", http://www.pc-ghana.org/university.html (accessed August 21, 2007).

[148] Wikipedia, "Pentecost University", http://en.wikipedia.org/Pentecost_University_College (accessed August 21, 2007).

[149] Central University College, "The Distinctiveness of Central University College", http://www.centraluniversity.org (accessed August 21, 2007).

[150] Valley View University, "About VVU", http://www.vvu.edu.gh/ (accessed August 21, 2007).

[151] Methodist Church Ghana, "Investment", http://www.methodistchurch-gh.org/investment.htm (accessed August 21, 2007).

and the youth would have been more vulnerable. If all these jobs had not been provided by the other Christian churches, the crime rate would have been predictably higher as well. Ghana might have gone the way of other countries in the sub-region which have been devastated by civil wars. As noted by the Minister-in-charge of the Mankranso Circuit of the Methodist church, Rev. Godfrey Augustine Gaisie, "The church has neither failed nor disappointed the country but it has rather been a partner in national development."[152]   To buttress his point, Gaisie highlighted the contributions made by church-sponsored educational institutions, health facilities and other social amenities. He went on to say, "the church has helped in preventing social vices such as alcoholism, drug addiction, indiscipline and teenage pregnancy through the spreading of the gospel."[153]

No one can dispute the fact that many Christian churches have responded to the crisis of the youth in Ghana in positive ways. However, as the Akans say, *entire nte ye a, yennyae ekye soa,*—So long as the head is there, the wearing of hats will continue. As long as the youth of Ghana are beset with all kinds of problem, the churches must commit themselves anew to the ministries of evangelization and human service.

Response from other Religions—Africa Traditional Religion (ATR) and Islam

ATR

As far as the plight of male youth is concerned the response of ATR must be seen in terms of how traditional religious values shape male youth from birth to death. ATR is not an individualistic religion. Rather, it goes to the very heart of the cultural roots of the people of Ghana.   People are born into it and its purpose is to enable the individual to live a descent and responsible life because the one must to give an account of one's stewardship after death to the Supreme Being.[154] Though more will be discussed about this in subsequent chapters I would like to make the observation that many of male youth in Ghana find themselves beset by difficulties in part because they have disregarded the time tested principles and values associated with ATR. In the

---

[152]   Ghana News Agency, "The Church has never disappointed the country", http://www.myjoyonline.com/archives/news/200703/2586.asp (accessed March 16, 2007).
[153] Ibid.
[154] Kwame Gyekye, *An Essay on African Philosophical Thought: The Akan Conceptual Scheme*, 68-84.

process of becoming infatuated with foreign cultures and materialistic individualism, they have become aliens to their own culture. Consequently, many have lost their real selves and have become double-minded and disoriented. To overcome this cultural vertigo and grow into mature and integrated human beings, male youth need to retrieve and re-appropriate their rich cultural values.[155]

Islam

The response of Islam towards the plight of male youth in Ghana can be viewed from two different perspectives. In Ghana, Muslims are mostly the Ahmadis and the Sunnis. The Ahmadis are very committed to education. They have established secondary schools and have set up an Islamic university.[156] They have contributed positively to the education and formation of male youth by fostering self-esteem and providing opportunities for gainful employment. As a consequence, many of them are found in positions of trust in the country.[157]

With regard to the Sunnis who represent majority of Muslims in Ghana the circumstances are different. Apart from attending the Arabic schools to learn the Koran by rote, the majority of young men do not enter into formal education. Many have very limited background. They tend to stay in the zongos[158] or live in the slums in urban areas where criminal activities such as mobile phone-snatching, petty robbery and property damage are usually high.[159] It is in this light that the former Vice President of Ghana, Alhaji Aliu Mahama, recently "urged parents in the zongos to encourage their children to go to

---

[155] Elom Dovlo, "Christianity, Nation-Building and National Identity in Ghana: Religious Perspective", in *Uniquely African? African Christian Identity from Cultural and Historical Perspectives,* eds. James L. Cox and Gerrie ter Haar (Trenton, NJ: Africa World Press, 2003). See also Mercy Amba Oduyoye, "Christian Engagement with African Culture" in the same book.

[156] Islamic University—Ghana, "Welcome", http://www.islamicug.com/ (accessed August 21, 2007).

[157] Some of the Muslims who occupied high positions in Ghana include: Alhaji Aliu Mahama, former Vice President of Ghana; Alhaji Yakubu Alhassan, former Second Deputy Speaker of the Parliament of Ghana and Prof. Rabiatu Amma, former Dean of the Religious Department of the University of Ghana.

[158] These are communities where people from the northern part of Ghana who are mostly Muslims stay. They are usually at the outskirts of towns and villages.

[159] Daily Graphic, "Nima battles negative image", http://www.myjoyonline.com/archives/news/200705/4494.asp (accessed May 12, 2007).

school so that in future, the Zongos could also boast of highly qualified intellectuals in all fields."[160]

One response that Muslim leaders have contributed to the plight of male youth in Ghana is reflected in their promotion of peaceful co-existence with Christians and other non-Muslims. Even after the Regensberg Lecture by Pope Benedict XVI which generated considerable anger among some Muslim communities, Ghanaian Muslims resisted any incitement to violence. For example, an unknown itinerant African-Arab from Mali was selling some videos in the streets of Accra depicting Osama bin Laden calling on all Muslims to rise up against the infidels or non-Muslims whom he described in Arabic as *Kafr*.[161] Having promoted peace and harmony in Ghana for a long time, the Executive Secretary of the National Chief Imam, Alhaji Mustapha Yahaya, issued a statement to counter-act the incitement to violence. He gave assurance that Muslims in Ghana would not be influenced by the videos of terrorist Osama bin Laden. He said that Muslims in Ghana were peace-loving and responsible and would not engage in anything violent.[162]

It is worth mentioning that earlier that same week, the National Chief Imam, Sheikh Osman Nuhu Sharabutu had spoken vehemently against the Malian preacher. He said that the preacher had been creating confusion among Muslims and Christians. He went on to point out that Muslims and Christians have been living together peacefully in Ghana and there was no reason why the preacher should be allowed to cause trouble and division. The chief Imam "advised all Muslims in Ghana to stay clear of the preacher."[163] He did not end there. As a National leader, he directed all Muslim leaders across the country to preach against the phenomenon in their mosques.[164] Unlike other African countries, efforts like these have gone a long way to promote peaceful co-existence between Muslims and non-Muslims in Ghana. As acknowledged by

---

[160]   Ghana News Agency, "Vice-President calls for tolerance", http://www.ghanaweb.com/GhanaHomePage/NewsArchive/artikel.php?ID=125048 (accessed June 3, 2007).

[161]   Joyonline, "Al-Qaeda propaganda surface on the streets of Ghana", http://www.myjoyonline.com/ghananews.asp?p=21&a=29847 (accessed October 6, 2006).

[162]   Joyonline, "Ghanaian Muslims won't be influenced by bin Laden videos", http://www.myjoyonline.com/ghananews.asp?p=3&a=30071 (accessed October 12, 2006).

[163]   Joyonline, "Chief Imam warns against alien Muslim preacher", http://www.myjoyonline.com/ghananews.asp?p=21&a=299031 (accessed October 6, 2006).

[164]   Joyonline, "Al-Qaeda propaganda videos disappear from the market", http://www.myjoyonline.com/ghananews.asp?p=21&a=30046 (accessed October 11, 2006).

the former Vice President of Ghana, Alhaji Aliu Mahama, at a papal award ceremony at the Holy Spirit Cathedral in Accra, "we, in Ghana should be grateful to God that Christians, Muslims, Animists and several other religious sects and beliefs continue to co-exist in peace and poverty irrespective of gender, ethnic or geographical divide."[165]

In sum, it can be said that both directly and indirectly Muslims in Ghana have had significant influence on the lives of young men in Ghana. Indeed, this fact has contributed to the peace and tranquility which the country enjoys in contrast to many of its neighboring states.

Summary

Chapter Two has been a discussion on the plight of male youth in Ghana. Many challenges and problems confront them day-in and day-out. Some of these are: illiteracy, streetism, unemployment, emigration, drug abuse, crime, imitation of foreign cultures and sexual promiscuity and disease. The challenges and problems do not help them to live their lives as human beings. However, they have not been left to their fate. The church as a sacrament of Christ has been working through its missionary activities to assist them so that they can live their lives as true human beings created in the image and likeness of God.[166] A lot has been done in this regard. However, more needs to be done. While the situation in Ghana may be better compared to other African nations, the young men in Ghana must be helped to be able to face the challenges of today's globalization. Secondly, they can become ambassadors and witnesses to other young men in the sub-region in order to consolidate and promote peace and progress.[167]

The next chapter discusses maturity and identity formation of male youth.

---

[165] Ghana News Agency, "Religious co-existence in Ghana is priceless", http://www.ghanaweb.com/GhanaHomepage/NewsArchive/artikel.php?ID=123939 (accessed May 12), 2007.

[166] David F. White, *Practicing Discernment with Youth: A Transformative Youth Ministry Approach*, (Cleveland, Ohio: The Pilgrim Press, 2005), 36-40; 42-61.

[167] Constance R. Banzikiza, *Consolidating Unity and Peace in Africa*, (Eldoret, Kenya: AMECEA Gaba Publication, 2004), 42-61.

CHAPTER THREE

"I am because we are and since we are, therefore, I am": Maturity and Male Identity Formation: Recovering an African Moral Vision for "Persons-in-Relation": Insights from Kwame Gyekye, John Macmurray and Augustine of Hippo

> You stir man to take pleasure in praising you, because you have made us for yourself,
> and our heart is restless until it rests in you
>
> Augustine.[1]

The human person for a long time has been described as a social being. No one person is an island. For this reason, human beings often bond together. Africa has been noted for its sense of community and solidarity.[2] In spite of this, the individual person cannot be neglected. The relationship that exists between the individual and community is a delicate one. In this chapter, I emphasize that the individual person was created by God in a unique way. However, one's existence is always co-terminous with the existence of others. This is to point out to male youth in Africa that individualism is not according to their nature. Consequently, they must always see themselves as persons in-relation. Three persons namely, Kwame Gyekye, John Macmurray and Augustine whose insights can help in the formation of male youth are discussed in this chapter.

The chapter is divided into three parts. The first part looks at Kwame Gyekye, a Ghanaian philosopher. It discusses African values and the individual and the community in African social politic.

---

[1] Augustine, *Confessions*, trans. Henry Chadwick (Oxford: University Press, 1991), Bk 1: 1.
[2] For more on African sense of community-living see, Polycarp Ikuenobe, *Philosophical Perspectives on Communalism and Morality in African Traditions* (New York: Lexington Books, 2006), 51-91.

The second part draws upon the insights of John Macmurray, a Scottish philosopher and theologian. Drawing upon two key texts *Self as Agent* and *Persons-in-Relation*, Macmurray is proposed to male youth and those who minister to them as a resource that supports their training to consider as they strive for the full humanization.

The third part looks at the life of Augustine. It sets him up as a model that male youth in Africa can look up to and emulate.

Kwame Gyekye (1931-)

Kwame Gyekye is a Ghanaian philosopher, born in 1931 in Kumasi, Ghana. From 1948-1952, he did his secondary education at Adisadel College in Cape Coast. After that he went to the University of Ghana. In 1958, he completed and went to Oxford University to study for the Bachelor of Philosophy degree.[3] He did his doctoral studies at Harvard University specializing in Graeco-Arabic Philosophy. He is currently a Professor of Philosophy at the University of Ghana and a Visiting Professor of African and African-American Studies at Temple University in Philadelphia. He is a Fellow at the Woodrow Wilson International Center for Scholars, the Smithsonian Institute, and a lifetime Fellow of the Ghana Academy of Arts and Sciences. Kwame Gyekye's interest is in the development of modern African Philosophy.[4]

African Philosophical Thought

In dealing with African Philosophical Thought, Kwame Gyekye points to the generally accepted notion that the African is religious. This is due to the numerous religious belief systems and practices. He observes that "some of these are philosophical in that they deal with such fundamental questions as the meaning of life, the origins of all things, death, and related questions. In religion, we seek answers to questions of ultimate existence; philosophy also is concerned with similar questions of ultimate existence."[5] According to Kwame Gyekye, some people have questioned whether there is any thing as African Philosophy. Such people are quick to accept African Theology, African Art and African Music. However, they shudder at the mention of an African

---

[3]   Global   Oneness   Commitment,   "Kwame   Gyekye",
http://www.experiencefestival.com/kwame_gyekye (accessed September 20, 2007).
[4] Wikipedia, "Kwame Gyekye", http://en.wikipedia.org/wiki/Kwame_Gyekye (accessed September 20, 2007).
[5] Kwame Gyekye, *An Essay on African Philosophical Thought*, 8.

Philosophy. He notes that "African Philosophical ideas are not to be found in documents, for traditional African Philosophy is not a written philosophy, although this does not mean that it cannot be written down."[6] He argues that "Socrates did not write anything, although he inherited a written culture; but we know, thanks to Plato, that he "philosophized."[7] Kwame Gyekye believes that "African Philosophical Thought is expressed both in the oral literature and in the thoughts and actions of the people. Thus, a great deal of philosophical material is embedded in the proverbs, myths and folktales, folksongs, rituals, beliefs, customs, and traditions of the people, in their art and symbols and in their sociopolitical institutions and practices."[8] This assertion of Kwame Gyekye is affirmed by Kwasi Wiredu, another Ghanaian philosopher, when he said

> Ghanaian culture is a highly philosophical culture. This is seen in the fact that 'traditional life in our country is guided by many points by conceptions that might broadly be called philosophical.' Thus, customs relating to procreation, work, leisure, death and sundry circumstances of life are based on or reflect doctrines of God, mind, goodness, destiny and human personality that most adult Ghanaians will articulate at the slightest prompting.[9]

In the opinion of Kwame Gyekye, African Philosophical Thought is not theoretical and abstract. Rather, it is experiential and practical. He observes, "African Philosophy is oriented toward action and practical affairs. For the traditional Akan thinker there is an intimate articulation of a concrete way of life, not just a tissue of well-laundered concepts."[10]

An important element of African Philosophical Thought that Kwame Gyekye points out is its dualistic nature. There is a strong belief in the spiritual world. However, there is no sharp distinction between the physical and the spiritual worlds. The two worlds are interdependent. People from this world enter the spiritual world after death while those in the spiritual world are

---

[6] Ibid., 10.

[7] Ibid. For more on his description of African Philosophical Thought see his book, *Tradition and Modernity: Philosophical Reflections on the African Experience* (Oxford: Oxford University Press, 1997), 3-34.

[8] Kwame Gyekye, *An Essay on African Philosophical Thought*, 3.

[9] Kwasi Wiredu, "The Ghanaian Tradition of Philosophy", in *Person and Community: Ghanaian Philosophical Studies*, 1, eds. Kwasi Wiredu and Kwame Gyekye, (Washington, D. C: The Council for Research in Values and Philosophy, 1992), 1.

[10] Kwame Gyekye, *An Essay on African Philosophical Thought*, 67.

interested in what goes on in the physical world. Thus, for him, "The Akan metaphysical world is thus a dual world, notwithstanding the fact that the activities of the inhabitants of the spiritual world extend to, and are "felt" in the physical world."[11]   Among the pantheon of spiritual beings in the African metaphysical world is God—the Supreme Being.[12]

Akan Concept of God

Among the Akans, the Supreme Being is called, *Onyame* or *Nyame*. Kwame Gyekye observes that

> *Onyame* is the Absolute Reality, the origin of all things, the absolute ground, the sole and whole explanation of the universe, the source of all existence. Absolute Reality is beyond and independent of the categories of time, space and cause. As *tetekwaframmua* (He who endures from ancient times and forever), and *odomankoma* (Infinite, Boundless, Absolute, Eternal), *Onyame* transcends time and is thus free from the limitations of time, an eternity without beginning, without an end.[13]

He goes on to say, "As the ultimate source of being, *Onyame* created the whole universe, including the deities or lesser spirits, out of nothing. He is the *oboadee*, the creator of the thing, the *borebore*, originator. At some point in the distant past, *Onyame* created the world, and having brought the world into existence, he sustains it with his infinite power (*otumfoo*). All things end up in him (*atoapem*), that is into him all things are dissolved."[14]   For Kwame Gyekye, among the Akans, the Supreme Being is not only the creator but also the sustainer of the world. The Supreme Being has interest in the world and is deeply involved in what goes on in the world. The Akans are aware of this and have a very close relationship with the Supreme Being.   For this reason, short prayers, invocations and references are constantly made to the Supreme Being. Some of these prayers are:

1.   At the start of any undertaking the Akan would say, "*Onyame*, help me" (*Nyame boa me*).

---

[11] Ibid., 69.

[12] For more on the spiritual world in ATR see Keith Ferdinando, "The Spiritual Realm in Traditional African Religion", in *Angels and Demons: Perspectives and Practice in Diverse Religious Traditions*, 21-41.

[13] Ibid., 70.

[14] Ibid., 71.

2. The expression "If it is the will of *Onyame*" (*se Onyame pe a*), is constantly on people's lips at the start, or in the course, of a pursuit.

3. If one inquired about another's health, the latter would almost invariably say, "By the grace of *Onyame*, I am all right" (*Onyame adom me ho ye*).

4. Salutations and words of farewell are couched in the form of prayer to *Onyame*. For instance, "May you go in the company of *Onyame*" (*wo ne Nyame nko*); "I leave you in the hands of Onyame" (*me de Nyame gya wo*).

5. If one narrowly escapes a disaster one would say, "If *Onyame* had not intervened... (*se Onyame ampata...*). "*Onyame* alone" (*Onyame nko ara*).

6. The priest at the shrine of a deity, when consulted in the case of illness would say: "if *Onyame* permits, I shall cure you" (*Onyame ma kwan a, mesa wo yadee*).[15]

These references and invocations are indicators of the Akan belief in the Supreme Being.

In Akan societies, all human beings are creatures of the Supreme Being. For this reason, the Akans say, *nnipa nyinaa ye Onyame mma, obiara ne ho a oye asaase ba*—All human beings are children of God and no one is a child of the earth. Human beings do not only relate to the Supreme Being, but also they relate to one another. Communitarianism is emphasized among many African societies including the Akans. In the next section, the relationship between the individual and the community is looked at.

The Individual and Community

One area that Kwame Gyekye's contribution has been greatly felt as far as African Philosophical Thought is concerned is the place of the individual in the community. African culture is noted for its communitarianism. It is for this reason that many African leaders in the past and today have advocated for

---

[15] Kofi Asare Opoku, "Aspects of Akan Worship", in *The Black Experience in Religion*, ed. C. Eric Lincoln (New York: Doubleday, 1974), 297-8, quoted by Kwame Gyekye, *An Essay on African Philosophical Thought*, 71.

Socialism instead of Capitalism since they believe the former is more in tune with the African culture.[16]

Kwame Gyekye does not doubt the fact that communitarianism or communalism is at the heart of African heart. He believes in the Akan saying that *se onipa firi soro besi a, obesi kurom*—When a person descends from the sky into this world, he/she comes into a town. He acknowledges that the human person's relationship with a community is a natural one. However, Kwame Gyekye challenges the idea that it is the community that gives the individual his/her personhood. Secondly, he is of the opinion that the community's rights cannot negate the rights of the individual. He argues that "at the practical level communitarianism must realize that allowing free rein for the exercise of individual rights—which obviously includes the exercise of the unique qualities, talents and dispositions of the individuals—will enhance the cultural development and success of the community."[17] He goes on to say, "if communitarianism were to shrug off individual rights, it would be not only show itself as an inconsistent moral and political theory, but in practical terms would also saw off the branch on which it was going to sit."[18]

In his book, *An Essay on African Philosophical Thought: The Akan Conceptual Scheme*, Kwame Gyekye discusses the individual and the social order. He believes that the social order in African societies does not fall neatly into either community or individuality. He points out that "it would be more correct to describe the African social order as amphibious, for it manifests features of both community and individuality. The African social order is, strictly speaking, neither purely communalistic nor purely individualistic."[19] He thinks that "the concept of communalism in African social thought is often misunderstood, as is the place of the individual in the communal social order."[20] In his opinion, "Communalism as conceived in African thought is not a negation of individualism; rather, it is the recognition of the limited character of the possibilities of the individual, which limited possibilities whittle away the

[16] Cf. Kwame Nkrumah, *Conscience: Philosophy and Ideology for Decolonization and Development with Particular Reference to the African Revolution* (London: Heinemann, 1964). See also Leopold S. Senghor, *On African Socialism*, trans. Mercer Cook (New York: Praeger, 1964). For more on the Socialist Agenda see Kwame Gyekye, *Tradition and Modernity*, 144–170.
[17] Kwame Gyekye, "Person and Community in Akan Thought", in *Person and Community: Ghanaian Philosophical Studies*, 1, 115.
[18] Ibid.
[19] Kwame Gyekye, *An Essay on African Philosophical Thought*, 154.
[20] Ibid.

individual's self-sufficiency."[21] It is for this reason that the Akans say, *baako were aduro a egu*—If one person scraps the bark of a tree for medicine, the pieces fall down. It is also said, *benkum dware nifa, na nifa nso adware benkum*—The left arm washes the right arm and the right arm also washes the left arm. Thus for the Akan, there is no competition between the community and individuality. It is not a matter of choice. In contributing to the community, the individual's welfare or well-being is catered for since the community is made of individuals. As each individual puts in his/her effort, the common good is served and the individual has his/her wishes fulfilled. So there is a reciprocal relationship between communality and individuality as far as Akan social order is concerned.

In the opinion of Kwame Gyekye, some scholars from non-communalistic backgrounds and mentalities think that there are no individual rights in Africa. They think that communality absolves individuality in African social order.[22] It is a mistake to think along those lines. In the Akan social order, it is said, *abusua te se kwae. Wowo akyire a, ebo mu. Woben ho a na wohunu se edua biara si dee esi*—The clan is a like a forest. When you are far away, you think it is crammed together. When you get closer then you will realize that they are individual and separate trees. The proverb does not mean that communality is a farce in Akan societies. Rather, it means that communality does not destroy individuality. The individual in the community still maintains his/her identity. As Kwame Gyekye notes again, "The concept of communalism, as it is understood in Akan thought, therefore does not overlook individual rights, interests, desires, and responsibilities, nor does it imply the absorption of the individual will into the "communal will" or seek to eliminate individual responsibility and accountability. Akan social thought attempts to establish a delicate balance between the concepts of communality and individuality."[23] Consequently, he concludes

> In Akan social philosophy, then individualism and communalism are not seen as exclusive and opposing concepts, as they are in capitalism and communist philosophies. There the two concepts are poles apart because both positions have, in my view, become unnecessarily exaggerated. On the one hand, the value attached to the idea of the individual has been so exaggerated in the capitalist system as to detach the person from the natural communal social environment. On the other hand, the communist system runs berserk, brandishing its sword indiscriminately against

[21] Ibid., 156.
[22] Ibid., 158.
[23] Ibid., 160.

practically any trace of individuality. Neither system appears to offer the greatest opportunity for the full development of the human spirit.[24]

For Kwame Gyekye, "The individual person has a life to live, and so must have plans. The attainment of the goal imposes on the self the responsibility or duty to develop his natural abilities. Therefore, the duty one has toward the community and its members do not—should not—enjoin him to give over his whole life and be oblivious of his personal well-being."[25] Kwame Gyekye summarizes his discussion on the individual and the community in this way:

> In African social thought human beings are regarded not as individuals but as groups of created beings inevitably and naturally inter-related and interdependent. This does not necessary lead to the submerging of the initiative or personality of the individual, for after all the well-being and success of the group depend on the unique qualities of its individual members—but individuals whose consciousness of their responsibility to the group is ever present because they identify themselves with the group.[26]

Kwame Gyekye, therefore, advocates against any form of radical or extreme communalism. He prefers a moderate communalism where community rights do not submerge individual rights.[27]

The mutual relationship between the individual and the community depends very much on good morality. The question is what is the source of African morality? Is it based on religion or not?

African Morality: Religious or Non-Religious?

It was indicated in Chapter One that Africans have a profound religious sense. They cannot live without religion. It is not for nothing that scholars have described the African with all kinds of terms: John Mbiti—"notoriously religious"[28]; Kofi Abrefa Busia—"intensely and pervasively religious"[29]; Malcom J. McVeigh—"Deeply religious"[30]; E. C. Parrinder—"incurably

[24] Ibid., 162.
[25] Kwame Gyekye, "Person and Community in Akan Thought", in *Person and Community: Ghanaian Philosophical Studies*, 1, 120.
[26] Kwame Gyekye, *An Essay on African Philosophical Thought*, 210.
[27] Kwame Gyekye, *Tradition and Modernity*, 61.
[28] John Mbiti, *African Religions and Philosophy*, 1.
[29] Kofi Abrefa Busia, *Africa in Search of Democracy*, (New York: Praeger, 1967), 1.
[30] Malcom J. McVeigh, *God in Africa*, 103. Quoted by Kwame Gyekye, *An Essay on Africa Philosophical Thought*, 204.

religious."[31] There is a strong belief in the Supreme Being. This strong belief in the Supreme Being has led scholars to argue whether morality in African societies is dictated by religion. Opinions are divided on this issue. People like Peter Sarpong and J. N. Kudadjie believe that religion is the motivating factor in African Morality. According to Peter Sarpong,

> The real source and norm of unrestricted universally recognized and binding moral values in the religion of West Africa is the Supreme Being, the Pure King, the Perfect King. In him alone can be resolved the problem of right conduct. In order to guide us, the Supreme Being has given each person an inner voice, a conscience by which we can judge our conduct. A person is good or bad inasmuch as he obeys or disobeys the inner voice![32]

For Kudadjie, "to neglect the role of religion in any attempt to create a moral community would be an exercise in futility."[33] He goes on to say, "the religious claim is that when the inner man is renewed and God's power dwells in the person, his desires change, his life is ennobled, and his moral sense is strengthened and toughened."[34]

Kwame Gyekye has a different opinion. He does not think that religion is the motivating factor in African morality. He notes that "in Akan moral thought the sole criterion of goodness is the welfare or well-being of the community."[35] He strongly argues that "The guiding principles of African morality originate not from divine pronouncements as such, but from considerations of human welfare and interest. Reverence for non-human entities is not necessary considered to lessen one's devotion to the welfare and interests of human beings in this life. The (alleged) religiosity of African people, even if true, is therefore not at variance with the pursuit of human welfare on earth."[36] This position of Kwame Gyekye is supported by Kwasi Wiredu's assertion that "African conceptions of morals would seem generally to be of a humanistic orientation… One important implication of the founding of value on human interests is the independence of morality from religion in the Akan

[31] E. C. Parrinder, *Religion in Africa* (Penguin: Hammondsworth, 1969), 9.

[32] Peter Sarpong, *Unpublished Lecture Notes*, 79.

[33] J. N. Kudadjie, "Towards Moral and Social Development in Contemporary Africa: Insights from Dangme Traditional Moral Experience", in *Person and Community: Ghanaian Philosophical Studies*, 1, 221.

[34] Ibid.

[35] Kwame Gyekye, *An Essay on African Philosophical Thought*, 132.

[36] Ibid., 208.

outlook.   What is good in general is what promotes human interests."[37] Furthermore, Kwame Gyekye's position is supported by many Akan proverbs. Some of these proverbs are:

1.   *Wo amma wo yonko antwa anko a, wo nso wontwa nko duru*—If you do not allow your neighbor to cross first, you also will never reach your destination.

2.   *Wode wonsa tea rekyere obi soo no, na enan no a aka no erehwe wo so*—As you use one finger to point to your neighbor, the rest of the four will be pointing to you.

3.   *Aba a wode boo Takyi no, wode bebo Baah*—The cane that was used to whip Takyi will be the same cane that will be used to whip Baah.

4.   *Dee yede ye wo a nnye wo de no, mmfa nye wo yonko*—Do not do what you do not like to your neighbor.

I would only agree with Kwame Gyekye that the initial motivating factor of Akan morality is the welfare or well-being of the person. However, it cannot be devoid of religion. They are inter-related since all human beings are considered as children of the Supreme Being. Therefore, it can be said that while the immediate cause of Akan morality is human welfare and interests, the remote cause is the belief in the Supreme Being—a religious factor.   This is a position that Kwame Gyekye assumes in his later writings when he says,

> The insistent claim that every human being is a child of God does seem to have some moral overtones or relevance, grounded, as it must be, in the conviction that there must be something intrinsically valuable in God. Human beings, as children of God, by reason of their having been created by God and possessing, in the African belief, a divine element called soul, ought to be held as of intrinsic value, as ends in themselves, worthy of respect. A concept of human dignity can be linked with, or derived from the concepts of intrinsic value and respects! Also implicit in the proverb is the equality of the moral worth of *all* human beings—of all the children of God. Concepts of human dignity, intrinsic value, and equal moral worth generate a motion of moral rights that, as deriving ultimately from God or as belonging fundamentally to every human being as a creature of God, could be linked with the notion of innate or natural rights, that is to say, a human rights concept can certainly be said to be already involved in conceptions

---

[37] Kwasi Wiredu, "Moral Foundations of an African Culture", in *Person and Community: Ghanaian Philosophical Studies*, 1, 194.

of human dignity. The conception of human dignity compels the recognition of rights not only in an individualistic but also in a communal setting.

It is thus possible to derive a theory of individual rights from conceptions of the intrinsic worth of a human being that are themselves based on theism.[38]

This first part has been a discussion on Kwame Gyekye, a Ghanaian philosopher. He has made significant contributions to an understanding of African Philosophical Thought, the relationship between the individual and the community and what motivates African morality. In all these, he tries to show how the way of life in traditional societies of Africa is affected by contemporary situations. As indicated at the beginning of the chapter, the second part looks at John Macmurray whose insights can help in the formation of young men in Africa.

The Man—John Macmurray (1891-1976)

John Macmurray was a Scottish philosopher. He was brought up in a home where religion was taken very seriously. He had wanted to become a scientist but was persuaded by his parents to study classics at Oxford. A year after attending Oxford, the First World War broke out. He served in the British army in France during the war. He said that two events happened in his life that deeply affected and changed his life. The first was his brush with death during the war. That really shook his life. The second was his decisive break with organized religion.[39]

After the war, Macmurray wanted to work for the League of Nations so that he might take part in activities that could prevent the recurrence of war. He decided against that option and instead went to Oxford to teach as a philosopher. The Oxford he returned to after the war was dominated by idealism and realism. Macmurray was not pleased with either two streams of thoughts. As a philosopher he was very much interested in the person and the personal. He authored *The Self as Agent* which was originally given as *The Gifford Lectures* he presented at the University of Glasgow in 1953–1954. Some of his books include: *The Form of the Personal, The Self as Agent* and *Persons in Relation.* Some of these reflections were presented on radio broadcasts as well.

John Macmurray's legacy and life contributed a great deal to the field of philosophy, theology, psychology, politics, ethics and education. In the

---

[38] Kwame Gyekye, *Tradition and Modernity*, 63.

[39] John Macmurray, *Search For Reality In Religion* (London: Headley Brothers Ltd., 1965), 17.

following section, I present some thoughts on the particular relevance of John Macmurray for the subject at hand, addressing the crisis of male youth in Africa.

The Self as Agent

In his book, *The Self as Agent*, John Macmurray attacks Rene Descartes' philosophical dictum, '*cogito ergo sum*'—I think, therefore, I am. According to Macmurray, "from the standpoint of the '*cogito*' which establishes a dualism of mind and body, sense perception is a mystery, because as sense it is bodily while as perception it is mental."[40] For him, the self is not "I think." Rather, it is "I do." He believed that "The Self as agent is an existent, and its correlative therefore, is also existent."[41] The correlative of the Agent-self he refers to as the other.[42] Macmurray argued that "The Self does not first know itself and determine an objective; and then discover the Other in carrying out its intention. The distinction of the Self and the Other is the awareness of both; and the existence of both is the fact that their opposition is a practical, and not a theoretical opposition."[43]

On sense perception, Macmurray made a distinction between tactual perception and vision experience. He pointed out that "tactual perception is *necessary* perception in action. To touch anything is to exert pressure upon it, however, slight, and therefore, to modify it. Visual perception, on the contrary, excludes any operation upon its object, and is a perception of passivity."[44] He went on to say, "Tactual perception is always perception in action." On the other hand, "all visual experience is the production of an image. Visual *perception* is the reference of an image to the other."[45]

On the implications of action, Macmurray pointed out that movement and knowledge are inseparable aspects of all action, not separate elements in a complex. To represent action as consisting of a cognition which is the cause of a movement is to misrepresent the unity of action radically."[46]

---

[40] John Macmurray, *The Self As Agent* (New York: Humanity Books, 1999), 104.
[41] Ibid., 106.
[42] Ibid.
[43] Ibid., 109.
[44] Ibid., 107.
[45] Ibid., 113.
[46] Ibid., 128.

Macmurray pointed out that "in action, then, the Agent generates a past of actualizing a possibility." For him, "The act, therefore, is to determine; and the Agent is the determiner. To determine is to make actual what is apart from acting, merely possible."[47] He believed that "to possess free-will is simply to be able to determine the indeterminate, that is, the future."[48]

Another implication for Macmurray was that "action is the actualizing of a possibility, and as such it is a choice."[49] He made a distinction between an "act" and an "event". "To call any apprehended change an 'act' is to refer it to a non-agent. To express the distinction between acts and events, therefore, we say: for an event there is a cause for an act there is a reason."[50]

He believed that "the long argument of modern philosophy has moved steadily in the direction of an atheistic conclusion; and with it the historical development of our civilization has moved towards irreligion."[51]

Given these propositions, I believe that Macmurray enables those concerned with the plight of male youth to see the human person always as a '*doer*'. This does not mean that thinking is not necessary. It is an important intellectual exercise always geared towards doing something better later on. Consequently, idleness and laziness among young men must be eschewed. They must be always concerned about doing something better to care for themselves, their families and their communities.

Analysis of *The Self As Agent*

John Macmurray's attack on the Descartes' maxim, '*cogito ergo sum*' was a brave attempt to go against the current of his time. In seeing the *Self*, not as a "thinker" but as an "agent" or a "doer" was a major break-through. It challenged and still challenges the kind of dualism that has dominated the world for some time. The human person is not in the mode of thinking all the time. Rather, the person is either sleeping, or walking, or working, or doing something. When the person moves away to be alone "to think", even the moving away "to think" is itself doing something.

Secondly, "the thinking" itself is an action. When somebody moves away "to think", the intention always is to do something better later on. So the art of

---

[47] Ibid., 134.
[48] Ibid.
[49] Ibid., 139.
[50] Ibid., 148.
[51] Ibid., 221.

"thinking" is for the purpose of action. Hence, Macmurray's argument that the *Self* is an agent.

Furthermore, in considering the *Self* as a thinker Macmurray argued that certain categories of persons are excluded from full personhood. For example, would those who are mentally handicapped or challenged, be denied personhood? In fact, some people may be mentally-challenged, however, they can do certain things to the amazement of many people. Moving from the *Self* as a "thinker" to the *Self* as an "agent" or a "doer" stretches the narrow confines of intellectually bound "selfhood" and personhood. Macmurray's contribution draws our attention to the fact that all action precedes thinking and the art of thinking is for the betterment of action.

Persons-in-Relation

According to the Macmurray, "the idea of an isolated agent is self-contradictory. Any agent is necessarily in relation to the Other. Apart from this essential relation he does not exist."[52]   In his opinion, "I exist as an individual only in a personal relation to the other individuals."[53] He went on to say, "I can know another *as a person* only by entering into personal relation with him. Without this I can know him only by observation and inference; only objectively."[54]

Macmurray made a distinction between personal and impersonal relationships. It is the latter when the person is treated not as a person but as an object. It is the former when the person is treated as a 'person'. Relations can be direct or indirect. "Direct relations are those which involve a personal acquaintance with one another on the part of the persons to relate. Indirect relations exclude this condition: they are relations between persons who are not personally known to one another."[55]

With regard to the mother and child relationship, Macmurray rejected the widespread belief that "the human infant is an animal organism which becomes rational and acquires a human personality, in the process of growing up."[56] He said, "We can dismiss at once any notion that we are born with a set of 'animal' impulses which later take on a rational form. There is no empirical evidence for

---

[52] John Macmurray, *Persons in Relation* (New York: Humanity Books, 1999), 24.

[53] Ibid., 28.

[54] Ibid.

[55] Ibid., 43.

[56] Ibid., 44.

anything like this, and it is inherently improbable."[57] According to Macmurray, "the infant has a need which is not simply biological but personal, a need to be in relationship with the mother, and in conscious perceptual relation with her."[58] He concluded, "The human infant, then being born into, and adapted to, common life with the mother, is a person from birth. His survival depends upon reason, that is to say, upon action and not upon reaction to stimulus."[59]

According to Macmurray, "the development of a person from infancy to maturity is a process of acquiring skills, or in other terms, of forming habits."[60] For him, "the first aspect of this development which we must notice might be described as the differentiation of the Other."[61] Macmurray was of the opinion that "the child has to learn to discriminate and to co-ordinate the manifold of feeling, sense and muscular movement: he has to learn to stand, to walk, to feed himself, to put his clothes on, to speak, and in general 'to acquire and establish in himself the mechanisms of personal activity."[62] "If a child is to grow up, he must learn stage by stage, to do for himself what has up to time been done by the mother."[63]

In the second part of *Persons in Relation* (chapters 6-10), Macmurray rejected Thomas Hobbes' concept of society that said that the persons, who composed society were by nature, isolated units, afraid of one another, and continuously on the defensive. For Macmurray, "the history of human society moves from original heterogeneity to an increasing homogeneity. Its continuity is a continuity of action, not of process. Any human society, however, primitive, is maintained by the intention of its members to maintain it."[64] He went on to say, "human beings have no instincts, and a human society is not a herd. Any human society is a moral entity. Its basis is the universal and necessary intention to maintain the personal relation which makes the human individual a person, and his life a common life."[65]

Macmurray, however, made a distinction between a society and a community. For him, a society "refers to those forms of human association in

---

[57] Ibid., 52.
[58] Ibid., 49.
[59] Ibid., 62.
[60] Ibid., 64.
[61] Ibid., 75.
[62] Ibid., 65.
[63] Ibid., 88.
[64] Ibid., 128.
[65] Ibid.

which the bond of unity is negative or impersonal." On the other hand, a community "rests upon a positive apperception by its members of the relation which unites them as a group. It is a personal, not an impersonal unity of persons."[66] He went on to say that "a community is for the sake of friendship and presupposes love… Society is maintained by a common constraint that is to say by acting in obedience by law."[67]

When it comes to religion, Macmurray rejected Karl Marx's and Sigmund Freud's criticisms against religion. According to him, "no human society, from the most primitive to the most completely civilized, has ever existed without a religion of some kind. This can only signify that the source of religion must lie in some characteristic of human experience which is common and universal."[68] He thought that "religion is the reflective activity which expresses the consciousness of community: or more tersely, religion is the celebration of communion."[69] This celebration of their fellowship is their religious activity.[70]

According to Macmurray, "religion as a mode of reflection is concerned with the knowledge of the personal other." He believed that "religious reflection universalizes its problem through the idea of a universal Person to whom all particular agents stand in an identical relation. This is the idea of God, and religious knowledge is rightly described as the knowledge of God. Such knowledge will apply universally to all instances of personal relationship."[71]

On devices of politics, Macmurray pointed out that "a separation of moral and political obligation could only be maintained theoretically. It is impossible in practice to divide my activities into two kinds—those which are to be judged morally and those which are to be judged politically."[72]

Analysis of *Persons-in-Relation*

The human person has been described as a social being. It is also said that no person is an island. The human person is always transcending himself/herself. Macmurray correctly attacked individualism. Individualism can lead to

---

[66] Ibid., 147.
[67] Ibid., 151.
[68] Ibid., 156.
[69] Ibid. 162.
[70] Ibid.
[71] Ibid., 169.
[72] Ibid., 196.

egocentricism. It can also lead to narcissism. As a social being, the person is always in relation. One cannot think of himself/herself without reference to others. The assertion of Macmurray that "I" always go with "You" resonates well with what John Mbiti said, "I am because we are, and since we are, therefore, I am."[73]   In Africa societies, communalism is greatly emphasized without neglecting the individual. One is always in relationship with others. There is always a sense of community and a sense of solidarity when one thinks of the *Self*.

The concept of *Persons in Relation* from Macmurray while emerging from the European context resonates well in the African context. For the cultured African, individualism is anti-society. It is un-African. It is un-Ghanaian.

Macmurray noted that the development of a person from infancy and maturity is a process of acquiring skills or habits. He believed that the first stage of this development process is the differentiation from the other. This parallels in some ways the thoughts of Erik Erickson's *Eight Stages of Man*.[74] If a child is to grow up, he/she must learn stage by stage to do for himself/herself what has up to that time been done by another.

Freedom in the Modern World

In his book, *Freedom in the Modern World*, Macmurray discussed the dilemma that was confronting Europe during the early part of the twentieth century. He was deeply convinced that it was not an economic or industrial one. They were mere symptoms. Underneath the crisis was something deeper. Macmurray said that they would never solve the economic troubles unless they solved the dilemma in their spiritual lives, which produced them. He pointed out that they had lost faith and when you lose faith, you lose the power of action and the capacity of choice. The result is that you lose the grip on reality and your sanity.[75]

Continuing his analysis of the crisis at that time, Macmurray juxtaposed science with religion. He blamed the emphasis put on science at the expense of religion. He pointed out that science could not provide faith for the modern world. It could only provide the means of achieving what they wanted to achieve. Macmurray was of the view that western science was rooted in Christianity and stood or fell with it. Therefore, if Christianity was thrown

---

[73] John Mbiti, *African Religions and Philosophy*, 108.

[74] Erik H. Erickson, *Childhood and Society* (New York: Norton, 1993).

[75] John Macmurray, *Freedom in the Modern World* (New York: Humanity Books, 1992), 6.

overboard in order to choose science the very basis of science was destroyed. So for him, it was impossible to choose between science and religion, since our faith in science was itself a religious faith.[76] This assertion of Macmurray that western science is rooted in Christianity is very debatable. Does it mean that before Christianity, there was no science?

On the dilemma in our emotional life, Macmurray indicated that all along the scale had been tilted heavily in favor of the intellect over the emotions. However, he was deeply convinced that unless the emotions and the intellect were in harmony, rational action would be paralyzed. For him, "knowledge is power, but emotion is the master of our values of the uses, therefore, to which we put our power."[77] He thought that emotionally human beings were primitive, childish, undeveloped. Therefore, we have tastes, the appetites, the interests and apprehensions of children.[78] Macmurray concluded that the source of the crisis that was confronting Europe at his time could only be traced to the emotional.[79]

According to Macmurray, "the roots of religion are in the emotional life. That is not to make the common mistake of saying that religion is simply a matter of feeling. It is emphatically not." Rather, "it is the response of the whole of our personality to the whole of life; and it, therefore, includes the intellectual side of our nature, of necessity."[80] He defined religion as "a way of living, and neither merely a set of beliefs about the world nor a set of feelings about the world—although because it is a way of living it includes both of these."[81]

In discussing reality and freedom, Macmurray said that unreal things were just non-existent.[82] However, he pointed out that unreal things could be real for us, because we think they are real. If we do so we think that they are real. He went on to say that when we took something unreal to be real, we thought that something was what it was not. There are lots of things which seem to be what they are not and which tend to deceive us, for example, a mirage. According to him, "the real is the significant, and therefore whenever we use our minds in a way that has no significance our thinking is unreal. This will

[76] Ibid., 18.
[77] Ibid., 24.
[78] Ibid.
[79] Ibid., 29.
[80] Ibid., 31.
[81] Ibid.
[82] Ibid., 75.

occur, in the first place, if the things we think about have no real significance."[83] Applying this to people, Macmurray said that unreal people are egocentric. They are out of touch with the world outside them and tend in upon themselves. Due to that they are highly self-conscious. Their interest is really in themselves and not in the world outside them.[84]

For Macmurray, to act freely means that the person acts without constraint and that the act is done quite spontaneously. In addition to that but more importantly, "freedom means freedom to do something."[85] Whatever is done must be done according to one's nature.[86] It is for this reason, that he said that material things, like a coin or a table, are not free. They do not do things. They are always used. He indicated that human freedom demands not merely free people, but relationship among free people. For him, the final basis of human freedom lies in real friendship. This is because it is only in friendship not friendliness that we ever find ourselves completely and so completely free.[87]

Macmurray emphasized the point that freedom is very bound up with morality. He believed that to be moral means that the person is completely human as he/she can be and our human nature is our capacity to think really and feel really for ourselves, and act accordingly.[88] For him, personal freedom is the basis of our true morality. It is a quality of a person's character. It does not depend upon his/her circumstances, neither upon his/her wealth not upon his/her political and social conditions, though these may circumscribe and limit the expressions of his/her freedom.[89]

Analysis of *Freedom in The Modern World*

The approach of Macmurray in discussing the crisis in Europe of the twentieth century is still relevant today. He believed that the economic and industrial crises were only mere symptoms of the real problem. He felt that the problem was deeper. It was more spiritual. People have the tendency to scratch only the surface of problems, instead of dealing with the root causes of them. It is all

---

83 Ibid., 91.

84 Ibid., 107.

85 Ibid., 113.

86 Ibid., 114.

87 For more on Friendship in Macmurray, see John Kobina Ghansah, *"Drink with Pleasure when it is aged": A Model of Friendship for Contextual Christian Ethical and Liturgical Life* STD Dissertation, Weston Jesuit School of Theology, Cambridge, MA. April, 2006.

88 Ibid., 128.

89 Ibid., 140.

because many a time the truth may hurt and so many people tend not to face the problem head-on. Problems, must be tackled head-on and holistically and not piece-meal.

According to Macmurray, human freedom is freedom *par excellence*. It cannot be substituted by any other type of freedom. Freedom is closely bound up with morality. He pointed out that to be moral is to be completely human as one can. He believed that personal morality is the ideal morality for human beings. It does not consist in obedience to a moral law. That is mechanical or organic morality both of which are false. If one lives by obedience to a law, it means that the one is not a free being. The person is like a robot. Robots cannot be held accountable for their actions. What Macmurray was saying is that laws are intended to guide human beings. They are for the maintenance of peace and harmony. Since these laws are good for the community or society, they are to be internalized to become part and parcel of human beings. Consequently, when a human being acts, the one does so not because of the existence of a law but because the one knows that it is good and it will help the one and the community. So whatever one does must be done out of love not because of the obedience of a law. Love becomes the bottom-line of everything and not the obedience of a law.

Drawing from Macmurray, freedom is not the license to do whatever one likes. However, whatever one does must conform to one's nature as a human being. It must be real. One must think of the other person and not only of oneself. Secondly, it must lead to genuine friendship.

The second part of this chapter has been a discussion on John Macmurray's notion of the 'Self' not as a 'Thinker' but rather as a 'Doer.' This 'Self' is never alone. It is always in relationship and it is only in this way that it realizes itself. The third part looks at Augustine and his insights for the formation and humanization of young men in Africa.

Augustine of Hippo (354–430)

Augustine was born on November 13, 354 in Tagaste, North Africa.[90] Born to a very strong and devout mother, Monica and a pagan father, Patricius,[91] Augustine struggled to discover his real self. At seventeen, his life took a wayward direction to the displeasure of his parents especially his mother. He

---

[90] Augustine, *Confessions*, xiii.

[91] He was later baptized on his death bed in 372.

fathered a son out of wedlock and named the boy Adeodatus. He lived with this boy's mother for fifteen years.[92]

Augustine was brilliant. From the age of nineteen until twenty-eight, he was fascinated by the Manicheans[93] who were considered as heretics by the church.[94] However, after some time he became disillusioned with their teachings and broke away from them.[95] After leaving the Manicheans, he left Carthage to teach rhetorics in Rome. In Rome, he heard of Ambrose (c. 338–397), the eloquent bishop of Milan. Augustine went to listen to the sermons of Ambrose, not out of any desire for a spiritual growth but because of the rhetorics of Ambrose.[96] It became the turning point in his life. The decisive moment of his conversion to Christianity came when he was in a garden and heard a voice say to him, "pick up and read, pick up and read." When he looked around he saw a bible and opened it randomly to Rom. 13:13-14.[97] The biblical text reads, "Let us live honorably as in the day, not in reveling and drunkenness, not in debauchery and licentiousness, not in quarreling and jealousy. Instead, put on the Lord Jesus Christ, and make no provision for the flesh, to gratify its desires." Augustine sought baptism afterwards together with his son, Adeodatus and his friends and became a Christian. When they were returning home to Africa, his mother, Monica, died.[98] Augustine became the bishop of Hippo in 396. He died in 430. The life of Augustine is more meaningful to male youth in Africa not as a bishop but rather before his conversion. I will, therefore, review his life in his autobiography, *Confessions*.

---

[92] Augustine, *Confessions*, xiii; Bk IV: 2 #2.

[93] Manichaeism was named after Mani (210–276) who lived in Babylon. It was a dualistic religion with a vast influence in Persia and its environs. It taught that two natures, light and darkness, existed from the beginning. It believed that the universe was the result of the attack of darkness on the light. Manichaeism taught that there is no omnipotent good power and denied the infinite perfection of God. It believed that the human person is the battleground between good and bad (soul and body) respectively. It taught that human beings are saved when they come to know who they are and identity themselves with their souls.

[94] Ibid., Bk IV: 1.

[95] Ibid., Bk V: 13.

[96] Ibid., Bk V: 23 #2, 24.

[97] Ibid., Bk VIII: 29.

[98] Ibid., Bk IX: 17 #2.

The *Confessions* of Augustine

Augustine's *Confessions* was published in 397 when he was 43 years old. He published it when he was the bishop of Hippo. Some people divide the book into two: his pre-conversion and post-conversion. However, a critical analysis of the book shows that it cannot be simplified in that way. The book has thirteen chapters and it can be divided into three main parts:

Part I begins from Chapters I–IX. In this part Augustine recalls his past experiences.

Part II is made up of Chapter X. In this chapter he discusses his then present conditions and so he uses the present tense.

Part III has Chapters XI–XIII. In this part, Augustine talks about what is to happen in the future. It can be said that in the *Confessions*, Augustine discusses the past, present and future. This constitutes his memories, awareness and expectations.

Analysis of *Confessions*

One must understand the *Confessions* in order to appreciate what Augustine is trying to teach. Augustine is now a bishop. He is writing not as an ordinary individual but as a leader of a Christian community. The essence of the *Confessions* is about Christian identity. What Augustine is teaching is that life is a pilgrimage. This pilgrimage begins from God and ends in God—"You have made us for yourself, and our heart is restless until it rests in you."[99]

In writing the *Confessions*, Augustine sets out his purpose right at the beginning. It is to acknowledge and glorify God—

> You are great, Lord and highly to be praised (Ps. 47: 2): great is your power and your wisdom is immeasurable' (Ps. 146: 5). Man, a little piece of your creation, desires to praise you, a human being 'bearing his mortality with him' (2 Cor. 4: 10), carrying with him the witness of his sin and the witness that you 'resist the proud' (1 Pt. 5:5). Nevertheless, to praise you is the desire of men, a little piece of your creation. You stir men to take pleasure in praising you.[100]

Peer Group Pressure

In Book II of the *Confessions*, Augustine talked about his adolescent life. He recounts his numerous escapades. In talking about them, he does not have

---

[99] Augustine, *Confessions*, Bk I, 1
[100] Ibid.

nostalgic feelings for them. Rather, the intention was to demonstrate his love for whom he later came to love. He said, "The recalling of my wicked ways is better in my memory, but I do so that you may be sweet to me, a sweetness touched by no deception, a sweetness serene and content."[101]   According to Augustine, what made him do certain things was peer-group pressure. As he testified, "Yet I went deeper into vice to avoid being despised, and when there was no act by admitting to which I could rival my depraved companions, I used to pretend I had done things I had not done at all, so that my innocence should not lead my companions to scorn my lack of courage, and lest my chastity be taken as a mark of inferiority."[102]

Gangsterism

It was not just peer-group pressure that made Augustine do certain things. He fell into a group of gangs. They went to steal things which were of no use to them. Their interest was in the act of stealing as gangs, "I stole something which I had in plenty and of much better quality. My desire was to enjoy not what I sought by stealing but merely the excitement of thieving and the doing of what was wrong."[103]   A particular instance was when he joined his gangs to go and steal some pears at midnight. After stealing them, they threw them away to pigs—"Even if we ate a few, nevertheless, our pleasure lay in doing what was not allowed."[104]   In one of his confessions, he said, "I had no motive for my wickedness except wickedness itself. It was foul, and I loved it. I loved the self-destruction, I loved my fall, not the object for which I had fallen but my fall itself."[105]   In acknowledging the influence of peer-group pressure and the dangers of gangsterism, Augustine said, "The theft itself was a nothing and for that reason I was the more miserable. Yet had I been alone I would not have done it—I remember my state to be thus at the time—alone I would never have done it. Therefore, my love in that act was to be associated with the gang in whose company I did it... But my pleasure was not in the pear; it was in the crime itself done in association with the sinful group."[106]   The lesson for young men in Africa is to be aware of the dangers of peer-group pressure and

---

[101] Ibid., Bk II, no. I

[102] Ibid., Bk II, no. 7

[103] Ibid., Bk II, no. 9

[104] Ibid.

[105] Ibid., Bk II, 9 # 2.

[106] Ibid., Bk II, 16 . See also Bk II, 17.

gangsterism. As Augustine complained about in the *Confessions*, peer-group was what made him to do things that he did which he later on regretted. One must be careful about the friends one chooses and moves with. This is because as Augustine said, "Friendship can be a dangerous enemy, a seduction of the mind lying beyond the reach of investigation. Out of a game and a jest came an avid desire to do injury and an appetite to inflict loss on someone else without any motive on my part of personal gain, and no pleasure in settling a score. As soon as the words are spoken, 'Let us go and do it; one is ashamed not to be shameless."[107]

Augustine as a bishop

During the time of Augustine, one of the functions of the bishop was to offer catechetical instruction to people. Augustine was very diligent about providing a proper formation to catechumens in the Christian life. It was in pursuance of this that he wrote De *Catechizandis Rudibus* (First Catechetical Instructions). I would like to suggest that this document merit retrieval by bishops and the clergy in Africa as it holds genuine possibilities for the faith formation of male youth in Africa.

De Catechizandis Rudibus—First Catechetical Instructions (FCI)

The FCI was written by Augustine at the request of Deogratias. Deogratias was a deacon at Carthage who wanted a plan for catechumens who were to be instructed in the faith. He wanted to know what constituted the subject matter of catechesis. The purpose of the FCI was, therefore, to enable catechists to have something in hand that they could refer to when educating people in the Christian faith. Augustine never intended it to be used as a rigid manual. He believed the instructions needed to be adapted for pastoral reasons. He said, "But before I do this, I would have you bear in mind that the aim of the one dictating a catechetical instruction with a future reader in view is different from that of one catechizing with the listener actually present."[108] He went on to say, "If this discourse, in which I have instructed a candidate if present seems long to you, you may treat the subject more briefly; I do not think, however that it should be longer. Though much depends upon what the actual case suggests

---

[107] Ibid., Bk II, 17.
[108] Augustine, *First Catechetical Instruction*, trans. Joseph P. Christopher (Westminster, Maryland: The Newman Bookshop, 1946), chap. 15. 23.

and upon what the audience present before you show that they not only endure, but even desire."[109]

Secondly, the purpose of FCI was to encourage Deogratias to be enthusiastic about his work as a deacon and not to be dismayed because of his short-comings and failures.

Contents of FCI

The FCI is divided into two parts. The first part is the theory of catechesis. It consists of fifteen chapters. Chapters sixteen to twenty-seven constitute the second part which deals mainly with the practice of catechesis.

The Significance of Salvation History

According to Augustine, the whole economy of our salvation should be the subject matter of catechesis. This means that the catechist must begin from God's dealing with people from the creation of the world to the present moment of human history and the development of the church. To this should be added the church's doctrine on the last things of human beings. Augustine also believed that catechumens should also be instructed regularly on temptation and scandals that they are likely to face during their catechumenate and after becoming Christians. According to Augustine, this information should be presented "in a general and comprehensive summary, choosing certain of the more remarkable facts that are heard with greater pleasure and constitute the cardinal points in history."[110] Nonetheless, the catechist "Ought not present (these) as a parchment rolled up and at once snatch them out of sight, but we ought by dwelling somewhat upon them to unite, so to speak, and spread them out of view, and offer them to the minds of our hearers to examine and admire."[111]

The Love of God and the Motive of the Candidate

Augustine, in giving the subject matter of what to teach, put strong emphasis on the love of God.[112] He admonished the catechist to have this in mind all the time and it should be the motivating factor in doing catechesis "With this love,

---

[109] Ibid., chap. 26. 51.
[110] Ibid., chap. 3. 5.
[111] Ibid.
[112] Ibid., chap. 4. 7.

then set before you as an end to which you may refer all that you say, so give all your instructions that he to whom you speak by hearing may believe, and by believing may hope, and by hoping may love."[113]

Augustine taught that candidates should be screened so as to know their motives in desiring to become Christians. If they were becoming Christians in the hope of deriving some benefit or to escape from an injury from people whose displeasure or enmity they dread, then in reality they did not want to become Christians. If they were becoming Christians out of fear of God, then they were to be instructed on the love of God. On the other hand, if they were becoming Christians because they desire true rest and true happiness, then they were to be instructed to raise their hopes from things that perish and pass away and to place them in the Word of God; so that cleaving to that which abides forever, they may also together with it abide forever.[114]

Exhortation

Augustine offered great encouragement to Deogratias to do his catechesis with enthusiasm in spite of his inadequacies. In Augustine's estimation teachers under-estimate the great impact that they have on their students because teachers are often seeking perfection. He said, "But as regards your reflections on your own case, I would not have you be disturbed because you have frequently seemed to yourself to be delivering a worthless and wearisome discourse. For it may very well be that it was not so regarded by him whom you were endeavoring to instruct to have something better for your hearers, on this account what you were saying did not seem worthy of other's ears."[115] Augustine offered himself as an example to Deogratias. He said that many times the eagerness of those who desired to hear him revealed to him that his discourse was not as dull as it seemed to him. From the joy they manifested, he could gather that they had derived some benefit from his instruction even though he himself felt unworthy.[116]

Style of FCI

It is worth noting that Augustine did not have one pedagogical style. He always adapted his pedagogy to the needs of the audience. So he wrote to Deogratias,

---

[113] Ibid., chap. 4. 8.
[114] Ibid., chap. 16. 24.
[115] Ibid., chap. Chap. 2 .3.
[116] Ibid., chap. 2 .4.

"It likewise makes a great difference, even when we are speaking under these circumstances, whether there are a few present or many; whether learned or unlearned, or mixed audience made up of both classes; whether they are townsfolk or countryfolk, or both together; or a gathering in which all sorts and conditions of men are represented."[117] Augustine's pedagogy of the educated classes was different from that of the uneducated. With regard to the educated, he suggested brevity and advised not to dwell with annoying insistence upon those things which they know, but teach with discretion and delicacy.[118] To this end, the catechist should inquire about the books they had read. If these books were written by 'Catholic' writers of note, then the catechist should reinforce what they had read, on the other hand, if the authors were considered 'heretics', then the catechist must earnestly instruct the student regarding the teachings of the universal church and those of other most learned writers renowned for their disputations and expositions concerning the truth of the church's teaching.

On students from schools of grammar and rhetoric, Augustine had this to say,

> When, therefore these men, who seem to surpass all other men in the art of speaking, come to be made Christians, we ought to convey to them more fully than to the illiterate an earnest warning to cloth themselves in Christian humility, and learn not to despise those whom they know as shunning more carefully faults of character than faults of diction; and also that they should not even presume to compare with a pure heart the trained tongue which they had been wont even to prefer.[119]

Augustine, no doubt, was speaking from personal experience. For being a rhetorician himself and having embraced that lifestyle before, he knew that *knowing God* was completely different from *knowing about God*. Secondly, he knew that some students from schools of grammar and rhetoric tended to be proud and looked down on others who were less capable.

In teaching, Augustine pointed out that the comfort level of those being taught should be taken into consideration so as to make learning more engaging and satisfying. He said to Deogratias,

> It often happens, too, that one who first was listening gladly becomes exhausted either from listening or standing, and now opens his mouth no longer to give assent but to yawn, and even involuntary gives signs that he was to depart. When we observe this,

---

[117] Ibid., chap. 15. 23.

[118] Ibid., chap. 8. 12.

[119] Ibid., chap. 9. 13.

we should either refresh his mind by saying something seasonal with a becoming liveliness and suited to the matter under discussion, or something calculated to arouse great wonder and amazement, or even grief and lamentation.[120]

Augustine emphasized narration as the preferred instructional method. Nonetheless, he did not mean to reduce catechesis to a mere intellectual exercise. The catechist must allow the catechumens to examine and admire whatever they have been taught. Augustine's style of educating people (*De Catechizandis Rudibus*) can be summarized in these words, "And since the same medicine is not to be applied to all, although to all the same love is due, so also love itself is in travail with some, becomes weak with others; is at pains to edify some, dreads to be a cause of offense to others; is gentle to some, stern to others; and enemy to none, a mother to all."[121]

Analysis of FCI

Even though Augustine's FCI was written about fifteen hundred years ago, there are many things that the Roman Catholic religious educators can retrieve when educating young men in Africa today. Some of these include:

1. Christian Life is communal: One cannot become a Christian and live an individual private life and cut off from others. To be a Christian is to belong to a community and participate in its life. The Christian community has an identity. To be identified with the Christian community, one must be familiar with the history of the community. For this reason Augustine noted that the subject matter of catechetical instruction should include salvation history which begins with the creation of the world to the second coming of Christ, including the doctrines of the church. Centuries later, Luther expressed similar concerns about people who were supposed to be Christians did not know about the fundamentals of their faith. He complained, "although the people are supposed to be Christians, are baptized, and receive the holy sacraments, they do not know the Lord's Prayer, the Creed, or the

---

[120] Ibid., chap. 13. 19.
[121] Ibid., chap. 15. 23.

Ten Commandments, they live as if they are pigs and irrational beasts."[122]

2.   The candidate's motive must be pure: Augustine's scrutiny of candidates in order to know why they desired to become Christian is still relevant today. People should become Christians voluntarily, and not out of compulsion or coercion. They should become Christians not for any earthly benefits or out of fear of God. Rather, as Augustine said, they must seek to become Christians because they want to find true happiness and true peace in God.

3.   Catechists need to be motivated and encouraged: Today catechists are in need of ongoing formation. Just as Augustine encouraged and supported Deogratias in spite of his failures and inadequacies so too pastoral leaders must closely accompany their catechists. In that way, catechists will minister with enthusiasm. Without enthusiasm, the catechist may burn out easily if the ministry becomes routine and unfulfilling.

4.   Instruction must be student-centered: Augustine's student-centered approach is key to catechesis. This does not mean that the contents of instruction should be neglected. Rather, it simply means that young men must be the subject or the main focus of the education process, if the educational process is to enable male youth to acquire the necessary skills and knowledge needed to have a good life and meaningful relationships with others. The catechist cannot use the same approach for everyone and must be attuned to the background of each student. As Augustine suggested, the approach and discourse need to be adapted to the audience. This suggestion to Deogratias is most relevant today.

In sum, for Augustine, the preacher or the catechist is central to the instructional process. The person must be properly motivated both spiritually and psychologically. In a situation where the one is downhearted, he/she must take inspiration from the mystery of the Incarnation. It was out of love for humanity that Jesus descended from heaven to enable humanity to ascend to heaven. The catechist must not think only of his/her interests, but rather, in an

---

[122] Martin Luther, "The Small Catechism", in *Creeds of the Churches*, ed. John H. Leith (Atlanta: John Knox Press, 1982), Preface, 108.

imitation of Christ, the interest of those seeking instructions must be paramount. Consequently, like Jesus, love of God and love for the student must motivate the catechist to offer catechetical instruction.

As a convert and later on as a bishop, Augustine, in addition to offering catechetical instructions, gave an insight of what the Christine life is about.

Christian Identity—The Approach of Augustine

In the opinion of Augustine any attempt to understand the human person without reference to God was an exercise in futility. Augustine asserted that there is a special bond between humanity and God. Though human beings have been unfaithful, God remains faithful to the relationship despite humanity's sinfulness.

For Augustine, the initial cordial relation between humanity and God has been strained but never severed.[123] This is because God, in God's infinite mercy, in the person of Jesus Christ, humbled himself in order to negate the pride exhibited by humanity thereby redeeming humanity. Augustine sums up his conviction with these words, "a proud humanity is a misery, but a still greater mercy is a humble God."[124] Augustine's assertion resonates well with Paul's conviction that "where sin abounds, grace abounds all the more." (Rom. 5: 20) As Augustine says of God, "you have made us for yourself, and our heart is restless until it rests in you."[125] Not only is God the creator but God is also the sustainer of all that exists. For Augustine, everything created by God was good. This is because God is the source of goodness. Nothing evil can come from God. Human beings were created in the image and likeness of God. So how are we to understand humanity's sinfulness and the gift of God's salvation? According to Augustine, "Through the sin of the first man, which came from his freewill, our nature became corrupted and ruined; and nothing but God's grace alone, through Him who is the Mediator between God and men: our Almighty physician succors it."[126]

Humanity depended on God for sustenance. However, driven by pride, humanity thought it could stand on its own independently of God. Instead of choosing God, humanity chose itself. This, in the opinion of Augustine, was a distortion of the nature of being. By refusing to choose God, the source of all

---

[123] Augustine, *De Trinitate*, trans. Edmund Hill (Hyde Park, New York: 1991), Bk IV, Chapt. 1.

[124] Augustine, *De Catechizandis Rudibus*, 4.8.

[125] Augustine, *Confessions*, Bk 1: 1.

[126] Augustine, *On the Grace of Christ and On Original Sin*, Bk 1, Chap. LV.

life, humanity turned its back on the very source of life. Once that happened, humanity's life trajectory was marked by disaster and death. Left to our own devices, human beings could not turn back to God without assistance. Their nature had been corrupted. Ruined by concupiscence, the tendency was to choose things and paths that were not beneficial.

The Incarnation

Out of love for a proud and sinful humanity, Jesus Christ humbled himself and came to our aid. (Phil. 2: 6-9)   As Augustine acknowledged, "God's designs were thus accomplished, that the blood of the Innocent should be shed for the whole world, and the sins of all who believe in Him be bloated out... We were all debtors by the debt, which we inherit at birth, and to wipe out the debt of sin, he who was without guilt poured out His blood."[127]   For Augustine, our strained relationship with God was repaired and restored. Humanity's *No* was rectified by Jesus' *Yes*. Consequently, humanity was again reconciled with God. There was no way this could have been done, had not the Word been made flesh and dwelt among us.[128]

The Human Person as Pilgrim and Exile

According to Augustine, human life on earth is a pilgrimage. But human persons are not only pilgrims, they are also exiles. Being in exile connotes experience of sorrow, loss, anguish and nostalgia. Exiles are homesick. They are insecure. Augustine used the image of fragile spider as a metaphor for the human condition. For Augustine, humanity will be safe and secure only in heaven.[129]

The Presence of God

In spite of humanity's basic insecurity on this pilgrimage amidst temptations and treacherous paths, Augustine is convinced that the human person is not alone. God is a faithful companion on this journey. This is because God is everywhere.[130]   Augustine pointed out, however, that the presence of God is

---

[127] Augustine, *Easter Homilies*, Sermon 18, 2.

[128] Augustine, *Homilies of 1 John*, First Homily, I; See also *De Trinitate*, Book IV, Chap. 1, no. 4.

[129] Augustine, *Homilies on the Psalms*, Ps. 122, no. 6 #2.

[130] Augustine, *Letter 187*, Chapt. 16.

not experienced by some people.[131] He believed that it is only those with clean heart who can see and experience God interiorly. [132] These individuals he referred to as the saints. Characteristically, Augustine used a metaphor to illustrate his point. The image that he used was that of a sound. He said that when sound is made, those who are deaf do not hear it at all. Those who are half-deaf hear it partially. However, those with no hearing impediment hear it clearly and distinctly. In the same way, God is seen and experienced by those who are humble and do not put any impediment in their ways. They are the clean of heart. They are the saints.

Discipleship

Augustine's views on humanity's status as pilgrims and exiles serve as a reminder that people must seek not to get stuck or be attached to things in this world. As a disciple, one cannot simply do what he/she likes. The disciple must follow the master for the journey, who in the mind of Augustine is Jesus Christ. Humility and obedience are key elements necessary for this journey. As one goes on this journey, one must make use of the things in the world without becoming attached to them. Everything in the world is transient. All things reflect the goodness and the beauty of God. In order to enjoy something *in the world*, Augustine asserts that it must be enjoyed in and for God. The pilgrim must always love, desire and delight in God. For Augustine, it is only in the Triune God that real and everlasting happiness can be found.[133]

The Goal of Humanity

Before his ascension, Jesus prayed: "Father, I desire that those also, whom you have given me, may be with me where I am, to see my glory, which you have given me because you loved me before the foundation of the world." (Jn. 17: 24) For Augustine, the goal of human life is fullness of life in God. Believing that God is the source of all life, Augustine urges humanity to turn towards God in all humility, for this is our nature. By refusing to choose God, we become casualties of own pride. This pride does not lead us to the City of God but rather to the Worldly City. It does not bring us to the City of Life but rather to the City of death. Furthermore, by refusing to choose God, it leads us

---

[131] Augustine, Letter 147, Chap. 47, 53.
[132] Augustine, Letter 187, Chap. 17, 35, 38.
[133] Augustine, *On Christian Teaching*, trans. R. P. H. Green (Oxford: University Press, 1977), Book 1 no. 10.

not to the City of Truth but to the City of Lie.[134] For one to go to the City of God, where the Triune God dwells, one must descend in all humility just as Jesus did so that with the grace of God, one can assent to where Jesus is at the right hand of God. In the City of God, with the Triune God, nothing will be lacking. Humanity's desire for God will be fulfilled and fully satisfied.

To conclude, Augustine's assertion, "A proud humanity is a great misery, but still a greater mercy is a humble God", captures and answers the questions of young men who ask: Who are we? Where do we come from? What are we doing here? Where are we going from here?

Secondly, it gives a summary of humanity's whole life: past, present and future. This refers to our memory, our awareness and our expectations.

Thirdly, it gives us an idea of Augustine's anthropology, ecclesiology, Christology and Trinitarian doctrine as well as his spirituality as a bishop.

These are food for thought that the Roman Catholic church can make use of in forming male youth in Africa into mature and responsible person.

Augustine and Macmurray's insights for the humanization have been discussed. But how relevant are they in contemporary times? Are they applicable? How can they help to respond to the plight of young men in Africa? Has Kwame Gyekye anything in common with Augustine and John Macmurray? How can insights from the three persons respond to the crisis of male youth in Africa?

Comparison of the insights of Kwame Gyekye, John Macmurray and Augustine

In this section, key themes from the insights of Kwame Gyekye, John Macmurray and Augustine are discussed as a way of responding to the crisis of male youth in Africa. The key themes include: (1) God and Human Life; (2) Human Relationship and (3) Morality. It is to emphasize the fact that human life cannot be lived in isolation. It must always be in relationship with God—the creator of all that exists. Furthermore, since one's existence is co-terminous with the existence of others, human relationship must be always promoted. This will call for an ethical way of living.

---

[134] Augustine, *City of God*, Book XII, Chapt. 1 #4. See also Book XIV, Chapt. 4 #2; Chapt. 13 # 5; Book XIX, Chapt. 17 #3 & 4.

God and Human Life

God as a creator of the world is a fact that is strongly emphasized by Augustine. For him, there is nothing that exists in this world that was not created by God. All that exist belong to God—"without you, whatever exists would not exist."[135] According to Augustine, since God is the creator of the world, human life must always be anchored in God. Human life must always be lived in praising and glorifying God. It is only that way that the human being can enjoy happiness as seen earlier on. In his opinion, God does not live somewhere for the human being to seek God. Rather, God dwells in the hearts of human beings. He noted, "I was walking through darkness and 'a slippery place'. (Ps. 34: 6) I was seeking for you outside myself, and I failed to find 'the God of my heart'. (Ps. 72: 26) I had come into the depth of the sea. (Ps. 67: 23) I had no confidence, and had lost hope that truth could be found."[136]

Like Augustine, Macmurray also had a strong faith in religion. He believed that human life must be lived in harmony with God the creator of the world. To do otherwise would end in a disaster. It is in this light that he thought that the crisis confronting Europe in his time was neither an economic nor industrial one. For him, they were mere symptoms of the real problem. Macmurray believed that the real problem was a spiritual one. He noted that they had lost faith and when that happens, one loses the grip on reality and one's sanity.[137]

These assertions of Augustine and Macmurray resonate well with what Kwame Gyekye says in his treatment of Akan concept of God. *Nyame*, the Supreme Being of the Akans is the creator of all that exists. Since *Nyame* created all human beings, human beings are in a special relationship with the Supreme Being—*nnipa nyinaa ye Nyame mma, obiara nni ho a onye asaase ba*—All human beings are children of God, no one is a child of the earth. Consequently, human life cannot be lived independently of God. The human being in Akan society must always be mindful of the Supreme Being.

Kwame Gyekye also observes the immanent nature of the Supreme Being among the Akans as Augustine pointed out. The Supreme Being does not live somewhere independently of human beings, leaving human beings to their fate. Rather, the Supreme Being is experiential in Akan society and it is for reason that short prayers, invocations and references are frequently offered to the Supreme Being every now and then.

---

[135] Augustine, *Confessions*, Bk. 1. 2, 9, 10.
[136] Ibid., Bk. VI: 1.
[137] John Macmurray, *Freedom in the Modern World*, 6.

The theme of God and human life is to point to young men in Africa their identity and to inculcate into them the fact that they are special creatures. They are precious in the eyes of God. Secondly, it is to teach them that they are not on their own. As children of the Supreme Being, they are to live their lives befitting their status.

Human Relationship

The fact that the human person is a social being was emphasized by John Macmurray. For him, there is nothing like an independent 'self'. However, he believed that an 'I' always goes with a 'Thou'. In other words, one's existence is co-terminous with the existence of others. A person cannot live a solitary life without reference to a community. Macmurray, therefore, strongly advocated for persons to be in relationship. For him, the best way for persons to be in relation is in friendship.

John Macmurray's *Persons-in-Relation* harmonizes with Kwame Gyekye's Individual and Community in African Philosophical Thought. Gyekye notes that the human person is always born into a community. He believes that communitarianism is natural as far as human life is concerned. Consequently, a person cannot do without a community. However, according to Kwame Gyekye, this is not to say that it is the community that gives personhood to an individual.[138] Secondly, the fact that an individual person cannot do without the community does not mean that the community must trample on the rights of the individual. What he advocates for is a moderate or restricted communitarianism which "gives accommodation to communal values as well as responsibilities to oneself."[139]

These insights on *Persons-in-Relation* from Macmurray and Gyekye and Augustine's idea of Christian life as a pilgrimage with other Christians are to help in the formation and humanization of young men in Africa. They are to teach the young men to acknowledge their individual identities and uniqueness and to work to achieve their interests and goals. In doing this, they must be mindful of the fact that there is no 'lone-rangerism' in the African community. They must take into consideration the communities in which they live and have good relationship with others. However, they must be careful not to allow peer-group pressure to force them into gangsterism and do things that they

---

[138] Kwame Gyekye, *Tradition and Modernity*, 47-48.
[139] Ibid., 76.

would later on regret as it happened to Augustine in his earlier years. Young men in Africa must, therefore, always strive to live good moral lives.

Morality

Morality is something that human beings cannot do without. As persons in relations, human beings live in communities, although they live with themselves and their conscience. Every community has rules and regulations. These rules and regulations are not to take away human freedom. Rather, they are for the maintenance of peace and harmony. Furthermore, human beings are children of God. As a result, they cannot live as they want. They must always live as God created them for—according to one's nature. This is what Augustine realized later on his life: "I traveled very far from you, and you did not stop me. I was tossed about and split, scattered and boiled dry in my fornications. And you were silent. How slow I was to find my joy! At that time you said nothing, and I traveled much further away from you into more and more sterile things productive of unhappiness, proud in my self-pity, incapable of rest in my exhaustion."[140]

Living according to one's nature is a theme that John Macmurray picked up. For him, freedom is not a license to live as one wants. Rather, real freedom is to do something and whatever is done must be in accordance with one's nature.[141] This means that since human person is a religious being, whatever he/she does must be done in faith and geared towards the source of human existence—God.

These insights of Augustine and Macmurray resonate well with what Kwame Gyekye says on African morality. As seen earlier on, Gyekye first argued against the idea that African morality is motivated by religion. He thought that it was the welfare or well-being of the person which was the motivating factor in African morality. However, in his later writings, he modified his stance. He acknowledges that since all human beings are children of God and no one is a child of the earth, there is some truth in the view that religion is behind African morality.[142]

These insights from Augustine, Macmurray and Kwame Gyekye on morality are to help in the formation of maturity and identity of male youth in Africa. Young men in Africa must always see the dignity of each human being

---

[140] Augustine, *Confessions*, Bk. II. 2.

[141] John Macmurray, *Freedom in the Modern World*, 114.

[142] Cf. Kwame Gyekye, *Tradition and Modernity*, 63.

and seek their interests and welfare. Secondly, since all human beings are children of God and no one is a child of the earth, whatever they do must be done according to their nature and dignity as children of God.

Summary

Chapter Three has been a discussion on some philosophical and theological resources for the formation of maturity and identity of male youth in Africa. Insights from African culture, Augustine and John Macmurray were examined. These insights were juxtaposed with insights from Kwame Gyekye, a Ghanaian philosopher to see their relevance in Africa today. Key themes like God and Human Life, Human Relations and Morality were looked at. These, I believe, are very crucial in the humanization and formation of maturity and identity of male youth in Africa.

The next chapter looks at how the Roman Catholic church promotes solidarity and communion with young men in Africa with particular reference to Ghana.

CHAPTER FOUR

Communion and Solidarity with Male Youth: A Missiological Imperative for the Roman Catholic Church in Africa

Se abofra hunu ne nsa hohoro a, one mpaninfoo na edidie—If a child learns how to wash his hands, the child eats with his/her elders.

No society can neglect its youth. Any society which does places its future at risk. Over time, today's youth become tomorrow's adults. Seen in this light, the Roman Catholic church in Africa cannot neglect the next generation. Mindful of this urgency, this chapter examines some of the ways in which the church engages in communion and solidarity with male youth.

Among the Akans, it is said, *praee wo ho yi, woyi baako a na ebuo, wokabo mu a emmu*—One stick of broom is easily breakable but put together with others, it cannot be broken. This proverb gives expression to the insight that strength lies in unity. It reinforces Jesus' exhortation to his disciples to remain united. He forewarned his disciples about divisions and disputes within their ranks. He knew that a house divided against itself could not stand. In this light, as part of his farewell message, Jesus did not only give his disciples a commandment to love one another, (cf. Jn. 13:34-35) he also prayed for them so that they would always stay in unity. He wanted his disciples to be one just as he and the Father are one, (cf. Jn. 17:11; 20) Jesus was not naïve about the unpredictability and the changeability of human nature, for this reason, his message of unity was very important during his earthly ministry. It was something to which the disciples had to attend if they wanted to remain as a community. Through their witness of unity they too provided an example of *love in community*.

As a sacrament of Christ, the Church has been described by images and models that characterize its true nature. Some of these include: Bride of Christ, Mystical Body, Sacrament of Christ, Herald, Servant, People of God, and Family of God. One model that has received a great deal of attention in recent years is that of the church as "Communion."[1] As a community of believers,

---

[1] Cf. Avery Dulles, *Models of the Church*, Expanded Edition (New York: Doubleday, 2002), 39-54.

each person is as important as every other. Individuals exercise different functions or roles in the Church, and while the hierarchical nature of the Church cannot be denied, it must be properly understood, as a means for service in the Church.

Communion and Solidarity in The New Testament Church

The early Christian community of disciples carried forward the message of communion which Jesus entrusted to them. The Acts of the Apostles attests to some of the ways in which the followers of Jesus maintained communion and solidarity. They lived as a community. They prayed together. They broke bread together. They were described as having one heart and one mind. (cf. Acts 1:12-14; 2:1, 42–47) The communion that existed among them was evident to the people of Antioch who were the first to call the followers of Jesus, Christians. (cf. Acts 11:26) With the assistance of the Holy Spirit, their number began to increase and the gospel message spread to other places.

As the number of disciples increased, the message and witness of communion began to be put to the test. (cf. Acts 6:1-6) First the Hellenists began to complain against the Hebrews because their widows were being neglected in the daily distribution of food. The Twelve quickly dealt with this dilemma for the sake of communion. Seven people were appointed and prayed over. Their responsibility was to be responsible for the material welfare of the community so that the Twelve could concentrate on prayer and the preaching of the word. (cf. Acts. 6:1-6) Here, it can be seen that the Twelve could not do everything by themselves. They invited others to participate in the mission given to them by Jesus Christ. This was in furtherance of the message of communion and solidarity. It was a practical demonstration of division of labor. No special group had a monopoly on the gospel message or the resources of the community. All of the disciples of Jesus Christ had a part to play in the proclamation of the gospel. However, this could not be done disjointedly. It had to be done in concert and partnership. In this way, communion and solidarity became the benchmarks of discipleship.

Another instance when communion and solidarity among the early Christian community was put to the test took place at the Council of Jerusalem. (cf. Acts 15:1-35) A dispute had arisen concerning circumcision and salvation in the church at Antioch where Paul and Barnabas were ministering. Some were teaching that unless new converts were circumcised in accordance with the Mosaic Law, they could not be saved. When it could not be resolved in the local church, the case was referred to the apostles and elders in the Jerusalem. They sat on the case and finally made a decision. The decision was that no one should impose any further burden on the Gentile converts. Only the essentials were necessary. The Gentile converts were encouraged to abstain from meat that had been sacrificed to idols and from blood. Furthermore, they were to abstain from whatever was strangled and from fornication. In this way, communion and solidarity were upheld and maintained.

In addition to the Acts of the Apostles, expressions of communion among the followers of Jesus also can be found in the communities which Paul helped to establish. Wherever Paul went to preach, he set up communities. These communities gathered in people's homes. Elders were installed to see to the orderly manner of the community. These various communities were not entities unto themselves. They were linked to the church in Jerusalem. It was characteristic of Paul to take contributions from the communities that he founded and send the money to Jerusalem. (cf. 1 Cor. 16:1-4; 2 Cor. 8-9; Rom. 15:25-27)   In the opinion of Daniel J. Harrington, the taking of the contributions served two purposes. In the first place, it showed that the Gentile communities had connections to their Jewish roots. Secondly, it was an indication of the sense of communion that existed among the local churches.[2]

At one time when some new teachings were being introduced into the Christian community at Galatia, Paul vehemently spoke out against them. Among other things he said,

> I am astonished that you are so quickly deserting the one who called you in the grace of Christ and are turning to a different gospel—not that there is another gospel, but there are some who are confusing you and want to pervert the gospel of Christ. But even if we or an angel from heaven should proclaim to you a gospel contrary to what we proclaimed to you, let that one be accused! As we have said before, so now I repeat, if anyone proclaims to you a gospel contrary to what you received, let that one be accursed! (Gal. 1: 6-9)

In the opinion of Paul, communion and solidarity extended to one's relationship with Christ and with the church. For him, there was no such person as an *individual* Christian. One could not call oneself a Christian and live in isolation from other Christians. For one to be a Christian, it meant that the one was incorporated into Christ and this incorporation could not be uncoupled from the Church. This is because the Church exists for Christ and

---

[2] Daniel J. Harrington, *The Church According to The New Testament* (Chicago: Sheed and Ward, 2001), 57.

continues the ministry of Jesus in the world. To be incorporated into Christ means that one is incorporated into his Body which, is the Church. It is evident that Pauline Christology is closely linked with his understanding of ecclesial communion. As Thomas P. Rausch notes, "To be in Christ" for Paul is not just Christological, it is also profoundly ecclesial. It cannot be understood individualistically. Being in Christ means being a part of the Body of Christ; the Church."[3] (cf. Gal. 1:22; 3:28; Rom. 16:7; 1 Thess. 2:14)

In discussing communion and solidarity as presented in the Pauline letters, it is important to note that there was no strict uniformity among the various Christian communities founded by Paul. It is an acknowledged fact that while some of the Pauline Christian communities were charismatic; others were episcopal; still others were presbyteral.[4] For Paul, the word "church" almost invariably referred to a Christian community in a particular locale, for example, Corinth, Galatia, Ephesus or Rome. In order for a particular church to participate fully in the Body of Christ, it could not be closed in upon itself. These local Christian communities shared communion with other ecclesial communities. In other words, each particular church was linked to the church universal. According to Daniel J. Harrington, "the idea of the 'church universal' is based primarily on belief in the universal sovereignty of God and the universal significance of Christ."[5] In this light, Harrington concludes that "Ecclesiology is a consequence of theology and Christology."[6]

Mindful of the fact that there were some occasions during which communion in the New Testament churches was threatened, (cf. Acts 15:1- 35; I Cor. 1:10-17; 1 Jn. 2:18-20) communion and solidarity remained a value for early Christian communities because those who adhered to the message of Christ believed that "unity belongs to the essential nature of the Church; a divided Church is a deficient sign; its disunity negatively impacts its mission."[7]

This treasured sense of communion and solidarity has suffered in the course of the history of the Christian Church. Disagreements and disputes led to a schism in 1054 when the Christian church became divided into East and

---

[3] Thomas P. Rausch, *Towards A Truly Catholic Church: An Ecclesiology for The Third Millennium* (Collegeville, MN: Liturgical Press, 2005), 85.

[4] Daniel J. Harrington, *The Church According to the New Testament*, 69.

[5] Ibid., 85.

[6] Ibid.

[7] Thomas P. Rausch, *Towards A Truly Catholic Church*, 9.

West.[8]   Again in 1517, the Reformation began by Martin Luther weakened communion in the church universal.[9] Thanks to the ecumenical movement in the Church today, there have been attempts among the various Christian churches to work towards unity in an effort to redress the damage done to the Christian church.[10]

Communion and Solidarity in the Roman Catholic Church Today

An image that can be used to depict communion and solidarity in the Roman Catholic church today is the organ.   The organ keyboard is made up of black and white keys.   If one plays only the black keys or the white keys, the music produced is cacophonous.   However, if both black and white keys are played together, the music produced is harmonious.   In a similar fashion, the church inasmuch is made up of ordained and lay members alike, if any group of members is neglected or under-appreciated, the group does not function well. The church is a community of believers with different gifts and talents.   The church has struggled to grow in this understanding since its inception.   This understanding was deepened during the Second Vatican Council.   At the council, the special and indispensable role of the laity in the missionary activity was acknowledged.   In *Apostolicam Actuositatem*, the communion and solidarity that exist in the church was pointed out, "between the members of this body there exists, further, such a unity and solidarity (cf. Eph. 4: 16) that a member who does not work at the growth of the body to the extent of his possibilities must be considered useless both to the church and to himself."[11]   This was a complete departure from what had occurred in the Roman Catholic church previously.   Early on, the role and function of the clergy became an organizing principle for the church.   The laity ceased to be actors.   They became mere spectators.   At the time of the Second Vatican Council this way of proceeding was called into question as the Council Fathers reminded the faithful that: "on

---

[8] For more on the schism in 1054 see Irvin T. Dale and Scott W. Sunquist, eds. "Controversy and Crisis in Christendom", in *History of the World Christian Movement* (Maryknoll, NY: Orbis Books, 2001), 390-393.

[9] Cf. Scott Hendrix, "Martin Luther, Reformer", in *The Cambridge History of Christianity: Reforms and Expansion: 1500-1660*, vol. 6, ed. R. PO-Chia Hsia (Cambridge, U. K: Cambridge University, 2007), 3-19. See also McLaughlin R. Emmet, "The Radical Reformation", in *The Cambridge History of Christianity*, vol. 6, 37-55.

[10] *Unitatis Redintegratio*, no. 1, *Vatican Council II*, 452. See also Mary Reath, *Rome and Canterbury: The Elusive Search for Unity* (New York: Rowman & Littlefield Publishers, Inc. 2007).

[11] *Apostolicam Actuositatem*, no. 2, in *Vatican Council II, 768.*

all Christians, accordingly, rests the noble obligation of working to bring all men
[sic] throughout the whole world to hear and accept the divine message of
salvation."[12] By virtue of their baptism, the laymen and women also share in
the priestly, prophetic and kingly roles of Christ. For this reason, they "have an
active part of their own in the life and action of the church."[13] In order to
maintain and promote communion and solidarity, it is necessary for the laity "to
develop the habit of working in the parish in close union with their priests, of
bringing before the ecclesial community their own problems, world problems,
and questions regarding man's salvation, to examine them together and solve
them by general discussion."[14] The document goes on to say, "Bishops, parish
priests and other priests of the secular and regular clergy will remember that the
right and duty of exercising the apostolate are common to all the faithful,
whether clerics or lay: and that in the building up of the church the laity too
have parts of their own to play."[15] To the extent that young people make up a
significant percentage of the laity, their participation and presence in the life of
the church cannot be underestimated or ignored.

Young People in the Church (1965-2005): A Retrospective Overview

In deliberating about communion and solidarity in the church, church leaders at
the Second Vatican Council acknowledged the great influence that young
people have in the world. They are enthusiastic, energetic and full of youthful
exuberance. The participants were convinced that "if this enthusiasm is
penetrated with the spirit of Christ, animated by a sense of obedience and love
towards the pastors of the church a very rich harvest can be expected from
it."[16] The Council Fathers were very much convinced that there was no better
way to accomplish this active participation than by getting young people directly
involved in the life of the church. Accordingly, they said, "The young should
become the first apostles of the young, in direct contact with them, exercising
the apostolate by themselves, taking account of their social environment."[17]
Effectively, the Second Vatican Council highlighted the indispensable role that
young people have in the building up of the church. Underscoring the

---

[12] Ibid., no. 3 #3, 769.

[13] Ibid., no. 10, 777.

[14] Ibid., no. 10 #2, 777.

[15] Ibid., no. 25, 790.

[16] Ibid., no. 12, 780.

[17] Ibid.

importance of accompaniment and direction, the Council Fathers also noted that young people cannot be left unguided, the very nature of communion demands that pastoral leaders extend to young people a hand of solidarity and encouragement. They advised that :

> Adults should be anxious to enter into friendly dialogue with the young, where, despite the difference in age, they could get to know one another and share with one another their own personal riches. It is by example first of all and, on occasion, by sound advice and practical help that adults should persuade the young to undertake the apostolate. The young, on their side, will treat their elders with respect and confidence; and though by nature inclined to favor what is new they will have due esteem for praiseworthy traditions.[18]

Since the Second Vatican Council, successive popes have demonstrated great interest in the youth in the church and of the world.

Paul VI and the Youth in the Church

In 1967, Paul VI issued the encyclical *Populorum Progressio*. In it, he noted,

> True to the teaching example of her divine Founder, who cited the preaching of the Gospel to the poor as a sign of His mission, the church has never failed to foster the human progress of the nations to which she brings faith in Christ. Besides erecting sacred edifices, her missionaries have also promoted construction of hospital, sanatoriums, schools and universities. By teaching the native population how to take full advantage of natural resources, the missionaries often protected them from the greed of foreigners.[19]

Paul VI believed that human development contributed to the conditions for peace in the world. He stated, "Extreme disparity between nations in economic, social and educational levels provokes jealousy and discord, often putting peace in jeopardy."[20] Furthermore, he affirmed that peace goes hand-in-hand with justice.[21] However, for Paul VI, development cannot be restricted to economic growth alone. "To be authentic, it must be well rounded; it must

---

[18] Ibid. no. 12 #3, 780.

[19] Paul VI, "Populorum Progressio", no. 12 (Rome: March 26, 1967), http://www.vatican.va/holy_Father/Paul_VI/encyclicals/documents/hf_P-vi_enc-26031967-populorum_en.html (accessed March 10, 2007).

[20] Ibid., no. 76.

[21] Ibid., no. 77 #2.

foster the development of each man [sic] and of the whole man [sic]."[22]   In concluding the encyclical, Paul VI acknowledged the role of the youth.[23]   He commended a number of them who offered their services to public and private organizations that seek to aid developing nations.   He prayed that all those who profess to be followers of Christ heed His plea: "I was a stranger and you took me in; naked and you covered me; sick and you visited me; I was in prison and you came to me."[24]

In *Evangelii Nuntiandi*, Paul VI emphasized again the link between evangelization and human development.   Among other things he said, "Between evangelization and human development—development and liberation—there are in fact profound links.   These include links of an anthropological order, because the man who is to be evangelized is not an abstract being but is subject to social and economic questions.   They also include links in the theological order, since one cannot dissociate the plan of creation from the plan of Redemption."[25] He went on to say,

> Evangelization would not be complete if it did not take account of the unceasing interplay of the Gospel and of a man's concrete life, both personal and social. This is why evangelization involves an explicit message, adopted to the different situations constantly being realized, about the rights and duties of every human being about family life without which personal growth and development is hardly possible, about life in society, about international life, peace, justice and development… a message especially energetic today about liberation.[26]

In sum, for Paul VI, evangelization loses much of its force and effectiveness, if it does not use the language, the symbols and signs of the people to whom it is addressed; if it does not answer the questions that they ask and if it does not have an impact on their concrete lives.   No where was this truth more evident than in the church's ministry to youth.   Embodying the spirit of the Council, Paul VI set a course concerning the church's commitment to young people in the modern world.

---

[22] Ibid., no. 14.

[23] Ibid., no. 74.

[24] Ibid.

[25]   Paul   VI,   "Evangelii   Nuntiandi,   no.   31   Rome: December   8,   1975, http://www.vatican.va/holy_Father/Paul_VI/apost_exhortations/documents/hf_P-vi_exh_19751208_evangelii-nuntiandi_en.l (accessed March 11, 2007).

[26] Ibid., no. 29.

John Paul II and the Youth

Following the example of his predecessors, Pope John Paul II placed the youth apostolate at the center of his papacy of twenty-six years. Through his travels around the world, he acknowledged the exuberant energy of young people and believed that if it was permeated with the message of Christ it would be a great asset to the church, the world and young people themselves. Ever ready to demonstrate his affection for young people, it is important to note that he not only referred to them as "my sons and daughters", but also as "my friends". John Paul II loved to be with the young people and he took every opportunity to communicate this fact.[27] He was energized by them and placed enormous confidence in them. His efforts to promote communion and solidarity with young people were buttressed by his institution of an annual World Youth Day in the life of the Church universal. Even in the midst of declining health, he always welcomed opportunities to meet young people from around the world.

John Paul II and the World Youth Day: An Example
of Communion and Solidarity

John Paul II inaugurated the first World Youth Day in Rome in June1986.[28] It was designated to be held every year on Palm Sunday. Its purpose was to recognize young people and to acknowledge their presence in the church and in the world. Furthermore, it was intended to promote and maintain communion between church leaders and youth. This kind of papal outreach to youth was unprecedented in the history of the Roman Catholic church. At that time, there were many people who were very skeptical about this initiative and its value over time. Skeptics were surprised to find that by 2002 it was estimated that about one million youth from around the world attended the World Youth Day

---

[27] John Paul II, Address to Seminarians in Ghana (Kumasi, May 9, 1980), http://www.vatican.va/holy_father/john_paul_ii/speeches/1980/may/documents/hf_jp-ii_spe_1980509_seminarians-ghana (accessed November 4, 2007). See also his address to Young People in Nigeria in 1982 (Onitsha: Nigeria, February 13, 1982), http://www.vatican.va/holy_father/john_paul_ii/speeches/1982/february/documents/hf_jp-ii_spe_19820213_giovanni-nigeria (accessed November 5, 2007).

[28] John Paul II, "Message to Youth of the World on the occasion of the Second World Youth Day-1987", http://www.vatican.va/holy_father/john_paul_ii/messages/youth/documents/hf-jp-ii_mes_30111986_11-world-youth-day_en (accessed August 5, 2007).

in Toronto, Canada.[29]   It was said of John Paul II that "he is virtually the only world figure who calls young people to bear burdens and make sacrifices, and his trust tapped into the young people's thirst for the heroic and their search for God. He does not modify his message so it will be well received. He speaks the truth candidly, and young people seem to like that."[30]

The following year World Youth Day was held in Buenos Aires, Argentina. The theme for 1987 was "We ourselves have known and put our faith in God's love towards ourselves." (1 Jn. 4:16) Prior to this gathering, John Paul II sent a message in anticipation of the event on November 30, 1986. In this document, he dealt with the subject of what the world at that time purported to give to youth for their satisfaction. He pointed out that what the world offered could not lead to full satisfaction. No matter what the world supplied, a void would remain inside of young people. John Paul II went on to admonish young people to avoid getting caught up in themselves. He encouraged them to open themselves up to others and reach out to those in need. This was the essence of what it meant to be fully human. He said to them,

> You know very well, in the depths of your heart, that the satisfactions afforded by a superficial hedonism are ephemeral and leave nothing but emptiness in our soul; that it is illusory to enclose ourselves in the shell of our egoism; that all indifference and skepticism contradict the noble aspirations of a love that know no frontiers; and that the temptations of violence and of ideologies which deny God can only lead to a dead end.[31]

After speaking against the illusory and transitory nature of what the world offers, he explained to them that finding satisfaction involved responding to God's offer of love. He appealed to them saying,

> To grow in humanity, to give absolute priority to the values of the spirit and to transform yourselves into "new man" by increasingly recognizing and accepting the presence of God in your life; the presence of a God who is love; of a father who loves each one of us from the whole of eternity, who created us by love and who loved us so

---

[29]   Daughters   of   St.   Paul,   "John   Paul   and   World   Youth   Day", http://www.daughtersofpaul.com/johnpaulpapacy/meetsjp/thepope/jpworldyouthdays.html (accessed March 11, 2007).

[30] Ibid.

[31] John Paul II, "II World Youth Day", 1987 – Buenos Aires, http://www.vatican.va/holy_father/john_paul_ii/message/youth/documents/hf_jp-ii_mes_30111986_ii-world-youth-day-en (accessed March 30, 2007).

much that he gave up his only Son to forgive us our sins, to reconcile us to Him, and to enable us to live with Him in a communion of love which will never end.[32]

By cautioning youth against putting their trust and hope in the things of the world, he urged them to recognize that ultimately material things will not lead to true happiness. God is the creator and the sustainer of the world. In God we live, move and have our being. (cf. Acts 17:28) In their search for real happiness, he invited young people to recognize that God must be at the center of their lives.

By instituting the World Youth Day, John Paul II took account of the fact that communion and solidarity not only need to be fostered between church leaders and youth but also among the youth themselves. Thus, by bringing young people from all around the world together, he wanted them first and foremost to know one another, 'become one another's keeper' and support one another in love and justice. Reflecting upon the communal dimension of World Youth Day, among other things John Paul II said, "It is a call that strengthens and renews the bonds by which the young people are united. In these conditions, it is essential that the bonds that unite them be particularly strong and operative with the young who are suffering from unemployment, who are living in poverty or solitude, who feel themselves marginalized or who bear the heavy cross of sickness."[33] Throughout his papacy, John Paul II believed in young people. He had confidence in them and showed over and over again that he loved them. He took delight in being among them and listened attentively to whatever they had to say.[34] It is reported that in Catania, Sicily in 1994, he said "Young people always rejuvenate me." Later on he is reported to have said, "I am always happy to meet with young people; I don't know why, I am…"[35] Without mincing words, he sought to give young people a voice and help them find their voices. In *Ecclesia in Africa*, he noted the indispensable role that the youth can and ought to play in the work of evangelization. He said, "It is thus necessary to help young people to overcome the obstacles thwarting their development: illiteracy, idleness, hunger, drugs. In order to meet these challenges, young people themselves should be called upon to become the evangelizers of their peers. No one can do this better than they."[36]

---

[32] Ibid. no. 2 #2.

[33] Ibid., no. 3.

[34] Ibid.

[35] Ibid.

[36] John Paul II, *Ecclesia in Africa* (Vatican City: Libreria Editrice Vaticana, 1995), no. 93.

Through his efforts to persuade young people to eschew individualism and isolationism, the pope challenged them not be closed in upon themselves. He encouraged them to recognize that the world had become a global village. He urged them to be concerned with world events. He reminded them that those who are in positions of privilege and advantage must be concerned about the welfare of their brothers and sisters in poor countries who lack the basic necessities of life. He emphasized that this was not only a call to Christian charity but Gospel justice. By bringing young people from the world together, the pope endeavored to address xenophobia, prejudice and racism. By creating the conditions for relationships of mutual reverence and respect, the pope sought to promote peace and the desire for reconciliation among a new generation of witnesses for Christ and ambassadors of joy in the world.

Benedict XVI on Communion and Solidarity with Youth in the Church

Before he became pope, Benedict XVI bemoaned the decline of Christian roots and the move towards secularism and relativism in Europe. For him, "A world without God has no future."[37] He noted that God is the ultimate good, beauty, and truth, the source and fountain of all life... The importance task in life is to seek God, and to find him, and to develop a loving relationship with him, because this leads human beings to the deepest and most lasting happiness they can experience.[38] Deeply convinced that "the crisis facing the world today is 'absence of God'"[39], Benedict XVI argues that certain basic values, principles and institutions are to be upheld and defended. Among these are: human dignity, hetero-sexual marriage and family and respect for other religions.[40] He notes that "The church does not wish to impose on others that which they do not understand, but it expects that others will at least respect the consciences of those who allow their reason to be guided by the Christian faith."[41]

In an effort to address the issue of secularism and relativism in the world with particular reference to Europe, Benedict XVI on assuming the office of pope, continued the legacy of communion and solidarity with the youth

---

[37] Joseph Ratzinger and Marcello Pera, *Without Roots: The West, Relativism, Christianity and Islam*, trans. Michael More (New York: Basic Books, 2006), 80.
[38] Robert Moynihan, ed. *Let God's Light Shine Forth: The Spiritual Vision of Pope Benedict XVI* (New York: Doubleday, 2005), 79.
[39] Ibid., 4.
[40] Joseph Ratzinger and Marcello Pera, *Without Roots: The West, Relativism, Christianity and Islam*, 94.
[41] Ibid., 134.

initiated by his predecessor, John Paul II. During the homily at his inaugural mass, he ended it by speaking directly to the youth. He echoed some statements which John Paul II used during his inauguration on October 22, 1978,—"Do not be afraid! Open wide the doors for Christ"! He extended an invitation to the youth of the world by saying, "And so today, with great strength and great conviction, on the basis of loving personal experience of life, I say to you, dear young people: Do not be afraid of Christ! He takes nothing away, and he gives you everything. When we give ourselves to him we receive a hundredfold in return. Yes, open, open wide the doors to Christ—and you will find true life."[42]

Later that year in August 2005, he met the youth from around the world at the 20th World Youth Day in Cologne, Germany under the theme: "We have come to Worship Him"—(Mt. 2:2). In his homily during the Sunday liturgy, Benedict XVI shared with the young people a reflection on the Eucharist. He told them to make the Eucharist the center of their lives.[43] He said to them, "Do not be deterred from taking part in Sunday Mass, and to help others to discover it too. This is because the Eucharist releases the joy that we need so much, and we must learn to grasp it ever more deeply, we must learn to love it."[44] He went on to say, "Let us discover the intimate riches of the church's liturgy and its true greatness: it is the living God himself who is preparing a banquet for us."[45]

In the opinion of Benedict XVI, communion and solidarity with youth is first and foremost an acknowledgement of their role in the church. Secondly, it is a recognition of the fact that they must be formed in Jesus Christ in order to become witnesses of the Christian faith. During his visit to Brazil in May, 2007 on the occasion of the Fifth General Conference of the Bishops of Latin America and the Caribbean, Benedict XVI requested a special meeting with young people. When he met them, he praised them for all that they were doing

---

[42] Benedict XVI, "Homily during Inaugural Mass" (Rome, April 24, 2005), http://www.vatican.va/holy_father/benedict_xvi/homilies/dpcuments/hf-ben-xvi_hom_20050424_inizio-pontificato_en.html (accessed November 8, 2007).

[43] Benedict XVI, "Homily during Sunday Eucharistic Celebration" (Cologne, August 21, 2005), http://www.vatican.va/holy_father/benedict_xvi/homilies/2005/documents/hf_ben-xvi_hom_20050821_20th-world-youth-d. (accessed November 8, 2007). See also Benedict XVI, *God's Revolution: World Youth Day and Other Cologne Talks* (San Francisco: Ignatius Press, 2005), 56-62.

[44] Ibid.

[45] Ibid.

in their parishes, ecclesial communities, universities, colleges, schools, and places of work. He urged them to realize that it was necessary to go even further.[46] He said to them, "My appeal to you…is this, *do not waste your youth.* Do not seek to escape from it. Live it intensely. Consecrate it to the high ideals of faith and human solidarity."[47]

Mindful of the role in the missionary activity of the church, Benedict XVI exhorted young people to remember that "anyone who has discovered Christ must lead others to him. A great joy cannot be kept to oneself. It has to be passed on."[48] He went on to say, "Help people to discover the true star which points out the way to us: Jesus Christ! Let us seek to know him better and better, so as to be able to guide others to him with conviction."[49] The same message of World Youth Day in Cologne was reiterated two years later when he met young people in Brazil. He said,

> You are the youth of the church. I send you out, therefore, on a great mission of evangelizing young men and women who have gone astray in this world like sheep without a shepherd. *Be apostles of youth.* Invite them to walk with you, to have the same experience of faith, hope, and love; to encounter Jesus so that they may feel truly loved, accepted, and able to realize their full potential. May they too discover the sure ways of the commandments, and by following them, come to God.[50]

As a way of demonstrating communion and solidarity with youth in the ongoing work of evangelization in the church, Benedict XVI took the initiatives of his predecessor a step further by acknowledging the importance of vocational identity "so that the vocational dimension would truly emerge in all of its importance, since it plays an evermore important role."[51] In a meeting with young seminarians during World Youth Day 2005, Benedict XVI said to

---

[46] Benedict XVI, "Meeting with Young People" (Paceambu, Sao Paolo, Brazil, Thursday May 10, 2007), no. 2 #2. http://www.vatican.va/holy_father/benedict_xvi/speeches/2007/may/documents/hf_ben-xvi_spe_20070510_youth_brazil_en. (accessed November 9, 2007).

[47] Ibid., no. 7 #1.

[48] Benedict XVI, "Meeting with Young People" (Cologne, Germany).

[49] Ibid.

[50] Benedict XVI, "Meeting with Young People" (Paceambu, Sao Paolo, Brazil), no. 5 #4.

[51] Benedict XVI, "Meeting with Seminarians" (Cologne, Saint Panteleon, Friday, August 19, 2005), http://www.vatica.va/holy_father/benedict_xvi/speeches/2005/august/document/hf_ben-xvi_spe_20050819_semianrians (accessed November 9, 2007).

them, "The seminary years are a time of journeying, of exploration, but above all of discovering Christ. It is only when a young man has had a personal experience of Christ that he can truly understand the Lord's will and consequently his vocation."[52] He concluded his meeting with the seminarians by saying, "The seminary years are a time of preparation. Like the Magi, you too, after your long, necessary programme of seminary formation, will be sent forth as ministers of Christ; indeed each of you will return as an *alter Christus.*"[53]

In the first part of this chapter attention was given to the place and the role of youth in the Roman Catholic church since the Second Vatican Council. Emphasizing the importance of communion and solidarity with youth since the time of Vatican II, these have been reviews in brief of appeals and initiatives of Paul VI, John Paul II and Benedict XVI. In the next section the contextual application of what the Church and the three popes have said about communion and solidarity with youth in general will be examined in terms of the reception of these Church teachings and exhortations in the church of Ghana.

Reaching out to Youth: Pastoral Strategies for incorporating Male Youth into the Roman Catholic Church in Ghana

When one considers the past, present and future of the Roman Catholic church in Ghana, a key tool for analysis can be found in one simple yet profound question: "How is 'communion' and solidarity with youth to be lived out?" Mindful of the position taken by the Second Vatican Council that "the church is not truly established and does not fully live, nor is a perfect sign of Christ unless there is a genuine laity existing and working alongside the hierarchy,"[54] how does the church in Ghana enable all of its members—especially its youth—to carry out their rightful and legitimate obligations as Christian witnesses by virtue of their baptism? More specifically for the purposes of this book, how does the church in Ghana engage male youth, while at the same time opening itself to the challenges posed by these young men to the church as institution and its leaders, especially bishops and priests?

Among the post-resurrection experiences recounted in the Gospel, one is particularly important for reflection on the church's concern for youth. In the twenty-first chapter of John's Gospel, Peter tells the apostles that he is going

[52] Ibid.
[53] Ibid.
[54] *Ad Gentes*, no. 21, *Vatican Council II.*

fishing. (Jn. 21:1-19) They tell him that they will go with him. Unfortunately, the night-long fishing expedition yields nothing. As day is breaking, they decide to return home. When they come near to the shore, a man asks them if they have caught anything. They reply in the negative. He tells them to cast the net on the right side of the boat and they will catch something. They do so and they are amazed with the number of fish that they catch. The beloved disciple whispers to the apostles that it is the Lord. Peter immediately puts on some clothes and jumps into the water and swims to shore. Sitting by a charcoal fire, Jesus asks them to prepare some of the fresh fish for breakfast. Nobody asks who Jesus is for they know it is the risen Lord.

After breakfast, Jesus asks Peter whether he loves him more than the rest. He does so three times. Peter is disturbed by the fact that Jesus asks him three times whether he loves him. In the first instance, Jesus tells Peter that if he truly loves him then he must feed his lambs. In the subsequent injunctions, Peter is told by Jesus to feed his sheep. "Feed my lambs", suggests a mandate to take care of the young ones. Mindful of this mandate, leaders of the Roman Catholic church in Ghana are called to shepherd the youth entrusted to their care.

Inspired by the Akan culture, where youth occupy an important place and they play an indispensable role in the community, the church has made the incorporation of youth in positions of leader an important part of the process of inculturation. Among the Akans, every community has *mmerantee hene*—Chief of the youth. The *mmerantee hene* has a seat in the highest council of every community. When the youth are to be mobilized for any action, it is always done through the *mmerantee hene*. The place and the importance of the leadership of youth in Akan society have not been lost on the church. As the Third Synod of the Archdiocese of Kumasi acknowledged,

> Over the years, the local church of Kumasi has accorded the youth its rightful place concerning their formation and roles in the church. Indeed, section six of the 1984 synod was on the youth. It was also a pastoral concern of the 1994 synod. It could be said that every pastoral plan in this Archdiocese begins and ends with the youth in mind since they are the future of the church. They constitute a large percentage of the faithful in the Kumasi church.[55]

The youth are an integral part of community life in the various parishes in Ghana. This is reflected in the activities of various youth groups of dioceses

---

[55] *Acts and Declaration of The Third Synod of the Catholic Archdiocese of Kumasi*, 34.

and parishes. The youth council plays an active part in parish life. Represented at the parish council, they have a voice in the running of the parish. Such action and incorporation lends credibility to the church's expressed commitment to be in communion and solidarity with young people.

In the 1994 Post-Synodal Apostolic Exhortation, *Ecclesia in Africa*, Pope John Paul II acknowledged the importance which the church in Africa places on the youth in view of their roles as future leaders. For this reason, as noted earlier, he pointed out that "it is thus necessary to help young people to overcome the obstacles thwarting their development: illiteracy, idleness, hunger, drugs. In order to meet these challenges, young people themselves should be called upon to become the evangelizers of their peers. No one can do this better than they."[56] He went on to admonish that

> The pastoral care of youth must clearly be a part of the overall pastoral plan of Dioceses and parishes, so that young people will be enabled to discover very early on the value of the gift of self, and essential means for the person to reach maturity. In this regard, the celebration of World Youth Day is a privileged instrument for the pastoral care of the youth, which favors their formation through prayer, study and reflection.[57]

In 2004, at the Third Synod of Archdiocese of Kumasi, the Youth Apostolate in the Roman Catholic church was a focus of concern. Among some of the Acts and Declarations of the Synod, the following capture the spirit of such consciousness:

1. A well-coordinated youth policy is put in place. The Archdiocesan Youth Office, consequently, shall ensure that within one year of the promulgation of the Acts and Declarations of this Third Synod, the existing youth policy, as outlined in earlier synods which specifies areas of formation and elaborate structures needed to realize the vision of the Archdiocese for our young people, is complied with.

2. Strong character formation, respect for human dignity, and tolerance for cultural, religious and ethnic differences shall become an integral part of the annual formation programmes at both diocesan and parish levels. The Youth office shall ensure that this is done.

---

[56] John Paul II, *Ecclesia in Africa*, no. 93.
[57] Ibid.

3.   Ecumenical youth programmes shall be intensified to help the Catholic youth interact well with other Christian youth.

4.   Parents are not only to encourage their children to belong to groups and societies in the church but also encourage ecumenical programmes that will expose their children to other religious denominations.

5.   Inter-diocesan youth programmes shall also be encouraged by the youth office, at least once in a year.

6.   Since the media also could exert undue influence on the youth, youth programmes shall educate the youth to be circumspect of the media, be it electronic (especially the internet), or printed.

7.   The Youth Office shall publish a Youth Apostolate Handbook. This Handbook shall be published within two years of the promulgation of the Acts and Declarations of this Third Synod. It shall promote Catholic identity.

8.   Parents shall particularly take interest in creating the awareness of the members of HIV/AIDS, emphasizing on the need to avoid premarital and extra-marital sex.

9.   Pastors and the Youth Office shall identify young people who, for various reasons, are not organized or have not been reached. This is especially for those who are not in institutions. When they have been identified, parish priests shall show interest in these people and respond to their needs by organizing periodic programmes for them.

10. Parents, priests and parish councils shall give recognition to the youth, for example, through award schemes and allowing them to be members of parish councils which play active roles in the decision-making process of the parish.[58]

It must be pointed out that these Acts and Declarations on youth have not remained mere theories on paper. It is gratifying to note how they are being executed in the Archdiocese of Kumasi and in the parishes of the diocese.

The Akans say that *abofra a onyini a, obeto kaa no, onam a na orebisa tae boo*—A child who will buy a car in future, asks for the price of a tire as he/she goes

---

[58] *Acts and Declaration of The Third Synod of the Catholic Archdiocese of Kumasi* (December 3-12, 2004), 36.

around. The meaning is simple: the youth are the future leaders. However, they do not assume leadership positions out of the blue. They need to be prepared and trained for such responsibilities and relationships within the faith community. In making sure that youth participate actively and fully in the activities of the church, the Roman Catholic church in Ghana has committed itself to guaranteeing that almost all the adult groups present in the parish have their junior counterparts. Examples of such engagement can be found in Corpus Christ Catholic church in New Tafo, Kumasi. These include the Youth choir, the Junior Praesidium of the Legion of Mary, the 'Evangelicals of the Catholic Charismatic Renewal, the Tarcisians of the Sacred Heart Confraternity and Catholics for Social and Religious Advancement.

Youth Choir

At the Corpus Christi Catholic church, the adult choristers have formed a youth choir. It has a membership of over one hundred. The choir sings at the youth masses. At certain times, when the senior choir travels or is engaged somewhere else, the youth choir sings at other masses as well. On special occasions and parish celebrations the youth choir joins the adult choir. Apart from leading in the singing in the church, the youth choir also undertakes excursions to educative sites and important places. On occasion, they do exchange programs with other youth choirs in other dioceses throughout the country.

Legion of Mary—Junior Praesidium

This is a society that promotes devotion to the Blessed Virgin Mary. They have a weekly meeting. At the end of the meeting, members are assigned particular ministries. Some are sent on home visitation. Others visit the hospitals. Still others visit lapsed Catholics. Members give a report of their ministry assignments at the next meeting. Through this society, the Roman Catholic church keeps in touch with those who are sick and those who have not been coming to church. Through these assignments, the catechist and the priest are informed about any further actions that may be needed. These may include the baptism of new converts and older adults; communion to the sick and anointing of the sick. This society engages youth in active ministry in the church while making them partners in mission with priests and adult catechists.

Charismatic Renewal Movement—The Evangelicals and Youth Camp

The Catholic Charismatic Renewal Movement has brought new energy and vitality into the Roman Catholic church in Ghana. Though the movement has been met with some criticisms and concerns, the fact remains that it has enriched the lives of members empowering them with the Holy Spirit through prayer as well as reading and reflection on the Word of God which is at the core of the movement. There is strong emphasis placed on living a life of repentance, renewal and reconciliation with God and with one another. This has led to a deepening of the faith of many Catholics.

This movement has devoted itself to the formation of young people. The group is called the 'Evangelicals'. Every year during the long vacation, all members throughout the Archdiocese of Kumasi gather in one place for Youth Camp. For one week, young people engage in all kinds of programs; educative, religious and social.[59] The long term effects of youth camp are illustrated by the increase of young people in the church in Ghana and an increase in vocations to the priesthood and religious life.

Sacred Heart Confraternity—Tarcisians

The Sacred Heart Confraternity is a society in the church that promotes devotion to the Most Sacred Heart of Jesus and the Immaculate Heart of Mary. Devotions include: reception of communion, especially on the First Friday of every month. This is preceded by a one-hour adoration of the Blessed Sacrament on the first Thursday of the month. On the first Saturday of every month, they participate in devotions to the Immaculate Heart of Mary. The Sacred Heart Confraternity has a junior group, referred to as Tarcisians. The purpose of this group is to inculcate in the youth devotions to the Most Sacred Heart of Jesus and Immaculate Heart of Mary.

Apart from those mentioned above, other societies like the Knights of Marshall and St. John's Auxiliary have all formed junior ranks. These youth groups are autonomous. They have their own leaders and meet at their own level. They are, however, supported by the senior groups and the parish council when the need arises. They form an integral part of the church's mission of communion and solidarity.

---

[59] There have been several occasions that I have been invited to preside over masses for them and as a confessor during the administering of sacrament of reconciliation. These Youth Camps are always well attended. In 2003, there were about 850 participants.

Catholics for Social and Religious Advancement (COSRA)

Catholics for Social and Religious Advancement is a society for those young people who have moved into young adulthood. They hold prominent positions in schools, businesses and corporations. Some of them are Chief Executives of District Assembles and Regional Ministers. COSRA is the fastest growing youth organization in the Roman Catholic church in Ghana. It exists at both diocesan and national levels. Every year among others things, members of COSRA come from all over the country to visit the major seminaries. Through these encounters, young lay leaders engage and are engaged by their peers preparing for priesthood. Through such encounters mutual support, understanding and union is promoted.

As noted in the previous section, the Roman Catholic church in Ghana has high regard for the youth because it believes that

> Most of the conflicts and the so-called "ethnic cleansing" in many parts of the world today are the results of xenophobia. The future of any group of people, whether ecclesiastical or secular depends to a large extent on how we form our youth, and pass on our values and cultural patrimony to them. Above all, we need to educate them to accept who they are in terms of their culture. Yet at the same time respecting other's differences. It would be a delusion and indeed a naiveté to disregard the youth especially in this respect. Every pastoral plan in the church, to a large extent could be said to begin and end with the youth in mind.[60]

Despite such positive efforts, however, much more needs to be done, especially with regard to disaffected male youth in Ghana. For this reason, the youth who take on leadership roles need to be well equipped and formed to be ambassadors and witnesses of the Lord Jesus Christ, especially among their own peers in Ghana and in the sub-region.

Male Youth: A Missiological Challenges for the Roman Catholic Church

In Chapter One, it was noted how the initial attempts to plant Roman Catholicism in the Gold Coast did not yield good results due in part to the missiological approaches adopted at that time. Later missionaries took different approaches. These included: the recognition and acceptance of the culture of the indigenous people in propagating the gospel of Christ and calling forth lay members of the church to become actively involved in the overall missionary

---

[60] Ibid., 12.

activity of the church.[61] Furthermore, the youth were encouraged to play an integral and indispensable role in the work of evangelization. As seen above, the youth in the Roman Catholic church in Ghana have not been neglected. Many have been actively involved and their involvement has yielded positive results. It has contributed immensely to upholding the peaceful co-existence that distinguishes Ghana from countries like Liberia and Sierra Leone, where years of civil wars have destroyed human lives and lots of property throughout the sub-region, and given rise to a refugee crisis in neighboring countries. Mindful of these realities, the Roman Catholic church in Ghana has a responsibility to be proactive with promotion and maintenance of peace in the country. Key to this responsibility is attending to its ministry and outreach to young men who typically are both the agents and victims of social unrest and civil strife.

Witness for Peace: Promoting Peace among the Youth in Ghana

At the Second Vatican Council, the bishops noted that "Peace is more than the absence of war: it cannot be reduced to the maintenance of a balance of power between opposing forces nor does it arise out of despotic dominion, but it is appropriately called "the effect of righteousness."[62] (Is. 32: 17) They went on to say, "Peace will never be achieved once and for all, but must be built up continually. Since, moreover, human nature is weak and wounded by sin, the achievement of peace requires a constant effort to control the passions and unceasing vigilance by lawful authority."[63]

Ghana has enjoyed relative peace in the West African sub-region. However, the peaceful co-existence among Ghanaians cannot be taken for granted. It has been the fruit of long years of working at it. The Roman Catholic church and the other churches have played and continue to play indispensable roles as far is peace in Ghana is concerned. They have been pro-active in this regard from the beginning of Christianity in Ghana.[64]

---

[61] *Ad Gentes*, no. 21 #4. *Vatican Council II*, 839.

[62] *Gaudium et Spes*, no. 78, *Vatican Council II*, 986.

[63]Ibid.

[64] Cf. Bob-Milliar, George & Gloria, "Christianity in the Ghanaian State in the Past Fifty Years", http://www.ghanaweb.com/GhanaHomePage/features/artikel.php?ID=119921 (accessed April 27, 2007). This is not to overlook the Nanumbas and Kokumbas conflict in 1994; the Dagbon Crisis in 2002 and perennial conflict between the Mamprusis and Kusasis in Bawku, all in Northern Ghana.

As indicated earlier, unlike some other African countries, Ghana is not made up of rivaling ethnic groups like Tutsis and Hutus in Rwanda and other Central African countries. There are many ethnic groups in Ghana who exist in relative harmony. The Akans are made up of different ethnic groups such as the Asantes, Fantes, Nzemas, Akyems, Akuapems and the Ahafos. From their foundations, the churches in Ghana took the integration of people seriously. Missionary activity was not confined to one area. The Christian message spread across the whole of the country and was embraced by the different ethnic groups. Today, as churches hold their annual conventions, congresses, synods and other celebrations, people from various ethnic groups come together to deliberate and to socialize. In this manner, the Christian churches in Ghana have advanced integration through participation and mutual understanding. Despite these initiatives, nothing has contributed more to this process than the legacy of schools and the education of youth.

As noted earlier by Lamin Sanneh, one of the means of evangelization adopted by the early missionaries was the setting up of schools.[65] The churches established boarding schools which pupils from different ethnic backgrounds and various regions from all over the country attended. In this way, the students were brought together. At very tender ages, they began to know and learn from one another. In this way, suspicions and biases against some ethnic groups were challenged early on in life. These students grew up having known one another. They made friends at school and these friendships led to collaboration that has continued over time.[66] As they grew up and assumed leadership roles in the country, they were students familiar with one another as school mates. These relationships have gone a long way to promote ethnic differences and advance communion and solidarity among the various young people from different ethnic groups in Ghana.

Christian Education: Evangelization, Peace-Making and Human Development

Today, Christian churches in Ghana continue to establish and run schools: secondary, vocational, technical and other third cycle institutions. These

---

[65] Sanneh, *West African Christianity*, 120.

[66] Alumni Net, "Mfantsipim Old Boys Association", http://www.alumni.net/Africa/Ghana/Cape_Coast/mfantsipim_Old_Boys_Association, (accessed December 8, 2007). See also, http://www.accraacaalumni.com, (accessed December 8, 2007).

mission schools are considered the best in Ghana.[67] The churches do all this with the view to promoting Gospel values among the populace, recognizing that mutual reverence and respect is key to guaranteeing peace and harmony in the country.

Prophecy and Social Responsibility: Youth for Political Action

The Roman Catholic church in Ghana has made use of its prophetic voice by helping to shape the moral imagination of Catholic citizens through the issuance of statements, related to social responsibility and political action. There have been many instances when the church has become the voice of the voiceless in the history of Ghana. The church has been pro-active on many occasions by identifying ways of proceeding that promote justice and social responsibilities. Along with other churches, the Roman Catholic church has participated actively and fully in all the consultative and constituent assemblies that have been called in the history of Ghana to draw up new constitutions after military interventions.[68]   In all cases, the churches endeavored to guarantee broad representation throughout the country. In all the various constitutions that have been drafted in Ghana, the churches in Ghana have made sure that political parties are not determined on the basis of ethnicity or religion. The current constitution guiding the Fourth Republic of Ghana was drawn and promulgated in 1992. In the 1992 Constitution, it is illegal to establish a political party on ethnic or religious grounds. In addition, all political parties must have at least ten representatives from the two hundred and thirty constituencies in the country. It states, "Every political party shall have a national character, and membership shall not be based on ethnic, religious, regional or other sectional divisions."[69] According to the 1992 Constitution, for a party to be registered in Ghana, it means that "The party has branches in all the regions of Ghana and is, in addition, organized in not less than two thirds

---

[67] For example, in 2004, the Ghana Education Service released a league table of the performance of secondary schools in Ghana in the final examinations. Among the first ten schools seven were managed and run by the Roman Catholic church. It has been on record that Catholics in the Roman Catholic schools in Ghana constitute only about 30% of the student population. See Ghana News Agency, "Ghana needs successful people to be prosperous", http://www.myjoyonline.com/archives/education/200703/2633.asp (accessed March 19, 2007).

[68] "Statement of the State of the Nations - 1982", *Ghana Bishops Speak*, 73.

[69] Cf. 1992 Ghana Constitution, Chap. 7, Article. 55, Section 4, http://www.ghanaeview.com/Gcons7.html, (accessed November 12, 2007).

of the districts of each region.”[70]   In furtherance of integration among the populace, political appointments by the president, especially the cabinet, have ethnic and regional balance.

In sum, one can say that the Roman Catholic church together with the other Christian churches in Ghana have played important roles towards the full humanization of the people of Ghana. The young men in Ghana have been direct beneficiaries of this action.   In view of globalization and the free movement of people among the Economic Community of West Africa States (ECOWAS), church leaders must continue to be vigilant regarding the proper formation of young Ghanaian men's social responsibility and sense of citizenship grounded in Gospel values and cultural identity. Failure to do so will have serious consequences for the youth in particular and the society at large. This is discussed in the next chapter.

As bishops, clergy, religious, lay leaders and faith communities of the Roman Catholic church in Ghana work together to address the plight of young men, they are made aware of the fact that they are not alone in this effort. In communion and solidarity, they stand together with other Catholic Bishops in the sub-region of West Africa as well as Catholics from around the world.

The Ghana Catholic Bishops' Conference has played and continues to play an indispensable role in Ghana and in the sub-region of West Africa by becoming a voice for the voiceless.   It has done so by promoting and maintaining a sense of social consciousness regarding the problems that affect the people of Ghana, and the sub-region of West Africa, the African continent and indeed the world.   Among other things, it is important to remember the gathering of the Association of Episcopal Conferences of Anglophone West Africa (AECAWA) that took place in Enugu, Nigeria in November of 1995. At that time, civil wars in Sierra Leone and Liberia had claimed many lives and displaced many people in the sub-region.   There also was political unrest in Togo and the Ivory Coast. These upheavals displaced many people. Numerous refugee camps were set up in nearby countries. Those most affected by civil unrest and the refugee crisis were women and children. At the conclusion of their AECAWA assembly, the bishops issued a document entitled *Take Heart! AECAWA Bishops Speak.*[71]   In the document, they made a series of declarations. Included in these declarations were the following points:

---

[70] Ibid., Chap. 7, Article 55, Section 7, sub-section (b).
[71] Association of Episcopal Conferences of Anglophone West Africa, *Take Heart! AECAWA Bishops Speak* (Takoradi, Ghana: St. Francis Press, 1996).

1. The alarming and general debasing of the rights of human beings in our sub-region calls for our immediate, urgent action, as Christian leaders.

2. We resolve to be united as one body to condemn 'evils and injustices as part of that ministry of evangelization in the social field which is an aspect of the Church's prophetic role, bearing in mind, however, that proclamation is always more important than condemnation (EIA 70).

3. We realize the need for establishing, within limits of our financial strength, organs of justice, peace and human promotion within AECAWA.

4. Our realization of the blatant degradation and destruction of the person in our sub-region leads us to speak out clearly but in charity and humility, against such practices as torture, executions, manipulation of the judiciary, imprisonment without trial, discrimination against women and minority groups, religious militancy, corruption and exploitation in all their manifestations.

5. In our search for true peace, justice and humanity for our sub-region, we are convinced of the need to forge some sort of organic links with bodies such as the African Commission on Human and Peoples' Rights which are seriously pursuing similar objectives.[72]

The bishops realized how the youth were easily manipulated, recruited and used by opportunists in the sub-region to achieve their selfish interests. This accounted for the many child and teenage soldiers who were indoctrinated to participate in violent actions. In their deliberations, the bishops paid attention to the challenges before them. Consequently, they resolved "To take the apostolate of the lay faithful, with special reference to the young and women, seriously, knowing how easily the youth can lose their sense of direction and how vulnerable women can be to discrimination, exploitation and physical and sexual abuse."[73]

---

[72] Ibid., 27-29.

[73] Ibid., 28. It must be pointed out that it is not only AECAWA which is operating in the sub-region. There is the Episcopal Conferences of Francophone West Africa (CERAO). In the spirit of communion in the Roman Catholic Church the two bodies have now merged. It must be acknowledged that AECAWA together with CERAO have played very important roles in the stability and the gradual development of the sub-region. They worked and continue to work in

Furthermore, to forestall the re-occurrence of the atrocities which befell the sub-region, the bishops identified the need for proper education and formation most especially of the young men so that they would not be easily persuaded by war-lords for their self-interests. The bishops noted the need for the Roman Catholic church in the sub-region to be pro-active in preventing aggression and hostilities. The bishops continue to recognize that the formation of young men is crucial to the process of creating an infrastructure of Christian leaders who will be in a position to act as ambassadors of peace, liberation and salvation for all, especially the people in the sub-region of West Africa.

During his pastoral visit to Uganda from July 31–August 2, 1969 Paul VI among other things challenged Africans to be missionaries to themselves.[74] The Roman Catholic Church in Ghana has taken this challenge seriously and has sent young men as diocesan priests and Ghanaian priests in religious congregations and other lay missionaries to other places. Today, there are young Ghanaian priests and religious working as international ministers in United States of America, Canada, and Europe and in the Oceania in view of the missionary nature of the Roman Catholic church.[75]

---

concert with other world bodies to stop the atrocities that were being carried out in the sub-region of West Africa.

Today the civil wars in both Sierra Leone and Liberia have ended. Both countries have had constitutionally elected governments and are in the process of building their countries. The perpetrators of those heinous crimes are being tried in the U. N. tribunals in Freetown in Sierra Leone and The Hague in The Netherlands—BBC News, "Rebels face Sierra Leone tribunal", http://newsbbc.co.uk/2/africa/386591.stm (accessed August 9, 2007). See also United Nations Organization, "Two former militia leaders convicted by UN-backed tribunal in Sierra Leone", http://www.un.org/opps/news/story.asp?NewsID=23400&Cr=sierra&Crl=Leaone   (accessed August 9, 2007). Many refugees have begun to return to their countries. For instance, at the peak of the Liberian civil war, there were about 40,000 people who fled as refugees to Ghana. They were put into two different camps. As their country returns slowly to normalcy, some of the refugees are returning to their country under the supervision of the U. N. Refugee Agency. They are given aid and assistance to begin life afresh.

Today, a peace keeping force has been formed by the member countries of the sub-region to help to forestall the re-occurrence of the atrocities that befell the sub-region. It is known as Economic Community Monitoring Group (ECOMOG). It intervenes whenever there are political agitations in any member state in order to keep the peace.

[74] Paul   VI,   "Journey   to   Uganda"   July   31-August   2,   1069, http://www.vatican.va/holy_father/paul_vi/travels/sub-index_uganda.htm (accessed August 5, 2007).

[75] The nature of the Roman Catholic church is missionary—(*Ad Gentes*, no. 2). When the early Europeans brought the Christian religion to Africa, they were referred to as missionaries.

In May 8-10, 1980 Ghana was privileged to receive John Paul II during the centenary celebration of the Roman Catholic church in Ghana. During that pastoral visit, the pope interacted with different people including government officials, chiefs and leaders of other religions in Ghana. He met and addressed seminarians during his visit.[76] He told them that he was always delighted to talk to young men preparing for the priesthood. John Paul II emphasized that in spite of their youthfulness, they were able to teach the world a lesson by the way they live. For him, "it is a lesson of faith."[77] He went on to say that "the seminarians had demonstrated their desire to become followers of Jesus. In this way, they become shining examples to their own peers. John Paul II ended his address to the seminarians by saying, "Stay close to Jesus through prayer and Holy Eucharist. And so by the way you live, let everybody know that you really do have faith, that you really believe in our Lord Jesus Christ."[78]

It can be seen from the discussions that the Roman Catholic church in Ghana has been ministering mostly to young men in the church. What about those outside the church? Can young men who were once wayward be fully incorporated in the church?

Care for Male Youth in Prison

A category of male youth in Ghana that the Roman Catholic church cannot neglect are those who have fallen on the wrong side of the law and are in prison. As the sacrament of Christ, the good shepherd who always went after the lost sheep, the church cannot abandon young men in prison. It must go after them and minister to them. For this reason, the church must expand and intensify its prison ministries in the various Archdioceses and dioceses in the

---

However, today priests, religious and lay people from other countries working in America, Canada and Europe are referred to as International ministers and not missionaries. Each local church is a missionary church. As a missionary church, it must be prepared to send and at the same time receive missionaries. For more on International Priests and Missionaries see Margaret Eletta Guider, "From the Ends of the Earth: 'International Minister' or Missionary? Vocational Identity and the Changing Face of Mission in the USA: A Roman Catholic Perspective", in *Antioch Agenda: Essays on the Restorative Church in honor of Orlando E. Costas*, eds. Daniel Jeyaray, Robert W. Pazmino and Rodney L. Petersen (New Delhi: Academy Press, 2007), 329–346.

[76] John Paul II, "Address to the Seminarians" (Kumasi: Ghana), May 9, 1980, http://vatican.va/holy_father/john_paul_ii/speeches/1980/may/documents/hf_jp-ii_spe_19800509_seminarians-ghana, (accessed November 4, 2007).

[77] Ibid.

[78] Ibid.

country. In this way when they come from prison after serving their sentences, they would have been rehabilitated and formed to fit well into the society. Otherwise, they can relapse and be sent back into prison. As John Bosco admonished, "They are our sons, and in correcting their mistakes we must lay aside all anger and restrain it so firmly that it is extinguished in our minds entirely. There must be no hostility in our minds, no contempt in our eyes, no insult on our lips. We must use mercy for the present and have hope for the future, as is fitting for the true fathers who are eager for real correction and improvement."[79]

In sum, well-educated and properly formed young men in Ghana by the Roman Catholic church can be empowered to become self-confident persons. They can become ambassadors, messengers and witnesses in Ghana in particular and the sub-region in general. Furthermore, they cannot be easily manipulated and recruited by opportunists and war-mongers. This can help to eliminate civil wars and strives. It would promote peace and stability in the sub-region. This can help the African continent to develop and improve the conditions of its people. This may enable young men to have a descent standard of living. In this way, they can live their true lives as human beings created in the image and likeness of God. (cf. Gen. 1:26) This will go a long way to confirm what John O'Donohue says that "we cannot live without the infinite."[80] He argues that "an infinite that ignores the sacred becomes monstrous. The sense of proportion disappears. In its most sinister sense anything is possible."[81]

The Once Wayward Young Men in Ghana—Can they enter the Priesthood and Religious Life?

When he came into the world, Jesus said that he came not to call the righteous but sinners. (cf. Mt. 9:13) He, therefore, invited people to repent and believe the goodness because the Reign of God was near. (Mk. 1:14-15) In the course of his ministry, he associated himself with all categories of people including the poor, the marginalized and those who were considered as sinners and outcasts. (Mt. 9:9-13) As a sacrament of Christ, the Roman Catholic church in Ghana cannot neglect those on the fringes of the society especially young men who have fallen foul to the laws of the country and are in borstals and prisons. As

---

[79] John Bosco, "I have always laboured out of love", The *Liturgy of the Hours*, Vol. III, 1338.

[80] John O'Donohue, *Eternal Echoes: Celtic Reflections on our Yearning to Belong*, 80.

[81] Ibid., 82.

seen earlier, the church has not neglected these young men but more needs to be done. Can the church rehabilitate or reform some of these young men to play active roles in the church and society? Can they be admitted into seminaries and religious houses in order to prepare for leadership positions in the church as religious brothers, priests, even bishops? In the "Decree on the Training of Priests", the bishops at the Second Vatican Council said, "Each candidate should be subjected to vigilant and careful enquiry, keeping in mind his age and development, concerning his right intention and freedom of choice, his spiritual, moral and intellectual fitness, adequate physical and mental health, and possible hereditary traits."[82] They went on to say, "notwithstanding the regrettable shortage of priests, due strictness should always be brought to bear on the choice and testing of students."[83] Furthermore, according to the 1983 *Code of Canon Law* of the Roman Catholic church, "The diocesan bishop is to admit to the major seminary only those whose human, moral, spiritual and intellectual gifts, as well as physical and psychological health and right intention, show that they are capable of dedicating themselves permanently to the sacred ministries."[84] In view of these criteria of admission to the priesthood and religious life, can there be a "second chance-attitude" for young men who have once fallen foul of the law? Or is it a case of 'one strike and you are out policy?'[85] Can those who have spent some time in correctional institutions be admitted into seminaries and religious houses to be formed and trained as priests and religious brothers in the church? History abounds with people who once served prison terms but later on become leaders of their countries.[86] In

---

[82] *Optatam Totius*, no. 7, *Vatican Council II*, 712.

[83] Ibid.

[84] *The Code of Canon Law* (Grand Rapids, MI: Williams B. Eerdmans Publishing Company, 1983), Can. 241, #1.

[85] For more on giving the youth a second chance in their growth and development see The World Bank, "World Development Report 2007: Development and the Next Generation", http://web.worldbank.org/WEBSITE/EXTERNAL/EXTDEC/EXTRESEARCH/EXTWDR S/EXTWDR2007/0, menuPK:1489865~pageF (accessed December 15, 2007).

[86] Kwame Nkrumah of Ghana and Nelson Mandela of South Africa are examples. As pointed out earlier, Kwame Nkrumah was the first President of Ghana. He was imprisoned for causing political agitation for independence after over two hundred years of British rule. He won elections while in prison and was released to form the next government. For more on Kwame Nkrumah see his autobiography, *Ghana: The Autobiography of Kwame Nkrumah* (Edinburgh: Thomas Nelson and Sons, 1957). Nelson Mandela was imprisoned for about twenty-seven years for his opposition against the apartheid system of government in South Africa. He was released from prison in 1994 and became the President of South Africa after winning elections. For more on

his book, *Sacraments of Healing*, Christopher Gower makes a point which is very relevant to this discussion. He says that "allied with the desire to begin again is the hope of a second chance in life, which is another basic human need that arises from time to time."[87] People who were given a second in life who later on became great include: the examples of Paul and Augustine which are instructive in this regard.

The Experience of Paul

In Christianity, Paul is regarded as one of the great pillars of the church. He established many Christian communities through his missionary activities. He is credited to have written a number of the books in the New Testament.[88] However, Paul did not begin on a bright note before he became a Christian. He persecuted the members of the Christian religion before his conversion. After his conversion, he assumed an important position when it comes to Christianity. In all this, Paul realized that it was not due to his own efforts and prowess but through the grace of God. As he himself testified, "I am the least of the apostles, unfit to be called an apostle, because I persecuted the church of God. But by the grace of God I am what I am, and his grace toward me has not been in vain. On the contrary, I worked—harder than any of them—though it was not I, but the grace of God that is with me." (1Cor. 15: 9-10) Paul, in spite of his previous life has influenced many people in the course of the history of the church after his conversion to Christianity. An example of one of his great admirers is Augustine, another convert to Christianity.

The Experience of Augustine

In Chapter Three, Augustine's earlier life of debauchery and licentiousness was considered. He converted and became a Christian. He later became a bishop. Today, Augustine is considered as a noted theologian and a doctor of the church. In setting up Augustine as a model for young men, can the Roman Catholic church in Ghana learn from his experience? Can it give other young men a second chance as Augustine had in his time? Are there not many other

---

Nelson Mandela, See his autobiography, *Long Walk to Freedom*, (Boston: Little, Brown and Company, 1994).

[87] Christopher Gower, *Sacraments of Healing* (London: SPCK, 2007), 58.

[88] Out of the twenty-seven books in New Testament, thirteen are considered as having been authored by Paul. Seven of these books namely; Romans, 1 and 2 Corinthians, Philippians, Galatians, 1Thessalonians and Philemon are regarded as undisputed letters of Paul.

Augustines among the young men in Ghana who have once messed up their lives in pursuance of their youth exuberance? I am of the view that in an attempt to respond to the crisis of male youth in Ghana, the Roman Catholic church must pay serious attention to the marginalized ones and those who have fallen foul to the laws of the country. They must be helped to be fully integrated into the church. I argue that their former way of life should not be used to debar them from entering into the seminary and religious houses. I am of the view that once they have shown great remorse for their past lives and have taken the Lord Jesus as their personal savior, they must be accepted and adequately formed to become priests and religious brothers in the church. In this way, they would be in a better position to speak to delinquent youths and their messages would be more powerful since they would be speaking from personal experiences. I am of the opinion that the church is not a haven of saints. Rather, it is a place where people come in to encounter the Lord Jesus Christ in order to be formed so that they can be transformed into the image and likeness of God. (cf. Gen. 1:26) This image is beautifully captured by a signboard of a Baptist church in Waynesboro in Mississippi. On the signboard is written: "Be Ye Fishers of Men: You Catch Them: Jesus will Clean Them."[89]

Summary

This chapter has discussed Communion and Solidarity with male youth in Africa. It has traced communion and solidarity in the Roman Catholic church to the early communities in the New Testament period. It briefly looked at how communion and solidarity have been threatened in the course of the history of the church.

Since the Vatican Council II, the notion of communion and solidarity as understood by successive popes namely; Paul VI, John Paul II and Benedict XVI were considered. It was seen how especially John Paul II incorporated the youth into the communion of the church during his papacy by instituting the World Youth Day.

In a more particular way, it was seen how the Roman Catholic church in Ghana has promoted and continues to promote the concept of communion and solidarity among its members. It has paid attention to youth by giving them a place in the church through the various programs and forming them

---

[89] Joe York, *With Signs Following: Photographs from the Southern Religious Roadside* (Jackson: University Press of Mississippi, 2007), 14.

into groups in the church. In this way, they have become an integral part of the church as communion.[90]

Furthermore, communion and solidarity in the sub-region of West Africa as well as around the world were discussed. The next chapter explores how to form young men in Africa to become mature human beings and faithful Christians. Insights from African Philosophical thoughts set in dialogue with selected biblical narratives are used in this regard. They are to serve as a foundation for catechism and introduction to a life of virtue ethics for young men in Africa.

---

[90] This is one way of doing inculturation in Ghana since young people have their groups (for example, Asafo companies) and are recognized and represented in traditional African societies.

CHAPTER FIVE

Maturing in Faith and Virtue:
Towards an Inculturated Catechesis for Male Youth:
Insights from Traditional African Philosophy and Biblical Narratives

Se woma wowere fire wo kurom hene aben a, woyera adwabo ase —If you forget the whistle of the chief of your hometown, you may get lost at the durbar grounds.

The holding of durbars[1] is very common in Ghanaian traditional societies. During such durbars, people from far and near congregate on the durbar grounds. In times past, transportation was difficult to come-by. A passenger vehicle would leave a village in the morning for the city and return only in the evening. If one missed a returning vehicle, it meant that one had to spend the night in the city or be prepared to walk many kilometers. It meant that when one boarded a passenger vehicle for the durbar grounds, one always had to listen attentively for the village signal. The proverb alerts male youth always to the fact that they always must be conscious of their identity and remember from where they come. Failure to do so could result becoming lost in this fast changing world.

This fifth chapter is divided into two parts. Methodologically, it is constructive, practical and pastoral. Divided into two parts, my objective is to offer a template for engaging the cultural, moral and religious imagination of male youth in Africa. The first part of the chapter reasserts some of the essential beliefs of Africa Traditional Religion that inform and influence Ghanaian culture. If the Church is to assist male youth in setting a direction for their future, it must take seriously the importance of keeping young men connected to their origins as they embark on their life journeys. Building upon these foundational convictions about God, the human person and the world,

---

[1] Durbars are occasions during which a paramount chief summons all his sub-chiefs and citizens of his community for celebrations and deliberations on the development and progress of the community.

the second part of the chapter sets selected African proverbs in dialogue with some instructive biblical narratives. Since proverbs are modes of imparting moral truths and directives for ethical action in African societies, setting proverbs in conversation with the insights of provocative biblical passages puts in place the foundations necessary for an inculturated catechesis. If the formation of young men in faith and virtue is to be successful, I argue that this proposed approach to moral and religious instruction may be a productive way of contributing to the joint processes of full humanization and Christian identity formation.

Male Youth in Africa and the Formation of Cultural Identity: Coming to terms with ATR: The Challenge of Inculturation

For the African life is one. There is no dichotomy between the sacred and secular dimensions of life. As John Mbiti observes, "Belief and action in African traditional society cannot be separated."[2] Furthermore, for the African, religion is integral to life. It is not something that one learns; a person is born into it. It is for this reason that the African is sometimes described as "'notoriously' religious."[3] As Mbiti notes, "African people do not know how to exist without religion."[4] Consequently, my argument in the final chapter of this book is that if the church is to respond effectively to the plight of male youth in Africa, it must attend to the cultural dynamics of Africa Religious Tradition (ATR) mindful of the fact that having been born into the religio-cultural reality of ATR, young men are not well-served by denying this reality or relegating it to the background of their lives. In the past, ATR contributed to the formation of their ancestors, in the present its philosophical insights and traditional religious wisdom must be recognized as a critical component of their identity formation from birth to adolescence and from adulthood and to the grave.

Historically, ATR has been described in the West as primitive. Frequently, ATR has been associated with paganism, heathenism, fetishism, animism and ancestor worship.[5] Many of descriptions of ATR were used in a derogatory manner. ATR was understood in pejorative terms. However, these were not the terms used by the indigenes of Africa to describe ATR. These terms were used by outsiders to describe religious beliefs and cultural practices that they

---

[2] John Mbiti, *African Religions and Philosophy*, 4.

[3] Ibid., 1.

[4] Ibid., 2.

[5] See Peter Sarpong, *Some Notes on West African Traditional Religion: Advanced Level*, 4-8.

observed but did not understand. Repeatedly, outsiders have failed to capture the religious horizon of ATR in its entirety, including its Faith, Morality and Worship. As Kwame Bediako notes,

> For many years Africa theologians have refused to accept the negative view of African religion held by Western missionaries and have shown consistently the continuity of God from pre-Christian Africa past into the Christian present…They have, therefore, like the Apostle Paul, handed to us assurances that with our Christian conversion, we are not introduced to a new God unrelated to the traditions and cultural aspirations of our heritage. In this way the limitations in our missionary past need no longer hinder the growth of Christian understanding and confidence in our churches.[6]

Since the Second Vatican Council, ATR has been given a place of recognition along side of other religions of the world. Writing on ATR, Pope Paul VI observed,

> As a firm foundation, there is in all traditions of Africa, a sense of the spiritual realities. This sense must not be understood merely as what scholars of the history of religion at the end of the last century used to call animism. It is something deeper, vaster and more universal. As for the (African) man, he is not considered as mere matter or limited to this earthly life, but is recognized as having a spiritual active element, so that his moral life is seen as connected at every moment of his life even after death.[7]

He went on to say,

> A very important and common factor of this sense of spiritual realities is the notion of God as the first and ultimate cause of things. Such a notion is more experienced than described, more realized in life than apprehended by thought. It is expressed in many different ways according to the variety of cultural forms. In reality, a living sense of God as the supreme, personal and mystical being pervades the whole of African culture.[8]

About thirty years later in *Ecclesia in Africa*, John Paul II also spoke about ATR, saying "Africans have a profound religious sense, a sense of the sacred, of the existence of God the creator and of the spiritual world. The reality of sin in its individual and social forms is very much present in the consciousness of these

---

[6] Kwame Bediako, *Jesus and The Gospel in Africa: History and Experience* (Maryknoll, NY: Orbis Books, 2004), 21.

[7] Paul VI, *Africae Terrarum*, October 29, 1967.

[8] Ibid.

people, as is also the need for rites of purification and expiation."[9] John Paul II went on to say, "Africans show their respect for human life until its natural end, and keep elderly parents and relatives with them."[10] He noted that "African cultures have an acute sense of solidarity and community life…" He prayed that "Africa will always preserve this priceless cultural heritage and never succumb to the temptation to individualism, which is so alien to its best traditions."[11]

In the light of the recognition given to ATR by these two major popes of the late 20th century, I believe it is important to discuss briefly the cosmology, theology, creation, anthropology and eschatology of ATR so as to provide the cultural foundations necessary for a contextual construction of a contemporary catechesis for African male youth.

Cosmology in ATR

Africans live in a spirit-filled world. They hold strong convictions about the spiritual realm. The spirits who inhabit this realm can be divided into two groups: benevolent and malevolent. The latter spirits are believed to be evil. They do not seek the welfare or well-being of people; rather they tend to be destructive. Examples of malevolent spirits are often identified with curses. The former spirits are believed to be good. They are protective of human beings. Among these are the Supreme Being and other entities.[12] Oliver A. Onwubiko described this comic vision in the following way:

> Ideologically speaking, the African world is a world of inanimate, animate and spiritual beings. The African is conscious of the influence of each category of these beings in the universe. Their existence, for the African is reality; so also is the fact that they interact as co-existent beings in the universe. This idea of the world is accepted by the African and is passed on from one generation to another. It forms the basis of the African ideology in relation to his existence in the world. This idea helps the African to define and explain intelligibly, the rationale behind all that he does, wants to do, what he can or, is expected to do in life. Africans, in general, have their own ideas and beliefs about life in the world, the world and the life outside it.[13]

---

[9] John Paul VI, *Ecclesia in Africa*, no. 42 #2.

[10] Ibid.

[11] Ibid., no. 43 #2.

[12] Peter Sarpong, *Peoples Differ: An Approach to Inculturation in Evangelization* (Accra-Ghana: Sub-Saharan Publishers, 2002), 95-103.

[13] Oliver A. Onwubiko, *African Thought, Religion and Culture* (Enugu-Nigeria: Snaap Press Ltd., 1991), 3.

Monotheism in ATR

ATR is not polytheistic. Rather, it is monotheistic. The Supreme Being has no equals or rivals. All the other divinities and spirits are under the authority and control of the Supreme Being. The name of the Supreme Being is mentioned either first or last but never in the middle among the other divinities during the pouring of libation.[14]

Some scholars[15] use the triangle to depict the place of the Supreme Being in ATR. The Supreme Being is put at the apex. The divinities are put on one side of the triangle and the ancestors on the other. At the base are the animate and inanimate objects associated with witchcraft, juju men, sorcery, charms and amulets.[16] I am of the view that this is not an accurate depiction of ATR. Such a description puts the ancestors on a par with the divinities. Ancestors are people who once lived and have died. Divinities are not human beings. They never experienced death. Consequently, to use the triangle to describe ATR is misleading. It wrongly equates the ancestors and the divinities inasmuch as the divinities are more powerful than the ancestors.

The existence of the Supreme Being is taken for granted in ATR. Viewed from this perspective, one might argue that atheism is "un-African." The Akans say *Obi nkyere abofra Nyame*—Nobody points out God to the child. The presupposition is that God dwells in every human being so there is no need to teach somebody what he or she inherently knows.

In ATR, the Supreme Being is described in terms of both what the Supreme Being *does* and who the Supreme Being *is*. Among the Akans some of the names and attributes associated with the Supreme Being are: *Onyankopon*—One-Great-Friend; *Totorobonsu a oboo nsuo, boo awia*—Creator of the rain and the sun. As Peter Sarpong points out,

> The fact is that belief in the Supreme Being is central to ATR. He has a name in all the African societies; he is unique; he is creator of everything, including all the spirits, human beings, indeed the universe. He is a just judge and holy. He is the provider of everything; he is eternal, our Father, our Grandfather, our Consoler, our everything.

---

[14] This is to indicate that the Supreme Being has no equals. The Supreme Being is the first and the last of everything in the world.

[15] Peter Sarpong, *Some Notes on West African Traditional Religion*, 9. See also E. G. Parrinder, *African Traditional Religion*, Third Edition (London: Sheldon Press, 1974), 24.

[16] Peter Sarpong, *Peoples Differ*, 94.

> Our approach to God is practical. Hence most of the names and attributes we give
> him describe what he does for us rather than what he is in himself.[17]

It also must be pointed out that among the Akans the Supreme Being is neither a male nor a female. Therefore, both female and male images and symbols are used to describe the Supreme Being.[18] The Supreme Being is sometimes called *Nyame, obaatan pa*—God, the good mother among the Asante. God is *obaatan a onim dee ne mma bedie*—a mother who knows what her children will eat.

Creation in ATR

In ATR, creation is attributed to the sole action of the Supreme Being and no other divinity. However, the Supreme Being can delegate a divinity to help in the work of creation. The Yorubas of Nigeria like many other societies in Africa have a fascinating creation myth. According to Yoruba belief, *Olodumare*, the Supreme Being among the Yoruba people, is the creator and the sole giver of life. The Yoruba believe that at the outset of creation, *Olodumare* delegated *Orinshanla,* one of the deities to create human bodies. After the creation of the human bodies *Olodumare* came and gave life to the created bodies enabling them to become living beings. This went on for some time. *Orinshanla* thought of spying on *Olodumare* to see how the giving of life was done. One day after creating the human bodies, *Orinshanla* hid among them to see how *Olodumare* gave life to the created bodies. *Olodumare,* being omnipresent and omniscient, was aware of the thoughts of *Orinshanla*. Before giving life to the bodies, *Olodumare* cast a spell on *Orinshanla* making him fall into a deep sleep. When *Orinshanla* woke up, *Olodumare* had finished giving life to the bodies.[19] The morale of this creation myth is that *Olodumare* is the sole Giver of Life. Like those of the Yoruba, many creation stories among the different tribes in Africa depict the Supreme Being as the only one who gives and sustains life. In a similar fashion only God can take life away. This is attested to by the Akan saying, *se Nyame nku wo a, oteasefoo bere kwa*—If God does not take away your life, the human being does so in vain.

---

[17] Peter Sarpong, *Peoples Differ,* 95.

[18] See Molefi Kete Asante and Emeka Nwadiora, eds. Spear Maters: *An Introduction to African Religion* (New York: University Press of America, Inc. 2007), 4.

[19] Bolaji E. Idowu, *Olodumare, God in Yoruba Belief* (London: Longman, 1962).

Anthropology in ATR

According to the Akan creation myth, the world created by the Supreme Being was harmonious, but something went wrong. Initially, the Supreme Being was very close and attentive to human beings. Due to their persistent disobedience and refusal to heed the directives of the Supreme Being, the Supreme Being decided to distance himself. The proximity of the Supreme Being is depicted in the well-known narrative of an old lady who used to pound *fufu*.[20] She used a long pestle for pounding and in the process the pestle kept hitting the Supreme Being. After directing the woman to use a shorter pestle but to no avail, the Supreme Being withdrew into the skies.

Another traditional myth says that in the beginning, the Supreme Being was very close to human beings. However, children used to wipe their hands on the face of the Supreme Being after eating. After persistent protests by the Supreme Being and the continual disregard and disobedience of the children, the Supreme Being withdrew further into the sky. These myths are reflections on the strained-relationship between the Supreme Being and human beings.

Another way of looking at these creation myths among the Akans is to illustrate both the transcendent and immanent nature of the Supreme Being. The Akans say, *Nyame biribi wo soro ma no ebeka me nsa*—God, there is something in the sky, let it reach me. The Akans do not only point out the transcendent nature of the Supreme Being, they also believe in the immanent nature of the Supreme Being as depicted in the song:

> *Yenam ko ba nyinaa, Nyame ne yen na enam*
> *Yen abisadee nyinaa, wobeye ma wo siabotre*
> *Yei nti nya gyidee, se Nyame beye*
> *Obeye ma wo, se wogyedie, Nyame beye ama wo.*

> As we move to and fro, God is with us
> God will provide for our needs, what is needed is patience
> Because of that, have faith that God will do it
> God will do it, if you have faith, God will do it.

The song emphasizes the immanent nature of the Supreme Being. The individual is never alone. The Supreme Being is always present at all times. Even in difficult times what is needed is patience and faith because the Supreme

---

[20] Fufu is a Ghanaian dish. It is a very popular food among the Asantes, one of the groups of the Akans.

Being, the greatest of all friends, will provide for the individual and never abandon the person.

Belief in the immanent presence of the Supreme Being in ATR, serves to remind human beings that they are not alone. They are in relationship and partnership with the Supreme Being. Furthermore, it is because of this relationship that they are set in relationship with other human beings. A person's existence is co-terminous with the lives of others. The person is always a person-in-relationship. As mentioned previously, John Mbiti, drawing upon ATR wisdom relates the following saying: "I am because we are, and since we are, therefore, I am."[21]

Speaking on human existence among the Igbos of Nigeria, Ferdinand C. Ezekwonma asserts that "the Igbo concept of the human person cannot be isolated from the community. It is only in relation with the community that the identity of the individual is perceptible."[22] This point is further developed by Cardinal Francis Arinze when he noted, "For the Igbo, as for many Africans, to exist is to live in a group, to see things with the group, to do things with the group. Life is not an individual venture, each one for himself."[23] This is not to say that the individual person has no value in African societies. Rather, valuing the individual concern for the common good as illustrated by responsibilities toward the family or community does take precedence over the particular needs of the individual. For example, if an individual owns a cocoa farm and there is a need to construct a road for the community so as to facilitate the easy movement of goods and services, the individual will be expected to sacrifice part of the cocoa farm so that the road can be constructed for the collective benefits of his/her neighbors.

Eschatology in ATR

Community life in Africa does not only consist of the living. It also includes the unborn and the dead. Ancestors are an integral part of the ATR structure of belief. As pointed out by Ezekwonma, "we must make it clear from the

---

[21] John Mbiti, *African Religions and Philosophy*, 108. This assertion resonates with Zachary Hayes when he said, "each individual pertains to the whole; and the whole is incomplete without the individuals that make up its fullness", Zachary Hayes, *Visions of a Future: A Study of Christian Eschatology* (Collegeville, MN: The Liturgical Press, 1989), 96.

[22] Ferdinand C. Ezekwonma, *African Communitarian Ethic: The Basis for the Moral Conscience and Autonomy of the Individual: Igbo Culture as a Case Study* (Berlin: Peter Lang, 2005), 63.

[23] Francis Arinze, *Sacrifice in Ibo Religion* (Ibadan, Nigeria: Ibadan University Press, 1970).

outset that one cannot talk of African community without mentioning the ancestors. Although the ancestors are presumed to be physically dead, for Africans they are still spiritually alive and share in the community life and the life of their respective families."[24] He notes that the Igbo people have great respect for their ancestors. They see them as elders of the community. As elders, they continue to have interest in their communities after death. They wish the community good. It is because of this that when an elderly Igbo dies, the body is buried in proximity to the compound. The reason for this is a relational connection that continues in spite of death.[25] Conscious of this fact, some scholars in the past characterized ATR as ancestor worship. It must be noted, however, that the ancestors are not worshipped. Sacrifices are not offered to them. They are profoundly revered and respected in ways comparable to the saints in the Christian tradition.[26]

Different societies in Africa have different criteria for according ancestorship to people. Among the Akans, for example to be found worthy of being an ancestor, one must have fulfilled certain conditions. These include:

- The person must have died. Consequently, there cannot be a physically living ancestor. Death is, therefore, the first criterion.

- The person must have had a good death. It means a natural death. People who are killed do not qualify. In addition, death through accidents and suicide referred to as *atofowuo* among the Akans excludes a person from being an ancestor.

- The person must have led a good and decent life. Criminals do not quality to be ancestors.

---

[24] Ezekwonma, *African Communitarian Ethic*, 43.

[25] Ibid., 47.

[26] The relationship between the living and the dead is emphasized by Benedict XVI in his encyclical, *Spe Salvi*. He believes that the souls of the departed receive "solace and refreshment" through the Eucharist, prayer and almsgiving offered by the living. He notes, "The belief that love can reach into the afterlife that reciprocal giving and receiving is possible, in which our affection for one another continues beyond the limits of death—this has been a fundamental conviction of Christianity throughout the ages and it remains a source of comfort today." Benedict XVI, *Spe Salvi*, no. 48 (Rome: Libreria, November 30, 2007), http://www.vatican.va/holy_father/ben-xvi_enc_20071130_spe-salvi_en.html (accessed January 12, 2008).

-        The person must have been an adult and married and preferably have had children. Exceptions are permitted to this condition.[27]

As mentioned elsewhere, rites of passage are very significant for ATR. They consist of birth (naming ceremony), adulthood (initiation or puberty rites) and death (final or funeral rites). Rites of passage are community affairs for family members and members of the community. When death occurs, funeral rites bring together members of communities from far and near. For the Akans, death involves a separation of the body and the soul. Since the soul comes from the Supreme Being, it goes back to the Supreme Being.

In this brief synopsis of African cosmology, anthropology and eschatology, it has been noted that there is a strong belief in spirits among African. These spirits are divided into good and evil spirits. There is strong belief in the Supreme Being who is considered to be the creator of the universe. This Supreme Being is very close to human beings who totally depend on the Supreme Being. With regard to anthropology, it was noted that Africans are communitarian. However, this does not negate individuality. Communitarianism and individuality re-enforce each other. In terms of eschatology, African belief in ancestor veneration is very strong in African communitarianism. It was emphasized that in the continuity of life on earth and after death, the African concept of community life includes the living, the dead as well as the unborn. As the Roman Catholic church attempts to cultivate the Christian message so that it might more deeply root itself in Africa, the church must be willing to retrieve the values and principles of ATR that resonate with the Christian tradition in its evangelizing ministry.[28]

Turning now to the second part of the chapter, I propose to set some essential elements of traditional African philosophical thought (as represented in selected proverbs) in dialogue with essential elements of the Christian faith (as represented in selected biblical narratives). As noted earlier, the purpose of this dialogue is to offer resources for the development of an inculturated catechesis for male youth that are able to contribute to a synthesis of moral wisdom and religious insight that is authentically African and authentically Christian. Drawing upon insights from Kwame Gyekye, John Macmurray and

---

[27] Peter Sarpong, *Peoples Differ*, 98.

[28] Some of the values may include: belief in the Supreme Being; the communitarian nature of African anthropology; African social ethics and belief in life after-death. These can be seen as "seeds" of preparation for the Christian message.

Augustine as discussed in Chapter Three, I have chosen to focus on the overarching theme of *relationship* as an organizing principle for understanding the three dimensions of human encounter: relationship with God, relationship with other persons, and relationship with the world. Under each of these three dimensions, a brief integrative reflection that deals with a particular theme is presented. Each process includes reflection on faith and virtue by setting in dialogue:

- an essential element of ATR cosmology
- an essential element of Christian doctrine
- a selected proverb
- a selected biblical narrative
- a specific virtue of African Christian manhood, and
- Relevant concerns and insights for an inculturated catechesis

See Table 1: Essential Elements of an Inculturated Catechesis for Male Youth.

Relationship: Divine and Human

Theme 1: Nyankopon—God, the One-Great-Friend Who Does Not Abandon

As indicated earlier on, the Akans refer to God as *Nyankopon*—One-great-friend. The implication of the African philosophical thought in this section is to inculcate in young men in Africa that even though they are individuals, they are always relational. They are most of all related to *Nyankopon*—the One-great-friend. Consequently, they must be helped to realize that they are never alone. In difficult and desperate situations, they must not despair and destroy themselves through suicide. Young men must be taught to approach God, the Supreme Being, confident that the Supreme Being, whose nature it is to love, will always come to their assistance.

The Akans believe that the individual is never alone. Even when family members and supposed-friends abandon an individual, *Nyankopon* always remains with the person. Mindful of this conviction, they say, *Aboa a, onni dua no Nyame na opra ne ho*—"It is God who drives away flies from the tailless animal." Since God is the Giver of Life, God is always there to protect and provide for the human being especially the defenseless. God does not abandon.

Table 1: Essential Elements of an Inculturated Catechesis for Male Youth

	Elements of ATR Cosmology: Fundamental Formative Insights for Life	Elements of Christian Theology: Formative Insights for Faith	Virtues for African Christian Manhood	Foundational Proverbs	Foundational Biblical Narrative	Relevant Social Issues and Pastoral Concerns
1	*Nyankopon* One-great-friend	God	Faith in an All-powerful God, the Origin of all	It is God who drives away flies from the tailless animal.	Ishmael and Hagar (Gen. 16:1-15; 18:1-13; 21:1-21)	Forces of Secularization-No sense of transcendence
2	*Borebore-Nyame* Creator-God	Creation	Stewardship Care for the earth & creatures, responsibility	God will demand accounts from you.	Creation Narrative (Gen.1:26-30)	Consumerism, Disregard of African culture, Seduction of globalization
3	*Daakye-abrabo* Life after Death	Eschatology	Integrity, Accountability	God does not die, for me to die.	Goal of Christian Life (Rom. 14:7-12)	No connection to roots, to ancestors, to the future
4	*Nyame- Bofoo* The Messenger of God	Jesus Christ	Fidelity, Loyalty, Commitment	May God's messenger accompany you.	Kenosis (Phil. 2:6-9)	Questionable discipleship, hypocrisy
5	*Wo wo nipa to abusua mu* *A human being is born into a family*	Anthropology	Fostering good human relationships, Friendship	Show me your friend and I will tell you your character.	David & Jonathan (1 Sam.18:1-15; 19:1-20; 2 Sam. 1:1-27)	Forces of dehumanization, peer-group pressure, gangsterism

6	*Nipa mua ne nipa* Communal existence	Christian Identity and Communion	Balancing individuality and communality	Two Siamese crocodiles with a common stomach	Jacob and Esau (Gen. 25:21-34; 27:1-40; 32-34)	Individualism, greed, egocentrism, corruption
7	*Nyame-sunsum* Spirit of God	Holy Spirit	Awareness of God's company	As we move to and fro, God is with us	Promise of the Holy Spirit (Jn. 15: 26; 16:12-15)	Distorted sense of direction, licentiousness, debauchery
8	*Nkwagyee* Salvation	Soteriology	Living life, seeking the good of all, mindful of Eternal Life	Use money to buy your life, do not use your life to buy money	The Rich Young Man (LK. 18:18-30)	Obsession with materialism, Unlimited craze for wealth
9	*Nipa firi soro ba a, obesi kurom* When a human being descends, he/she descends into a town	Solidarity with the world	Generosity, sharing, reaching out	Human beings need each other	The Prodigal Son (Lk. 15:11-32)	HIV/AIDS, streetism, drug addiction, incarceration

When life's situation becomes unbearable, young men must be encouraged to reflect upon the narrative of Ishmael and Hagar. (cf. Gen. 21:17ff)   This mother and son encountered difficulties and hardships during their lifetime. However, they did not commit suicide. They trusted and turned to God and, at the appointed time, God intervened and rescued them. They overcame their initial predicaments and became prominent figures in God's plan of salvation.

Ishmael and Hagar—Gen. 16: 1-15; 18: 1-13; 21: 1-21

In the Book of Genesis we read that Abraham was married to Sarah. They were both advanced in years and they did not have any children.   Sarah suggested to Abraham that he have sexual relations with her Egyptian maid-servant, Hagar, so that she could give him children and heirs. Abraham did so and Hagar became pregnant. When she became pregnant Hagar began to taunt and show disrespect to Sarah.   Sarah was offended and started to maltreat Hagar. As a result, Hagar ran away. She was, however, persuaded by an angel of the Lord to return to her mistress and serve her. (Gen. 16:7) Consequently, Hagar returned.   In time, she delivered a baby boy.   He was named, Ishmael—which means *God hears.*[29]

The story continues that one day Abraham was sitting in front of his tent. He saw three men coming towards him. Abraham went to meet and welcome them. He showed hospitality to them by catering to them. Before the men left, they promised to visit him again. By that time, they told Abraham that his wife Sarah would have given birth to a baby boy. Sarah, who was listening in, laughed at what was said since she thought she was long passed the age of child-bearing. When the men confronted her about her disbelief, she denied it. No sooner had the men left than Sarah became pregnant. She gave birth to a boy who was named Isaac. Isaac is the shortened form of the Hebrew name *yishaq'el* meaning *may God smile (on the child).*[30]

One day Sarah noticed Ishmael playing and laughing with Isaac. She was not pleased. Consequently, she asked Abraham to drive away the maid-servant Hagar and her slave son from the house. She did not like the idea that the son of a slave maid-servant would share the inheritance of her son, Isaac. Abraham did not take kindly to the idea. However, God spoke to Abraham and asked him to listen to his wife. He was assured that Hagar and her son would be

---

[29] Ricardo J. Quinones, *The Changes of Cain* (Princeton, NJ: Princeton University Press, 1991), 261.
[30] Eugene Maly, "Cain and Abel", Jerome *Biblical Commentary*, eds. Raymond E. Brown, Joseph A. Fitzmeyer and Roland E. Murphy (Englewood Cliffs, NJ: Prentice Hall, Inc. 1968).

taken good care of. On the basis of that revelation, Abraham asked Hagar and her son to leave the house after giving them some provisions.

Having left the house of Abraham, Hagar and her son headed towards the desert, not knowing where they were going or what they were going to do. When their food supplies were finished, Hagar could not bear the sight of her son dying. Therefore, she laid him down and sat at a distance. The boy began to cry. God heard the cry of the boy. An angel appeared and spoke to Hagar. The angel showed a well to Hagar. She drank some water from the well to quench her thirst and gave some to her son.

Angels feature prominently in the story of Ishmael and Hagar. As Richard Woods observes, "In Christianity, as well as Jewish and Islam belief, angels are immaterial spirits or pure intelligences created by God prior to human creation to regulate the order of the world and specifically to serve as messengers to human persons with respect to the divine plan of salvation."[31] According to Pope Gregory the Great, "the word "angel" denotes a function rather than nature. Those holy spirits of heaven have indeed always been spirits. They can only be called angels when they deliver some message."[32] When Hagar first ran away from her mistress, Sarah, it was an angel who comforted her and asked her to go back. Again when she was driven from the house together with her son into the desert and her son was crying, an angel appeared to comfort them and showed them what to do.[33] (cf. Gen. 21:19) "Like the proverb of the tailless animal, this narrative reveals that God does not abandon the human person. Even in desperate situations, the human person is never alone. God is present as God's angel gives comfort and support."[34] This is in fulfillment of

---

[31] Richards Woods, "Angels", in *The New Dictionary of Theology*, eds. Joseph A. Komonchak, Mary Collins and Dermot A. Lane (Wilmington: Michael Glazier, Inc., 1987), 18.

[32] Pope Gregory the Great, "The word "angel" denotes a function rather than a nature," *The Liturgy of The Hours,* vol. IV, (New York: Catholic Book Publishing Co., 1975), 1435.

[33] Elements of this narrative parallel what happened to Jesus in the Garden of Gethsemane: "When he reached the place, he said to them, 'Pray that you may not come into the time of trial." Then he withdrew from them about a stone's throw, knelt down, and prayed, "Father, if you are willing, remove this cup from me; yet, not my will but yours be done.' Then an angel from heaven appeared to him and gave him strength (Lk. 22:40-42).

[34] On the activities of guardian angels, Saint Bernard said, "Even though we are children and have a long, a very long and dangerous way to go, with such protectors what have we to fear? They who keep us in all our ways cannot be overpowered or led astray, much less lead us astray. They are loyal, prudent, powerful. Why then are we afraid? We have only to follow them, stay close to them, and we shall dwell under the protection of God's heaven." *The Liturgy of the Hours*, Vol. IV, 1454.

what God once said to the people of Israel, "I am going to send an angel in front of you, to guard you on the way and to bring you to the place that I have prepared. Be attentive to him and listen to his voice; do not rebel against him, for he will not pardon your transgression; for my name is in him. But if you listen attentively to his voice and do all that I say, then I will be an enemy to your enemies and a foe to your foes." (Ex. 23:20-22) The biblical narrative of Ishmael and Hagar serves to remind the young men of Africa who suffer that the Lord hears the cry of the poor. For this reason, they must be encouraged by church leaders never to despair, but always to keep hope alive. They must be encouraged to have faith in the all-powerful and loving God, the great Friend, who is the origin and protector of all that exists.

Relevant Concerns and Insights for an Inculturated Catechesis

Among the social issues and pastoral concerns confronting male youth in Africa, the forces of secularization and the gradual loss of the sense of transcendence easily contribute to despair and feelings of abandonment. The above quoted proverb of the tailless animal and the biblical narrative of Ishmael and Hagar can serve as important resources for hope in the midst of suffering. Both the proverb and the narrative encourage young men to have faith in the God who does not abandon, the One Great Friend, who, has a plan for them. "For surely I know the plans I have for you, says the Lord, plans for your welfare and not for harm, to give you a future with hope." (Jer. 29:11)

Theme 2: Borebore-Nyame—The God Who Creates

The Akans refer to God as *Borebore-Nyame*—the Creator-God. Creation has been given to human beings by God. As stewards of God's creation, they cannot destroy it without destroying themselves in the process. It is in the light of this observation that Nick Spencer and Robert White encourage those who identify as Christians to be concerned about the environment.[35] Following this line of thought, as part of their formation in faith and virtue, young men must be instructed to be concerned about the environment because:

- God cares about it.

- It is part of what it means to be human.

---

[35] Nick Spencer and Robert White, *Christianity, Climate Change and Sustainable Living* (London: SPCK, 2007), 75-120.

- It is part of obeying the commandment to love one's neighbor.

- It is our hope for the future.

This is due to the fact that God's plan 'to reconcile to himself all things' (Col. 1:20) really does include all things.[36] As indicated earlier on, everything in the world was created by God and entrusted to the care of human beings. Conscious of what humanity holds in trust, the Akans often say, *Nyame bisa wo*—God will demand accounts from you. Taking this African proverb as a starting point for fostering responsibility among young men for all that they have received from God, I now turn to the biblical account of creation.

The Genesis Creation Accounts (Gen. 1:1-31; 2:1-25)

According to the Book of Genesis, God created the world and all the things in it. Everything created by God was good. After creation, God entrusted everything to human beings saying,

> Be fruitful and multiply, and fill the earth and subdue it; and have dominion over the fish of the sea and over the birds of the air and over every living thing that moves upon the earth. See, I have given you every plant yielding seed that is upon the face of all the earth, and every tree with seed in its fruit; you shall have them for food. And to every beast of the earth, and to every bird of the air, and to everything that creeps on the earth, everything that has the breath of life. I have given every green plant for food. (Gen. 1:28-30)

According to Benedict XVI, the bible is not a natural science textbook. It is a religious book. "One can only glean religious experience from it. Anything else is an image and a way of describing things whose aim is to make profound realities graspable to human beings."[37] He argues that "the creation narratives represent another way of speaking about reality than that with which we are familiar from physics and biology… They say in different ways that there is only *one* God and that the universe is not the scene of a struggle among dark forces but rather the creation of his [God's] word."[38]

---

[36] Ibid., 78-89.

[37] Joseph Ratzinger, (Benedict XVI), *"In the Beginning…": A Catholic Understanding of the story of Creation and The Fall,* trans. Boniface Ramsey (Grand Rapids, Michigan: William B. Eerdmans Publishing Company, 1995), 4.

[38] Ibid., 25.

Relevant Concerns and Insights for an Inculturated Catechesis

When one considers the attitude of many of young men in Africa today, they are in a mad rush for money. They crave material possessions without giving any consideration to the consequences of getting rich quick. Seduced by globalization, their regard for African culture and tradition is diminishing more and more with every passing day. As the proverb and the biblical narrative suggest, the Church in Africa must inculcate in young men a sense of stewardship involving care for the earth and all its creatures. Key to moral and religious formation is the task of instilling responsibility for all that comes from Gods.

Theme 3. Daakye-abrabo—Life after Death with God

It was noted at the beginning of this chapter that Africans have a strong belief in life after death. The Akans refer to it as *Daakye-abrabo—Life after Death*. It is for this reason that they say, *Nyame nwu na mawu—*God does not die, for me to die. This proverb is an affirmation of the immortality of the soul and the lasting relationship between God and the human person for all eternity. As a complement to this proverb, is Paul's vision of the goal of Christian life is put forth as a resource for instruction on the meaning of life and death in God.

The Goal of Christian Life (Rom. 14:7-12)

According to Paul, the Christian does not live or die for himself or herself. He notes, "we do not live to ourselves, and we do not die to ourselves. If we live, we live for the Lord, and if we die, we die for the Lord; so then, whether we live or whether we die, we are the Lord's. For this end Christ died and lived again, so that he might be Lord of both the dead and the living… So then, each of us will be accountable to God." (Rom. 14:7-12) In the opinion of Paul, the Christian life begins with God and ends in God. Life in this world, therefore, always must be lived in anticipation of rendering account of one's stewardship to God at the end of one's early life.

Relevant Concerns and Insights for an Inculturated Catechesis

Many young men in Africa today are adopting attitudes of indifference towards life. They are losing all connections to their roots. They have no regard for the ancestors, much less those yet to be born. For them, their world is the 'present'. Consequently, they do not care about the past or the future. They question the possibility of any life after death.[39] If the Church is to teach male youth about the virtues of integrity and accountability, attention must be paid to both the temporal and eternal dimensions of life.

Theme 4. Nyame-abofoo—God's Messenger

In ATR, the Supreme Being has agents and messengers (*Nyame-abofoo*). Among the Akans it is common to find that when one is setting off on a journey or taking leave of somebody, the person says, *Nyame-Bofoo nfa (ene) wo nko*—May God's messenger accompany you. The belief is that even though, the Supreme Being is transcendent, the immanent nature of the Supreme Being cannot be disputed. According to the Akan, the Supreme Being comes to the people and lives with among the people through the Supreme Being's agents and messengers. While in ATR, there is no concept of Trinity, or of Jesus Christ or of the Holy Spirit, the proverb serves as a point of reference for understanding the mystery of 'God-With-Us.' It is from this perspective on the transcendence and immanence of God that the proverb is set in dialogue with the Paul's understanding of the *kenosis* of Jesus found in the Letter to the Philippians.

The Kenosis (Phil. 2:6-9)

According to Paul, the Christian's attitude must be like that of Jesus who, though He was in equality with God, did not claim equality with God. Rather, he emptied himself and became human and lived among us. He humbled himself to death and died on the cross. He rose again into glory. According to Daniel J. Harrington, this "Christ hymn" found in the Letter to the Philippians is perhaps the oldest source the Church has for understanding how the early Christians made meaning of the person of Jesus Christ. Speaking of him in very 'high christological terms,' the hymn points out the pre-existence of Christ, his incarnation, his saving death and resurrection and exaltation.[40] According to Gordon D. Fee, the text is significant for three main reasons. First, it acknowledges the divinity of Christ without negating his humanity through the incarnation. Secondly, it notes Christ as the second Adam. What Adam

---

[39] Benedict XVI, *Spe Salvi*, no. 48 (Rome: Libreria, November 30, 2007), http://www.vatican.va/holy_father/ben-xvi_enc_20071130_spe-salvi_en.html (accessed January 12, 2008). See also Stephen S. Smalley. *Hope for Ever: The Christian View of Life and Death*, (Waynesboro, GA: Paternoster Press, 2005), 43-63, 68-89.

[40] Daniel J. Harrington, *Who is Jesus? Why is He Important?: An Invitation to the New Testament* (New York: Sheed and Ward, 1999), 97.

destroyed through his pride and disobedience, Christ restores through his humility and obedience. Thirdly, the text is set up for all Christian to emulate Christ their leader.[41]

Relevant Concerns and Insights for an Inculturated Catechesis

Many young men in Africa today have no sense of the presence of God within them, much less the attitude of Jesus. For those who identify themselves as Christians, their lives and actions as Christians are often hypocritical. They are neither disciples of Christ, nor his imitators. They have no sense of how Jesus Christ, by becoming human and taking on the flesh of human beings, redeemed human beings from their sins, making possible their reconciliation with God and restoring them to right relationship with the Divine.[42] The proverb of the messenger and the biblical narrative of Jesus' kenosis are instructive to male youth in three ways. First, the proverb serves as a reminder that they are called to be *faithful messengers of Supreme Being*. Second, the passage from Philippians serves as a reminder to Christians of the self-sacrificial demands that a commitment to Christ entails. Third, taken together, these two sources call forth from male youth a sense of loyalty to God.

Mindful of the ways in which God and human persons relate, I turn now from reflection of the vertical relationship between the Divine and the Human, to reflection on the horizontal relationship among human beings. It is my intention to stress the significance of inter-personal relationships in the moral and faith formation of male youth.

Relationship: Person to Person

Theme 5. Wo wo nipa to abusua mu—A human being is born into a family

African anthropology emphasizes human relationship. The Akans say, w*o wo nipa to abusua mu*—A human being is born into a family. A human person cannot survive without relationship with others. This being the case, the challenge is to teach male youth in Africa how to promote good human

---

[41] Gordon D. Fee, *Pauline Christology: An Exegetical-Theological Study* (Peabody, Massachusetts: Hendrickson Publishers, Inc. 2007), 19.

[42] For why Jesus became human see, Anselm, "Cur Deus Homo", in *Anselm: Basic Writings*, ed. and trans. Thomas Williams, (Indianapolis: Hackett Publishing Company, Inc. 2007). See also Ela Nutu, *Incarnate Word, Inscribed Flesh: John's Prologue and the Postmodern* (Sheffield, U. K: Sheffield Phoenix Press, 2007).

relationship with family members, friends and neighbors. Such instruction must always take into account certain cautions regarding the types of relationships or friendships that young men enter into. As the Akans say, *kyere me wo yonko na menkyere wo wo suban*—show me your friend and I will tell you your character. Mindful of the insights of this proverb the accompanying biblical narrative is that of David and Jonathan.

David and Jonathan—1 Sam. 18: 1-5; 19: 1-20; 2 Sam. 1: 1-27

After the defeat of Goliath, David was introduced into the royal palace of Saul. The First Book of Samuel tells us that the "The soul of Jonathan was bound to the soul of David and Jonathan loved him as his own soul." (1 Sam 18:1) As a result, "Jonathan made a covenant with David, because he loved him as his own soul." (1 Sam. 18: 3) As a practical demonstration of his love for David, "Jonathan stripped himself of the robe that he was wearing, and gave it to David, and his armor, and even his sword and his bow and his belt." (1 Sam. 18: 4)

As a result of his military prowess, David came to live in Saul's house. He became more popular and won many accolades. Songs were composed in his honor, "Saul has killed his thousands and David his ten thousands." (1 Sam. 18: 7) The more popular he became the more jealous Saul became of him. He conspired with his son Jonathan and his servants to kill David. (cf. 1 Sam. 19: 1) Due to the covenant that he had established between himself and David, Jonathan revealed the plot to David. All attempts to eliminate David were made known to him by his friend Jonathan. At one instant, Jonathan put his life on the life in an attempt to save David. (cf. 1 Sam. 20: 1-42) When Jonathan realized that his father, Saul, was determined to kill David, he advised him to flee. Before they parted company, "they kissed each other and wept with each other; David wept the more. Then Jonathan said to David, "go in peace, since both of us have sworn in the name of the Lord, saying, 'the Lord shall be between me and you, and between my descendants and your descendants, forever." (1 Sam. 20: 41) With that they went their separate ways as friends forever.

After some time, David was informed that Saul and his son, Jonathan had been killed during a battle. The bible describes David's reactions on hearing of the death of Saul and his friend Jonathan. "He took hold of his clothes and tore them; and all the men who were with him did the same. They mourned and wept, and fasted until evening for Saul and for his son, Jonathan, and for the army of the Lord and for the house of Israel, because they had fallen by the sword." (2 Sam 1: 11-12) Furthermore, he intoned a lamentation over Saul and his son Jonathan. Among other things he said, "Jonathan lies slain upon your high places. I am distressed for you, my brother Jonathan; greatly beloved were you to me; your love to me was wonderful, passing the love of women. How the mighty have fallen, and the weapons of war perished!" (2 Sam. 1: 19-27) David never forgot his friendship with Jonathan and the house of Saul. Later on when he heard it was the people of Jabesh-Gilead who buried Saul, David sent messengers to them with these words, "may you be blessed by the Lord, because you showed this loyalty to Saul your Lord, and buried him! Now may the Lord show steadfast love and faithfulness to you! And I too will reward you because you have done this thing." (2 Sam. 2: 5) David, therefore, reciprocated the love and friendship of Jonathan.

An example of a true human relationship is the friendship between David and Jonathan. (cf. 1 Sam 18:1-5; 19:1-20; 2 Sam 1:1-27) It was a friendship that was well established in love and loyalty. Jonathan was from the royal house and heir to the throne, yet he associated himself with David, an ordinary citizen from the house of Jesse. He acknowledged the gifts and talents of David and celebrated them with him. He did not become envious and jealous. Instead, he entered into a lasting friendship with him.

"Come, let us go out into the field" (1 Sam. 20:11), this was the invitation from Jonathan to David. It is very similar to the invitation that Cain extended to his brother Abel. (cf. Gen. 4:1-16) In the case of Cain, however, it was with an evil intention. As it turned out, it was when they were in the field together that Cain killed Abel. In the case of Jonathan, he did not have any evil intention. He had a clear conscience. His objective was to strategize as to how to save David's life. Cain's going out with Abel in the field resulted in the destruction of life, for David and Jonathan, it led to the saving of a life. While the latter was for establishing a faithful friendship, the former led to fratricide.

"For as long as the son of Jesse lives upon the earth, neither you nor your kingdom shall be established" (1 Sam. 20:31)—this is what Saul said to his son, Jonathan when the latter excused David from attending the meals for the celebration at the king's palace. Saul knew that Jonathan had established a deep friendship with David. What he was trying to do was to incite Jonathan to turn against David but he did not succeed. Saul could not persuade Jonathan to join the conspiracy to eliminate David. For this reason, he became angry with him and insulted him—"You son of a perverse, rebellious woman! Do I not know that you have chosen the son of Jesse to your own shame and to the shame of your mother's nakedness?" (1 Sam. 20:30)   "Saul threw his spear at him to strike him" (1 Sam. 20:33) when Jonathan insisted on David's innocence. This episode shows the character of Jonathan. He had a strong personality. He had a sense of his own manhood. He could not allow himself to be pushed around. He was a person of convictions and principles.

The story of the friendship between David and Jonathan indicates that one must be prudent when it comes to friendship. One must pick and choose friends who are selfless and eager to help them to achieve their dreams. This is the mark of true friendship. As Blessed Aelred noted, "This is what truly perfect, stable and lasting friendship is, a neither tie that envy cannot spoil, nor suspicion weaken, nor ambition destroy. A friendship so tempted, yielded not an inch, was buffeted but did not collapse. In the face of so many insults, it remained unshaken."[43]

Relevant Concerns and Insights for an Inculturated Catechesis

Among the most urgent concerns confronting male youth in Africa today are the forces of dehumanization, peer-group pressure and gangsterism. The proverbs and the biblical narratives serve to remind young men of their relationships as brothers and friends. In this regard, the Church must find ways of instructing male youth to develop positive character traits that are humanizing and worthy of trust while cautioning them against negative traits that are dehumanizing and deceitful.

Theme 6. Nipa nua ne nipa—Communal Existence as a Sign of Identity and Communion

The Akans emphasize that the human person is never alone. This is because he/she is always in communion with others. This is fundamental to the identity of each and every person. The Akans speak of this reality as *nipa nua ne nipa*—neighborliness. In an effort to instruct male youth about identity and communion the African proverb used for this purpose is expressed in the following way: *Funtumfunafu denkyemfunafu, wonom nyinaa wo yeafunu koro nanso woredidi a, naworeko*—"Two Siamese crocodiles have the same stomach but they fight when eating." This proverb illustrates that community life need not destroy individuality. The proverb serves as an instruction about unity in diversity. I propose that the story of Jacob and Esau is also instructive in this regard.

---

[43] Blessed Aelred, "True, perfect and eternal friendship", *The Liturgy of the Hours*, Vol. III, (New York: Catholic Book Publishing Co., 1975), 400.

Jacob and Esau—Gen. 25: 19–34; 27: 1-45

In the biblical narrative we read that Isaac married Rebecca. Unfortunately, Rebecca was barren. Isaac prayed to God to bless his wife so that she could conceive a child and give birth. God listened to the prayers of Isaac. Rebecca became pregnant, however, it was a difficult pregnancy. She said, "If it is to be this way, why do I live?" (Gen. 25: 22) Through prayer, God revealed to her that she was carrying a set of twins who were struggling together within her. After some time, she delivered them. The first one to come out was Esau. The second one was Jacob who came out, "with his hand gripping Esau's heel." (Gen. 25: 26)

When they grew up, Esau became a hunter and worked on the field. Jacob, on the other hand, dwelt in tents. One day Esau was very hungry and went to Jacob for some food. Jacob agreed to give him some food on the condition that he sold him his birth-right. Esau agreed. An agreement was signed to that effect.

Isaac had grown old and had become blind. One day he called Esau and told him to go and hunt for a game. After that he told him to prepare him a meal. After the meal, he told him that he would give him his blessing before he died. When Isaac was saying this to Esau, Rebecca was listening in. Rebecca went and relayed everything that Isaac had said to Jacob who was her favorite. She asked Jacob to bring two kids from the flock so that she could prepare a meal for him to set before his father. Thus, Jacob received his father's blessing. Jacob was hesitant because he thought his father might recognize him that he was not Esau. Rebecca advised him to wear the cloths of Esau and put on some skins of the goat-kids so that when his father felt his hands, it would be hairy as Esau's.

Jacob did as his mother said and sent the food to his father Isaac. Isaac sensed something unusual. He questioned Jacob for some time. He was still not totally convinced. At the end, he said, "the voice is Jacob's voice but the hands are the hands of Esau." (Gen. 27: 22) After eating the food, Isaac gave his blessings to Jacob. Among other things, he said, "Let the peoples serve you, and nations bow down to you. Be Lord over your brothers, and may your mother's sons bow down to you. Cursed be everyone who curses you, and blessed be everyone who blesses you!" (Gen. 27: 29)

No sooner had Jacob left than Esau came in. When he prepared the food and sent it to Isaac, he was told that his brother had already received the blessing. Esau became furious and thought of killing his brother after their father's death. (Gen. 27: 41) When Rebecca realized that Esau was furious and had planned to kill Jacob, she advised Jacob to go into exile and live with her brother until Esau's anger abated.

Relevant Concerns and Insights for an Inculturated Catechesis

It is a well-known fact that African social ethics puts great emphasis on communalism. However, in recent times, a growing the trend among young African men is individualism. This trend results in greed, corruption and egocentrism. The instruction to be taken from the proverb and the biblical narrative is straight forward: young men in Africa must be helped to rediscover the fact that human life is communal and not individualistic. Observing that communality does not in any way negate individuality, young men in Africa must be encouraged to recognize that unity does not mean uniformity. Their individuality and identity are enriched by communality and vice versa. Communal existence constitutes the relational capacity to cultivate the virtues that challenge the tendencies towards individualism, greed, egocentrism, and corruption. This identification with others is at that heart of the African concept of personhood as well as the heart of Christian solidarity.

The next part of this reflection considers the dimension of relationship that exists between the human person and the larger world. Since human beings come from different backgrounds with different biases and preferences, there exists the need to take into account of the complexities of moral living in relationship with the world in ways that promote and maintain peace and tranquility in the human community.[44]

Relationship: Persons and the World

Theme 7. Yenam ko ba nyinaa, Nyame ne yen na enam— As we move to and fro, God is with us.

As previously noted, in the African world view, the human person is never alone. Always and everywhere, the Supreme Being is in relationship with humanity. In and through the world, the Supreme Being is actively engaged in

---

[44] For more on the importance of morality in the world see Vincent McNamara, "On having a Religious Morality, in *Contemporary Irish Moral Discourse*, ed. Amelia Fleming, (Blackrock, Co. Dublin: The Columba Press, 2007), 88-103 and Enda McDonagh, "A Discourse on the Centrality of Justice" in the same book, 104-116. See also Jerry Z. Muller, "Three Hundred Years of Positive Moral Effects of the Market", in *Markets, Morals and Religion*, ed. Jonathan B. Imber, (Brunswick, U. S. A: Transaction Publishers, 2008), 23-28 and Mara Einstein, *Brands of Faith: Marketing Religion in a Commercial Age* (New York: Routledge, 2008).

the lives of human persons as they relate to one another. It is in this light that the Akans say that *Yenam ko ba nyinaa, Nyame ne yen na enam*—As we move to and fro, God is with us. Mindful of this proverb, the notion of being in the world and being in God's company readily leads to connections being made with the biblical narrative recounting the promise of Jesus to send the Holy Spirit.

The Promise of the Holy Spirit (Jn. 15:26; 16:12-15)

During the Last Supper, Jesus shared with his disciples many parting thoughts. Among other things, in his farewell discourse, he told the disciples that he was not going to leave them alone as orphans rather he would send them the Holy Spirit, who would be with them and guide them in all things. What is the significance of this promise and its fulfillment in today's world?

Relevant Concerns and Insights for an Inculturated Catechesis

As church leaders take a critical look at the lives of many young men in Africa today, they discover the many ways in which male youth are lacking a sense of direction. They are licentious and live lives of debauchery. The proverb and the biblical narrative cited above offer reminders of the fact that they need to allow themselves to be guided by the Spirit of God as they engage and are engaged by the larger world.[45]

Theme 8. Nkwagyee—Salvation

The concept of *Nkwagyee*—Salvation is something that features prominently in ATR. As noted previously, the fact that the African looks forward to a better life after death does not mean that life in this world is not taken seriously. The African is very committed to life in all of its many dimensions. Daily prayers of thanksgiving and petitions are directed to God in the hope of having a good quality of life. The African believes that life is precious and that one must do everything in one's power to secure and safeguard one's life, the life of one's family, the lives of one's neighbors and so on. It is for this reason that the Akans say, F*a sika to wo nkwa, nfa wo nkwa nto sika*—Use money to buy your life, do not use your life to buy money. In the efforts of church leaders to help male youth in Africa to commit themselves to the defense and promotion of life and the quest for eternal life, the biblical narrative most indicated to be set in dialogue with the proverb cited above is the story of the rich young man.

---

[45] For more on the workings of the Holy Spirit, see Kirsteen Kim, *The Holy Spirit in the World: A Global Conversation* (Maryknoll, NY: Orbis Books, 2007).

The Rich Young Man—Lk. 18: 18-30

The narrative of the Rich Young Man is a story that is common to all three of the Synoptic gospels. In Matthew's gospel, it is recorded that someone came to Jesus and said, "Teacher what good deed must I do to have eternal life?" (Matt. 19:16) In Mark's gospel, it is said that as Jesus was setting out on a journey, a man ran up and knelt before him and asked him, "Good teacher, what must I do to inherit eternal life?" (Mk. 10: 17) In the Lukan account, it is said that a certain ruler asked him, "Good teacher, what must I do to inherit eternal life?" (Lk. 18: 18) In response to the question, Jesus referred him to the commandments of God. He encouraged the young man to observe these commandments. Such adherence would enable him to have eternal life. The man replied that he had been doing so since he was young. In reply, Jesus told him that there was something more he needed to do. Jesus asked him to go and sell all that he had, to give the money to the poor and then to come and follow him. The man left the presence of Jesus sad because he was very rich. Offering an interpretation of the encounter, Jesus said to his disciples, "how hard it is for those who have wealth to enter the kingdom of God! Indeed, it is easier for a camel to go through the eye of a needle than for someone who is rich to enter the kingdom of God." (Lk. 18: 24) This saying of Jesus led many people to wonder whether anyone could be saved. However, Jesus reminded them of the fact that "what is impossible for mortals is possible for God." (Lk. 18: 27)

Being concerned about eternal life, Peter questioned Jesus about what they were going to get in view of all the sacrifices they had made to become his disciples. Jesus said to them, "Truly I tell you, there is no one who has left house or wife or brothers or parents or children, for the sake of the kingdom of God, who will not get back very much more in this age, and in the age to come eternal life." (Lk. 18: 29-31)

The question of the rich young man, "what must I do to inherit eternal life?" (Lk 18:18) reveals the importance of humanity's quest for eternal life. As John Paul II noted in the encyclical *Veritatis Splendor* "For the young man, the *question* is not so much about rules to be followed, but *about the full meaning of life*. This is in fact the aspiration at the heart of every human decision and action, the quiet searching and interior prompting which sets freedom in motion. This question is ultimately an appeal to the absolute Good which attracts us and beckons us; it is the echo of a call from God who is the origin and good of man's life."[46]   In the encyclical, he goes on to say, "It (the question) is an essential and unavoidable question for the life of every man, for it is about the moral good and which must be done, and about eternal life. The young man senses that there is a connection between moral good and the fulfillment of his own destiny."[47]

In Luke's gospel, Jesus refers the questioner to the observance of the commandments of God. (cf. Lk. 18: 20) This is to reaffirm that the commandments are not to be understood as restricting or taking away the freedom of human beings. Rather, they are to be understood as instructive guides for human beings as they journey towards eternal life. Simply put, they are the basic requirements for leading a good life and for entering into eternal life. According to Pope John Paul II, "The commandments of which Jesus reminds the young man are meant to safeguard the *good* of the person, the image of God, by protecting his *goods*...

... The commandments thus represent the basic condition for love of neighbor; at the same time they are the proof of that love. They are the *first necessary step on the journey towards freedom*, its starting-point."[48]

Another lesson to be taken from the encounter of Jesus with the rich young man is that human beings must not allow themselves to be overly attached to material things. Jesus said to the rich young man, "Sell all that you own and distribute the money to the poor... then come and follow me." Lk. 18: 22b This is the second injunction that Jesus put to the questioner. It is a call to discipleship. As Daniel J. Harrington notes, "It seems that there are two grades of religious observances: keeping the commandments and becoming, a committed disciple of Jesus. The young man refuses to take the step into the second grade. Nevertheless, Jesus indicates that if he keeps the commandments he will "enter into life."[49] Often, this text has been used to differentiate the obligations of ordinary Christians and those called to priesthood or religious life. This divides Christians into two categories and is not an accurate interpretation of the text. As Daniel J. Harrington, explains, "The rich young man was not a Christian! He was a Jew. When he asked about having eternal

---

[46] John Paul II, *Veritatis Splendor*, no. 7 (Rome: June 8, 1993, http://www.vatican.va/holy_father/john_paul_ii/encyclicals/documents/hf_jp-ii_enc_06081993_veritatis-splendor_en.html (accessed July 2, 2007).

[47] Ibid., no. 8.

[48] Ibid., no. 13 # 3, 4.

[49] Daniel J. Harrington, *The Gospel of Matthew* (Collegeville, MN: The Liturgical Press, 1991), 279.

life, the answer he got from Jesus was "keep the commandments, "if he does so, he will enter into life (Matt. 19:17-18). This text seems to envision the possibility of salvation for Jews apart from the route of Christian discipleship (to which the rich young man is nevertheless invited, if he wishes to be perfect)."[50]

According to John Paul II, "Jesus points out to the young man that the commandments are the first and indispensable condition for having eternal life; on the other hand, for the young man to give up all he possesses and to follow the Lord is presented as an invitation: "if you wish…"[51] What the story of the rich young man illustrates is the cost of discipleship. Regardless of one's state in life, following Jesus calls for sacrificial disposition. It must be noted that Jesus is not saying that rich people cannot enter the Reign of God. What he is saying is that wealth can become a hindrance towards eternal life. This happens when a person makes the amassing and possessing of wealth his or her primary objective in life. When Jesus asked the rich young man to sell all that he had and give the money to the poor and then become his disciple, Jesus was trying to bring him to the discovery that his life must be focused and dependent upon God, not on material wealth. Through his teaching, Jesus is alerting his followers to the dangers of wealth. His instruction is buttressed by Qohelet, the sage, who says, "One who loves gold will not be justified; one who pursues money will be led astray by it. Many have come to ruin because of gold, and their destruction has met them face to face. It is a stumbling block to those who are avid for it, and every fool will be taken captive by it." (Sirach 31:5-7) Similarly, Paul reinforces the point when he says, "For the love of money is a root of all kinds of evil, and in their eagerness to be rich some have wandered away from the faith and pierced themselves with many pains." (I Tm. 6:10) In the situation where the disciple remains faithful to the Lord, he or she will be rewarded. This is what Jesus meant when he said that those who had left everything to follow him would receive "very much more in this age, and in the age to come eternal life." (Lk. 18:30) This is the same answer Jesus gave to Peter when asked about what the disciples were to receive in view of the sacrifices that they had made to be his followers. Simply put, Jesus is teaching two things: sacrifices made for the sake of the Reign of God will be rewarded and that physical death is not the end of life, there is the promise of the resurrection, the promise of life after death.

---

[50] Ibid., 281.

[51] John Paul II, *Veritatis Splendor*, no. 17 # 2.

Relevant Concerns and Insights for an Inculturated Catechesis

Money is something that all human beings need in order to help them to acquire the basic necessities of life such as food, clothing, shelter and medical care. In spite of this need, obsession with materialism and unlimited cravings for material wealth cannot be promoted. Unfortunately, this is the trap in which young men in Africa frequently have been caught. The two key lessons to be learned from the proverb about life and money and the biblical narrative of the rich young man are the importance of avoiding the obsession to possess material things at any cost and the importance of sharing, of generosity, of hospitality, and of solidarity.

Young men in Africa must be helped to realize that a person's dignity does not lie in the amassing of wealth and other material things, but rather the dignity of each human person is to be found in their very creation in the image and likeness of God. (cf. Gen. 1:26) As persons in relation—with God, others and the world, male youth must be encouraged to assume responsibility for assisting others, especially the needy, in a spirit of solidarity. Thomas J. Massaro beautifully captures this when he notes that solidarity

> Calls attention to the simple and easily observable fact that people are interdependent; they rely on each other for almost all their biological and social needs… Using the term "solidarity" means that we recognize that human interdependence not only as a necessary fact but also as a positive value in our lives. We cannot realize our full potential or appreciate the full meaning of our dignity unless we share our lives with others and cooperate on projects that hold the promise of mutual benefit.[52]

In the opinion of Massaro, "Solidarity begins as an inner attitude and, when it has fully taken root within us, expresses itself through numerous external activities that demonstrate our commitment to the well-being of others."[53] He concludes that "the full features of our human nature and dignity come to maturity only in the context of community life, where many relationships develop and ripen."[54]

Still on the sense of solidarity among all human beings, Thomas J. Massaro together with Thomas A. Shannon argue that

---

[52] Thomas Massaro, *Living Justice: Catholic Social Teaching in Action* (Franklin, WI: Sheed and Ward, 2000), 120. See also Jeffry Odell Korgen, *Solidarity will transform the World: Stories of Hope from Catholic Relief Services* (Maryknoll, NY: Orbis Books, 2007).

[53] Thomas Massaro, *Living Justice*, 121.

[54] Ibid.

One quality we need to develop among all people is a spirit of internationalism. From a practical point of view, internationalism is already a reality because we are all mutually dependent on each other to care for and preserve the goods of this world. We are all bound to our planet by the workings of a delicate ecosystem, and the only way to preserve our resources and ourselves is to look to the good of all.

From a theological point of view, a spirit of internationalism is a very deep part of Christianity. Christianity, along with other religions, proclaims that God is the God of all. Since all are created in the image of God, all are equally brothers and sisters. Such an orientation leads very naturally to a spirit of concern for each other and to a way of seeing one another that can transcend race and nationalism.[55]

This sense of solidarity was the attitude of Jesus which Paul encourages Christians to emulate when he writes to the Philippians:

Let the same mind be in you that was in Christ Jesus, who, though he was in the form of God, did not regard equality with God as something to be exploited, but emptied himself, taking the form of a slave, being born in human likeness. And being found in human form, he humbled himself and became obedient to the point of death—even death on a cross. Therefore, God also highly exalted him and gave him the name that is above every name, so that at the name of Jesus every knee should bend, in heaven and on earth and under the earth, and every tongue should confess that Jesus Christ is Lord, to the glory of God the Father. (Phil. 2:5-11)

Following the example and the teachings of Jesus, young men in Africa must be helped to recognize the importance self-giving and self-sacrifice and the need to eschew self-centeredness.

Theme 9. Nipa firi soro ba a, obesi kuro mu— Becoming One with the World in Solidarity

Life is such that the human person cannot exist without the world. One's life and progress are dependent in many ways upon that which pertains to the world. Taking an interest in the world is part of being human. The Akans say *nipa firi soro ba a, obesi kuro mu*—when a human being descends he/she descends into a town. The proverb is a reminder that people are born into a world, a real world where human persons need each other. Building on this proverb and its insights for discovering the meaning of oneness with the world in solidarity, the parable of the prodigal son serves as a resource for further reflection.

---

[55] Thomas J. Massaro and Thomas A. Shannon, *Catholic Perspectives on Peace and War* (New York: Rowman and Littlefield Publishers, Inc. 2003), 133.

The Parable of the Prodigal Son—Lk. 15: 11-32

A man had two sons. One day, the younger son asked the father to give him his share of the family inheritance. Some time after receiving his share, he traveled to a distant country. He spent his property through a life of debauchery and licentiousness. No sooner had he squandered all his property than a great famine affected the country. In his dire need, he became an employee of a rich man who sent him to take care of his swine. Filled with hunger, he desired to eat the food of the swine but he was not allowed. Reflecting upon his predicament, he decided to return to his father and apologize. While he was on his way home, his father saw him and ran to embrace him. The young man knelt down before his father and said to him, "Father, I have sinned against heaven and before you; I am no longer worthy to be called your son." (Lk. 15: 21) The father welcomed him by dressing him up and throwing a party for him because his son had returned to him safe and sound.

Meanwhile, the older son was in the fields taking care of the sheep. As he came closer to the house and heard the music and the dancing, he inquired about what was going on. He was informed of his brother's return and of the celebration prepared by their father. The older son became furious and refused to enter the house. The father came out and spoke to him. He said, "Son, you are always with me, and all that is mine is yours. But we had to celebrate and rejoice, because this brother of yours was dead and has come to life; he was lost and has been found." (Lk. 15: 31)

Relevant Concerns and Insights for an Inculturated Catechesis

As noted earlier, in spite of traditional communalism in Africa, individualism and greed are taking hold of a greater number of young men in Africa today. This has resulted in many of them not showing generosity or reaching out to the vulnerable and less fortunate people in the society, particularly those with HIV/AIDS, street children, drug addicts, and those in correctional institutions. There is the urgent need to inculcate in male youth the importance of being generous and sharing their talents, time and treasures with those in need.

Jesus speaks directly about the relationship between God and other human beings when he says that entrance into the Reign of God depends on one's actions towards other human beings: "Truly I tell you, just as you did it to one of the least of these who are members of my family; you did it to me… Truly, I tell you, just as you did not do it to one of the least of these, you did not do it to me." (Mt. 25:31-46) As the First Letter of John states, "Those who say, "I love

God and hate their brothers and sisters, are liars; for those who do not love a brother or sister whom they have seen, cannot love God whom they have not seen." (I Jn. 4:20)   In becoming aware of the fact that life is relational, young men in Africa must be taught that each person's existence is linked to the lives of others.   As such human existence has a vertical as well as a horizontal dimension.   No person can claim to have a relationship with God and neglect his/her relationship with other human beings or the world.

Having explored some of the ways in which integrative reflection on traditional African philosophy, Christian beliefs, African proverbs and selected biblical narratives can contribute to an inculturated catechesis that addresses relevant issues and pastoral concerns related to faith formation and moral education, the next section of this chapter discusses how some of the specific problems confronting male youth in Africa can be addressed by leaders in the Roman Catholic church.

The Formation of Male Youth: Challenges
Facing the Church & African Society

In spite of what the Roman Catholic church has done for male youth in Africa, more needs to be done both in terms of evangelization and education for citizenship. The Church must continue to bear in mind what John Paul II said to the young people of Nigeria during his visit to that country in 1982. Among other things he said, "will-power reinforced by humble prayer is essential to anyone who is trying to act in a fully human way."[56] The cultural and religious formation of the young men must contribute to their spiritual and social conscience. The elements of such formation must include: Personality Development, Respect for Human Life, the Promotion of Justice and Peace, Education for Citizenship and Authentic Christian Discipleship.

Personality Development

The Roman Catholic church must find ways of inculcating in young men the conviction that they are created in the image and likeness of God. (cf. Gen. 1:26)   In order for the dignity of the human person to be promoted, this value must be internalized. Young men must be led to discover that everything created by God is good. The cultivation of self-esteem among young men is critical to the development of a positive self-image that contributes to self-

---

[56] John Paul II, "Address to the Young People in Nigeria", no. 2.

confidence, positive thinking and respect for self and others.[57]   Male youth
must be taught to recognize that the fingers of a hand are not the same. People
are different and each person has a different role to play in this world. In a
similar fashion, every young man must be helped to discover that he was
created for a purpose. He must come to terms with the fact that he has a role to
play in the life of the church and society. Nobody can play that role except the
young man himself. For this reason, every young man needs to acquire skills
and abilities in order to be competent and capable enough to exercise his
unique and indispensable role in the community and in the society at large.[58]
Young men must be helped to acknowledge that at the end of their lives they
will be required to give account of their stewardship to their Creator. As Paul
notes, "We do not live to ourselves, and we do not die to ourselves. If we live,
we live to the Lord; so then, whether we live or whether we die, we are the
Lord's. For this end Christ died and lived again, so that he might be Lord of
both the dead and the living… So then, each of us will be accountable to God."
(Rom. 14:7-12) In paying attention to the personality development of young
men in Africa, the church is in a privileged position to foster their development
into mature adulthood and guarantee that their perspectives on human life and
existence will be positive and beneficial for the entire society.[59]

Respect for Human Life

Life is precious. It is inviolable. God is the giver of life. Consequently, it is
only God who can take it away. The Akans have many proverbs to talk about
the inevitability of death.   One is *otimfoo na oworo kawa fa batire*—It is the
Almighty who pulls a bracelet along the shoulders. They also say, *se Onyame nku
wo a, oteasefoo bere kwa*—If God does not take your life, no human being can
destroy your life. Mindful of these wisdom sayings, young men must be taught
to always respect and value human life. To destroy a human life is an affront to
God since it is God alone who determines who is to live and who is to die. If
respect for the value of human life is deeply inculcated and imbedded in male
youth, it will be difficult, if not impossible, for them to cause harm and do
violence to other human beings or themselves. Mindful of this value and belief
in the uniqueness of every individual, young men must be urged to recognize

---

[57] Terry D. Cooper, *Sin, Pride and Self-Acceptance: The Problem of Identity in Theology and Psychology*
(Downers Grove, ILL: InterVarsity Press, 2003), 14.
[58] Ibid., 87-110.
[59] Ibid., 139.

the insights so beautifully expressed by John O'Donohue: "There is something deeply sacred about every presence. When we become blind to this, we violate Nature and turn our beautiful world into a wasteland. We treat people as if they were disposable objects."[60] O'Donohue also notes that "We desperately need to retrieve our capacity for reverence. Each day that is given to you is full of the shy graciousness of the divine tenderness. It is a lovely practice at night to spend a little while revisiting the invisible sanctuaries of your lived day. Each day is a secret story woven around the radiant heart of wonder. We let our days fall away like empty shells and miss all the treasure."[61]

Proper personality development and respect for human life can enable young men to take care of themselves by avoiding self-destructive behaviors such as taking drugs, sexual promiscuity and corruption of every sort. An inculturated catechesis can help a young man to offer his entire self—body, mind and spirit to God. Rather than being conformed to the seduction of destructive forces, he can "be transformed by the renewing of his mind as he discerns what is the will of God—what is good and acceptable and perfect." (Rom.12:1-2)

Promotion of Justice and Peace

Akans say, *adidigya wo ho yi ene muna na enam*—If a person eats without thinking of his partner, the latter gets angry. Many of the conflicts and wars that have destroyed many countries in Africa are due to injustice, the failure and corruption of leaders, and disregard for the social welfare of all citizens. Many African leaders have become despots and dictators. They become inebriated by power, privilege and prestige. While the people suffer, starve and perish, the leaders become wealthier and more irresponsible.[62] Violence and injustice become the order of the day. Those who voice their feelings against such leaders are targeted. Some flee for their lives and go into exile. Those who remain are arrested, tortured, imprisoned and at times killed. In dealing with

---

[60] John O'Donohue, *Eternal Echoes: Celtic Reflections on our Yearning to Belong*, (New York: HarperCollins Publishers Inc. 1999), 76.

[61] Ibid., 77

[62] Cf. BBC News, "Charges mount against Chiluba", http://news.bbc.co.uk/2/hi/Africa/3125601.stm, (accessed December 8, 2007). See also, BBC News, "Liberia Police arrest ex-Leader", http://news.bbc.co.uk/2/hi/Africa/7133175.stm, (accessed December 8, 2007) and BBC News, "Nigeria ex-oil governor arrested", http://news.bbc.co.uk/2/hi/africa/7141047.stm (accessed December 12, 2007).

justice, John P. Bequette notes that justice is relational. He argues that "to be a person is to live in society, in relation to other persons. This relatedness carries with it certain rights and duties."[63] He goes on to say,

> In criminal justice, each person has the right to life and property, and is obligated to respect the person and property of his or her neighbor. In civil justice, each person has the right to be treated honestly in all business enterprises, labor arguments and basic community relationships, and each is obligated to conduct himself or herself honestly. In social justice, each person has the right to basic necessities of life in recognition of his or her vocational contribution to the good of society, this contribution comprising part of the obligatory aspect of social justice. Each is entitled to certain things, and each is obligated to contribute: "Each is entitled to his or her ability, to each according to his or her need.[64]

Heightening political consciousness and social responsibility is the best way to empower male youth to have a sense of justice and fair play.[65] In recognizing that "A hungry person is an angry person", and that "Justice delayed is justice denied", male youth must be taught to recognize that the denial of justice is always a threat to peaceful co-existence.[66] It is in this light that John Paul II in his address to young people in Nigeria during his visit in 1982, challenged them by saying,

> As young people, you should constantly strive to identify the ills of your society, such as bribery and corruption, the embezzlement of government or company funds, extravagant and unproductive spending, the parade of wealth, neglect of the poor and the friendless, nepotism, tribalism, political antagonism, denial of the rights of the poor, abortion, contraception and other evils which also ravage other countries. As true youth you will see, judge and then act according to the criteria of the Gospel of Jesus Christ.[67]

In order to promote justice and peace certain actions need to be taken. As Dafue Phou notes, "These actions involve the intervention of mediators of facilitators of people who encourage dialogue between the different parties as

---

[63] John P. Bequette, *Christian Humanism: Creation, Redemption, and Reintegration*, Revised Edition (New York: University Press of America, Inc. 2007), 88.

[64] Ibid.

[65] John A. Coleman, ed. *Christian Political Ethics* (Princeton, New Jersey: Princeton University Press), 2008.

[66] See Richard Gibb, *Grace and Global Justice: The Socio-Political Mission of the Church in an Age of Globalization* (Waynesboro, GA: Paternoster, 2006), 177-206.

[67] John Paul II, "Address to the Young People of Nigeria", no. 5.

well as of individuals who can console, sustain and accompany the victims of conflict and those who must make decisions related to it. People need to be trained at different levels of responsibility in this work for peace."[68] Phou thinks that "children, young people and adults can take part in experiments that help them to analyze their own behavior and envisage the kind of changes in themselves and their communities that will be needed to improve the situation."[69] In the opinion of Phou, working for peace, "Requires a sense of vocation and considerable courage, but also an open mind, adequate training and the conviction that working for peace cannot be separated from working for justice and equal opportunities. When a community adopts these values and put them into practice, it is possible to build the foundations for a culture of peace."[70] In order to promote peace in the sub-region of Africa, the approach recommended by Thomas Massaro and Thomas Shannon merits serious consideration. They observe that

> A new orientation suggests that peace be the beginning premise rather than the conclusion of one's methodology. Instead of seeing peace only as the end product of armed conflict, one must engage in the process of developing a theology of peace so that one may work actively toward establishing peace. The state of affairs produced by deterrence and the arms race may not be active conflict, at least at the present moment, but one would hardly describe it as a state of peace because of tensions and anxiety that the structure itself produces both nationally and internationally. Thus a primary part of a shift in attitude or a reevaluation of war would require that we begin with peace as a premise rather than as a conclusion.[71]

The promotion of justice and peace must be part of the cultural and religious formation of young men in Africa. In order to educate them for responsible citizenship, an understanding and appreciation of full humanization is necessary. As Massaro and Shannon note, "War is becoming more expensive. This cost is not exclusively financial. More and more of our brightest scientists and engineers are using their talents for the production of weapons of destruction rather than for the development of technologies that

---

[68] Dafue Phou. *Peace in Troubled Cities: Creative Models of Building Community amidst Violence* (Geneva: WCC Publications, 1998), 132.

[69] Ibid.

[70] Ibid., 133.

[71] Thomas J. Massaro and Thomas A. Shannon, *Catholic Perspectives on Peace and War*, 124.

will serve life. Not only our money but also our talent, our energy, and our creative thought serve war rather than life."[72]

Education for Citizenship

Leaders and members of the Roman Catholic church in Africa must be attuned to the lessons of history. The church cannot abandon its responsibility to educate young men for responsible citizenship. A person cannot be a good Christian and fail to assume social responsibility for his fellow citizens. Quoting again from John Paul II's address to young people in Nigeria in 1982, he made it clear that: "A good Christian is a good citizen. You must love your country, obey its laws, respect your leaders, and pay your taxes. You are called to take your due part in political, social, economic and cultural affairs. When you are eligible, you should vote and be voted for in political elections."[73] As the church engages in its mission of evangelization, it must enable male youth to become responsible citizens. John F. Kennedy, the former President of United States of America once said, "Do not ask what your country can do for you but ask what you can do for your country." This challenge is both a lesson and an eye-opener to young men in Africa.

In an effort to foster responsible citizenship among male youth, I believe the song writer Ephraim Amo[74] may serve as a model for male youth in Africa. Ephraim Amo, noted for his patriotic songs, highlights this message in *Yen ara yen asaase ni*—This land is ours. This song is so popular that it is like a second national anthem. It has been translated into many dialects in Ghana. The lyrics of the song are:

Yen are asaase ni
Eye abodenden ma yen
Mogya a nananom hwie gu, nya de too ho maa yen
Aduru me ne wo nso so
Se yebeye bi atoa so
Nimdee ntraso nkotokrane ne apesemenkomenya

---

[72] Ibid., 130.

[73] John Paul II, *Address to the Young People of Nigeria*, no. 4.

[74] Ephraim Amo was a citizen of Peki in the Volta Region of Ghana. He was a member of the Presbyterian church and wanted to introduce some forms of inculturation into the church. They were not accepted. Finally, he was expelled from the church because the leaders of the Presbyterian church at the time felt that the cultural elements he wanted to introduce in the church were 'pagan'.

Ato yen bra mo dem na ye'saase ho do atom se

Chorus 2 xs
Oman no se ebe ye yie oo
Oman no se enye yie oo
Eye se na ose, omanfo bra na yennkyere

This is our own land
It is a precious creation for us
Our ancestors shed blood to get it for us
It is now your turn and my turn
To work to continue it
Too-known-attitude and selfishness
Have possessed us so much
That our love for the land has been destroyed
Chorus 2 xs

Whether the country will progress
Whether the country will not progress
Whether it will be destroyed or not, it will depend on the lives of the citizens

One might ask: What if this song of Ephraim Amo were to become part of the church's evangelization efforts with young men? What if they were asked to reflect upon its message from time to time? Patriotic and theological, might it help them to live their lives as the socially responsible citizens and authentic Christians envisioned by John Paul II during his address to the young people of Nigeria?[75]

Authentic Christian Discipleship

The overall goal of the formation towards the full humanization of young men is to enable them to become disciples of Jesus Christ and authentic Christians. Pope John Paul II, quoting again from his address to the young people of Nigeria, said "Young people of Nigeria, I have come to encourage you in the great mission you have to help build a better world, to advance Christ's Kingdom of truth and life, of holiness and grace, of justice, love and peace. It is to him that I wish to direct your gaze."[76] Pope Benedict XVI said something similar when he noted, "Christ is totally different from all the founders of other

---

[75] For more on Christians and patriotism see Michael G. Long and Tracy Wenger Sadd, eds. *God and Country? Diverse Perspectives on Christianity and Patriotism* (New York: Palgrave Macmillan, 2007).
[76] John Paul II, *Address to the Young People of Nigeria*, no. 7.

religions and he cannot be reduced to a Buddha, a Socrates or a Confucius. He is really the bridge between heaven and earth, the light of truth who has appeared to us."[77] To comprehend this vision, young men must be helped to encounter and experience Christ in a mature way. This may involve enlarging their concepts and perceptions of God, in order that they might be opened to new insights from the Lord under the influence of the Holy Spirit.[78]

As previously noted, though the Roman Catholic church already has accomplished a great deal with and for young men in Africa, more still needs to be done in view of rapid cultural change and the pervasive effects of globalization.

Summary

The insights of Chapter Five offer the Church in Africa some essential elements necessary for an inculturated catechesis for young men. I have suggested throughout the chapter that a multifaceted catechesis of this sort provides concepts that they can hold on to and learn from in order that they can become fully human as God created them. Once church leaders and members form young men in the areas of Personality Development, Respect for Human Life, Promotion of Justice and Peace, Education for Citizenship and Authentic Christian Discipleship, young men in the sub-region will become respectable and responsible citizens and Christians for themselves, their families, their communities, and the world.

---

[77] Robert Moynihan, ed., *Let God's Light Shine Forth: The Spiritual Vision of Pope Benedict XVI*, 99.

[78] See Vincent MacNamara, "On Having a Religious Morality", in *Contemporary Irish Moral Discourse*, ed. Amelia Fleming, (Blackrock, Co. Dublin: The Columba Press, 2007), 88-103. See also Enda McDonagh, "A Discourse on the Centrality of Justice" in the same book, 104-116.

CONCLUSION

This book, entitled *Mission, Communion and Relationship: A Roman Catholic Response to the Crisis of Male Youths in Africa*, began by holding together the beauty and richness of Africa with an awareness of the fact that the majority of Africans live in abject poverty and malnourishment as ever growing numbers live and die with HIV/AIDS, and countless others live as refugees and exiles.

Chapter One focused on the missionary dynamics of the Church. It examined the background and contemporary context of this book and provided a Roman Catholic perspective on the relevance of this analysis for those engaged in ministry to male youth. The chapter began with an overview of Ghana. It discussed the people, the history, culture, religions and geography of Ghana. The chapter reviewed how the Christian religion was implanted in the then Gold Coast (now Ghana). It was noted that the first attempt to establish Christianity in Ghana in the fifteenth century was undertaken by Roman Catholics. However, this first attempt was not successful, in part because it was not well-planned. Subsequent efforts by Protestant churches like the Anglicans, the Presbyterians and the Methodists succeeded in introducing the Christian religion to the people. The Protestant churches succeeded in large part because they had a well-thought out plan to promote Christianity in the Gold Coast. Among other things the chapter examined how Protestant missionaries concentrated solely on the work of evangelization and did not get caught-up in the gold trade that thrived in the Gold Coast. Secondly, they were willing to learn the culture of the people which facilitated their ministry. Thirdly, they trained some indigenous people who in turn supported them in the work of evangelism. Last but not the least they established schools which went a long way to help in spreading the Christian message. Alongside Protestant efforts, Roman Catholic initiatives in the nineteenth century also bore fruit. The Chapter noted how the Christian religion continues to grow in Ghana today and observed the significance of African Indigenous Churches (AIC). These new churches together with the Roman Catholic church and Protestant churches in the region are working hand in hand to deal with the crisis confronting male youth in Ghana.

The Chapter ended with the review of some relevant documents of the United Nations and the African Union dealing with the plight of young men. My purpose in Chapter One was to discuss the early beginnings of Christianity in Ghana and to underscore the urgent need for the churches in Ghana to positively respond to the crisis confronting young men in Ghana and the sub-region mindful of the statistics presented by African and World organizations.

The title of Chapter Two gives expression to the heart of the book. "Beards on Fire": The Plight of African Male Youth as a Missiological Challenge to the Roman Catholic Church in Africa—A Ghanaian Analysis." The chapter identified and discussed the various crises confronting male youth in Ghana in particular and Africa in general. Arguing that these crises inhibit the development and progress necessary to be respectable and responsible citizens, the chapter identified the problems besetting young men, including: dislocation in the society, illiteracy, streetism, unemployment, emigration, crime, imitation of foreign cultures, drug abuse and sexual and reproductive health—HIV/AIDS. Statistics were given to buttress the crises confronting male youth in Ghana and Africa. It was argued that if these problems are not dealt with, the result will be a tragic social phenomenon in which young men become burdens and liabilities unto themselves, their families and the entire society.

The second part of the chapter looked at some of the ways that the various religious traditions in Ghana have been responding to the plight of male youth in recent years. In particular, it reviewed the many programs that the Roman Catholic church in Ghana has put in place to address some of the realities militating against young men in Ghana. Interventions noted included: the setting-up of schools at various levels in the educational ladder; the assignment of chaplains at both Catholic and non-Catholic schools; and a variety of youth programs designed to engage the youth in church-based activities including vacation camps, trips and gatherings. All these programs are geared towards formation of youth. The Archdioceses of Cape Coast and Kumasi were given as specific examples of the work being done by the Roman Catholic church as it responds to the crisis of male youth in Ghana. The chapter also observed that the Roman Catholic church is not the only entity interested in responding to the crisis of young men. Other churches in Ghana have proved equal to the task as far as youth formation is concerned. Also noted in the chapter was the fact that it is not only the Christians who are championing the cause of male youth in Ghana. Other religions like ATR and Islam are also stakeholders as far as the cultural and religious formation of young men in Ghana is concerned. In this way, it was observed that the churches in Ghana have worked in partnership in the spirit of ecumenism and inter religious-dialogue to promote development and progress among the citizenry of Ghana with particular reference to young men.

My purpose in Chapter Two was to diagnose some of the situations confronting male youth in Ghana and Africa. Secondly, it was to show that the churches in Ghana are not only concerned with the religious formation of male youth. They also are interested in the other areas of formation including the social, cultural and political. In this regard, the churches have adopted a holistic approach in dealing with young men in Ghana. This has helped to prevent many young men from going astray and being led into situations similar to those that have contributed to the start of civil wars and social strife in many other countries of Africa such as Sierra Leone, Liberia, Somalia, Darfur and recently in Kenya.

Chapter Three, entitled: "I am because we are and since we are, therefore, I am" dealt with maturity and male identity formation. In this chapter, I argued for the need to recover an African moral vision of 'Persons-in-Relation. To this end, I drew upon the insights of Kwame Gyekye, John Macmurray and Augustine of Hippo representing the past heritage, modern situation and Christian life respectively.

Under Kwame Gyekye, it was observed that Africans have a transcendent belief in the Supreme Being, the creator of all. It was also noted by Kwame Gyekye that African concepts of individuality and communality are not antithetical. Rather, they are reciprocal and even reinforce each other. Furthermore, Kwame Gyekye notes that African morality is under both religious and non-religious influences.

John Macmurray argued that the individual is not only a thinker but also an agent. This is because the individual is always doing something. However, the individual person is never alone but always in relation since one's existence does not make sense without the acknowledgement of the existence of others. John Macmurray further noted that the individual has freedom. However, the freedom of the individual is not a license to do whatever one likes. Whatever one does must conform to one's nature and it must not be injurious to others.

The section on Augustine discussed his past life of licentiousness and debauchery. It talked about how he got himself involved in peer-group pressure and gangsterism which made him do certain things which left to himself he would not have done. All these things changed when he converted and became a Christian and as a bishop wrote many books and letters and shared his life and goal as an example of Christian life on pilgrimage.

The last part of the chapter examined the conclusions of the three authors. The comparison centered on their views regarding (1) God and Humanity; (2) Human Relationships (3) Morality. My intention in Chapter Three was to argue that globalization is in some way negatively affecting young men in Africa. They are losing their cultural heritage and identity. Individualism is eating into the social fabric of their lives. I believe this is a dangerous phenomenon. It can disorganize and disorientate them as a people. Chapter Three underscored the fact that young men in Africa are individuals. However, their existence has meaning only in relation to the existence of others. Consequently, they must always see themselves as 'persons in relation'. This emphasis stresses the fact that in African anthropology, it is not a matter of choice between communality and individuality. Communality and individuality are symbiotic. They cannot be uncoupled.

Chapter Four sets forth a discussion on communion and solidarity with male youth. I argued in the chapter that communion and solidarity with male youth is a missiological imperative for the Roman Catholic church in Africa. The chapter examined the place of young men in the activities of the Roman Catholic church and explored how the church has empowered them to live their lives as true human beings. It started with communion and solidarity in the New Testament. It looked at how Jesus bequeathed these two virtues to his disciples and how they were promoted among the community of Jesus' disciples and in the churches founded by Paul and the other apostles. This was followed by a review of the evolution of communion and solidarity in the course of the history of the church.

The chapter acknowledged that since the Second Vatican Council, attempts have been made to repair the damage done to the Church's efforts to promote communion and solidarity. This has led to the ecumenical movement in the world today.

I observed in the chapter that in its recent years of promotion of communion and solidarity, the Roman Catholic church has paid greater attention to the youth in the church. Various popes since the Second Vatican Council, most especially John Paul II, have placed more emphasis on youth apostolate. Acknowledging the important role that youth can play in the missionary activity of the church, John Paul II established the World Youth Day. This has brought forth an enthusiasm and commitment on the part of many young people from around the world.

Again I observed in the chapter that communion and solidarity are not only carried out in the Universal church but also they are carried out at the local church in Ghana. As a practical demonstration of communion and solidarity in the Roman Catholic church, I used the Corpus Christi Catholic church, New Tafo, Kumasi as an example. In this parish, it was noted how the various adult groups in the parish have their junior counter-parts. Some of them include: Youth choir, the Junior Praesidium of the Legion of Mary, the Tarcisians of the Sacred Heart of Jesus, the Evangelicals of the Catholic Charismatic Renewal Movement and the Catholic Organization for Social and Religious Advancement. It was noted that the youth in the parish have their own Parish Youth Council and they are duly represented in the Parish Council. The youth in the parish form an integral part of the life in the parish. In this way, communion and solidarity with the youth are maintained and promoted.

At the end of the chapter, I argued that the Roman Catholic church must not be concerned only with young men affiliated with the church. The church must equally pay attention to those young men who are on the margins of the church and the society and those who have fallen foul with the laws of the country and find themselves in correctional institutes. Furthermore, I strongly argued that the Roman Catholic church must take a second look at its admission policies to seminaries and religious houses of formation. The church must give a second chance to young men who once fell on the wrong side of the laws of the country but have learned their lessons, repented and have been "born again." I cited Paul and Augustine as examples of people who had troubled pasts but later became great teachers and ministers for the church.

Chapter Five focused on the importance of theological imagination in the cultural, religious and ethical formation of male youth in Africa. This chapter used foundational insights from traditional African philosophy and biblical narratives as resources for an inculturated catechesis for the formation of young men in Africa. The chapter emphasized that if male youth can be helped to become respectful and responsible citizens and authentic Christians, they need to be formed culturally, religiously and ethically.

The chapter was divided into two parts. In the first part, I argued that young men in Africa have to know their origins and ends inasmuch as they come from a background that is rich both culturally and religiously. Consequently, I highlighted some selected concepts in Africa Traditional Religion that are foundational for the traditional African philosophy that informs and influences the culture into which the young men have been born.

These themes included: Cosmology, Monotheism, Creation, Anthropology and Eschatology.

In the second part, I made use of some selected African proverbs since proverbs are one of the ways of imparting knowledge in African societies. These proverbs were set in dialogue with selected biblical narratives. They were chosen to reinforce for young men teachings about God, Creation, Eschatology, Jesus Christ, Anthropology, Christian Identity and Communion, the Holy Spirit, Soteriology and Solidarity in the world. Secondly, these proverbs and biblical narratives were selected so as to identify those virtues that might be inculcated in young men in Africa, virtues that are necessary if an authentically African Christian manhood is to flourish in the next generation. The virtues that these proverbs and biblical narratives seek to reinforce are: faith in God as the origin of all things; stewardship and care for the earth and creatures; accountability; fidelity and commitment; good human relationships; individuality and communality; sense of God's accompaniment; quality of life; generosity and outreach to others.

The purpose for emphasizing these virtues was to address social issues and pastoral concerns which include: the forces of secularization; a limited sense of transcendence; consumerism, disregard of African culture; seduction by the forces of globalization; a frayed connection to cultural roots and identity; questionable capacity for discipleship; forces of dehumanization, peer-group pressure and gangsterism; egocentrism and corruption; misguided sense of direction; unlimited craving for wealth; HIV/AIDS, streetism and drug-addiction. I argued in this chapter that young men must be given opportunities for reflection if the Church is to form them—culturally and religiously—for Christian manhood and citizenship a culture and a country that is deeply religious. As John S. Pobee notes, "It is difficult to distinguish sharply between the religious and nonreligious; between the sacred and secular. In African societies, religion stares people in the face at all points—at birth, at puberty, at marriage, at death, and at national or tribal festivals. Thus, religion is as vocal as it is dynamic in African society and cannot be meaningfully sidestepped."[1] As a practical demonstration of this, he says, "a traditional Akan would not eat without putting the first morsel down for the ancestors; nor would he drink unless some of it had first been poured down to the ancestors."[2] I noted that if

---

[1] John S. Pobee, *Toward an African Theology* (Nashville, TN: Abington, 1979), 26.
[2] Ibid. 45.

these young men are not adequately mentored, they predictably will become burdens and liabilities to themselves, their families and the larger society.

In attempts to respond ecclesially and missiologically to the crises confronting male youth in Africa, I propose that the following topics merit serious consideration:

1. Good and credible leadership in the Church;

2. Adequate and proper formation in seminaries and religious houses;

3. Committed and dedicated laity in the church;

4. Responsibility on the part of young men for themselves.

Serving Youth: The Leadership of Good and Credible Men in the Church

As noted in the book, Jesus entrusted his sheep and lambs to Peter. (cf. Jn. 21:15-19) Young men in Africa, especially those who are on the margins of the Church and society need guides, models and mentors in their lives. The Roman Catholic church must help in this regard as it responds to the crises of male youth. Bishops, priests and religious men must live lives worthy of emulation. Moreover, they must be credible witnesses of Jesus Christ. They must avoid any form of behavior that reveals tendencies associated with corruption, egoism and the abuse of power as sometimes seen among some leaders in Africa. Speaking on the position of the bishop in relationship with his priests, the Second Vatican Council notes, "He should regard them as sons and friends. He should always be ready to listen to them and cultivate an atmosphere of easy familiarity with them, thus facilitating the pastoral work of the entire diocese."[3] To avoid authoritarianism in the church, bishops are encouraged, "to ensure an increasingly effective apostolate, bishops should be willing to engage in dialogue with his priests, individually and collectively, not merely occasionally, but if possible, regularly."[4]

With regard to priests, to ensure effectiveness in their ministry, priests are encouraged

> To cultivate those virtues which are richly held in high esteem in human relations. Such qualities are goodness of heart, sincerity, strength and constancy of mind, careful

---

[3] *Dominus Christus*, no. 16, #2. *Vatican Council II, 573.*
[4] Ibid., no. 28, #2, 580.

attention to justice, courtesy and others which the apostle Paul recommends when he says: "Whatever is true, whatever is honorable, whatever is just, whatever is pure, whatever is lovely, whatever is gracious, if there is any excellence, if there is anything worthy of praise, think about these things (Phil. 4:8).[5]

I argue that in responding to the crises of male youth in Ghana, bishops, priests and male religious must demonstrate that they are God-fearing, human-centered and approachable. In exercising their roles of leadership they must exhibit accountability and transparency in order to attract and serve young men in the Church.

Adequate and Proper Formation in Seminaries and Religious Houses

The Second Vatican Council noted the importance and the necessity for priestly training and the formation of men as religious.[6] I suggest that seminarians and aspirants in Africa must not see the priesthood and the religious life as stepping-stones towards a prosperous life. They must not enter the seminary and the religious houses because they have no options or because the priesthood or religious life offers future security. Rather, they must choose the priesthood and the religious life moved by the desire to serve God's people as priests and religious. Consequently, they must be formed in such a way that like St. Paul, they can say, "I have been crucified with Christ; and it is no longer I who live, but it is Christ who lives in me. And the life I now live in the flesh I live by faith in the Son of God, who loved me and gave himself for me." Gal. 2:19b-20   This calls for a greater emphasis on the four pillars of formation, namely: human, spiritual, intellectual and pastoral.[7] As noted by John Paul II,

> Today more than ever, there is need to from *future priests* in the true cultural values of
> their country, in a sense of honesty, responsibility and integrity. They shall be formed
> in a such a manner that they will have the qualities of the representatives of Christ, of
> true servants and animators of the Christian community…solidly spiritual, ready to

---

[5] *Presbyterorum Ordinis*, no. 3, #3. *Vatican Council II, 867.*

[6] *Optatam Totius*, no. 1, *Vatican Council II*, 707; See also *Perfectae Caritatis*, no. 1#2, *Vatican Council* II, 611.

[7] For more on the four pillars of formation, see John Paul II, *Pastores Dabo Vobis* (Rome: March 25, 1992), http://www.vatican.va/.../apost_exhortations/documents/hf_jp-ii_exh_25031992 (accessed February 15, 2008).

serve, dedicated to evangelization, capable of administering the goods of the church efficiently and openly and of living a simple life as befits their milieu.[8]

Committed and Dedicated Laity in the Church

The role of the laity in the missionary activity of the Church as it pertains to the formation of male youth cannot be over-emphasized. The bishops at the Second Vatican Council noted that

> The church is not truly established and does not fully live, nor is a perfect sign of Christ unless there is a genuine laity existing and working alongside the hierarchy. For the Gospel cannot become deeply rooted in the mentality, life and work of a people without the active presence of lay people. Therefore, from the foundation of a church very special care must be taken to form a mature Christian laity.[9]

I am of the opinion that the Roman Catholic church's attempts to respond to the crises of male youth in Africa cannot be successful without the active and full participation of the laity and more specifically, the commitment of mature lay men. Many ecclesial communities in Africa were started by lay people. They came together for fellowship and bible-sharing long before the clergy came in later on to minister to them. As bearers and transmitters of cultural values and Christian virtues, their leadership is essential in the development and growth of faith communities and formation. John Paul II recognized those who positively contribute to the education process of the church when he said, "How many of us have received from people like you our first notions of catechism and our preparation for the sacrament of Penance, for our first Communion and Confirmation! The fourth General Assembly of the Synod did not forget you. I join with it in encouraging you to continue your collaboration for the life of the church."[10] Bishops and priests celebrate the sacraments with people and later on leave for their homes and rectories respectively. It is the lay people who engage with young men on a day to day basis. While bishops and priests preach the gospel and teach the doctrines of the church, leading by example in ways that are important, it is the laity who put these teachings into practice in the context of daily life—at home, at work, and

---

[8] John Paul II, *Ecclesia in Africa*, no. 95.

[9] *Ad Gentes*, no. 21, *Vatican Council II, 838*.

[10] John Paul II, *"Catechesi Tradendae"*, no. 66 (Rome: October 16, 1979), http://www.vatican.va/.../apost_exhortations/documents/hf_jp-ii_exh_16101979 (accessed February 15, 2008).

in the market place. During the administration of the sacraments of baptism, confirmation and holy matrimony, the laity who serve as sponsors or God-parents, help in shaping the behavior of the individuals they sponsor and the families to which they belong. In view of these important roles, the laity must be continually empowered to play their indispensable role in the church. This must be done through the establishment of more institutions and more programs for the initial and ongoing formation (human and spiritual) of the laity. For example, while the bishops of Ghana have established two faculties of theology and three centers of philosophy to train people to become priests and religious, and in addition to these have built a new major seminary (2009) while sponsoring their own minor seminaries, church leaders must ask themselves: What are we doing to seriously educate the laity to actively and fully participate in the work of evangelization? I argue that a laity that is well-formed theologically will provide better direction and support for families and create more vibrant ecclesial communities. The possibilities for fostering more responsible fathers, sons and brothers may be the Church's most promising contribution to reduce streetism and other social vices confronting young men in Africa.

Responsibility on the Part of Male Youth Themselves

The Akans say, *obi nnom aduro mma oyarefoo*—no one takes medication for a sick person. Notwithstanding all that those who are ministering to male youth are doing, male youth themselves must be agents in the efforts aimed at responding to the crises confronting them. I suggest that they must be made aware of the need to help themselves through initiatives, cooperation and active participation. As it was noted in the Introduction, the majority of Africa male youth are energetic, resilient and hardworking. What they need is empowerment, not sympathy. I am of the view that the Church is well-positioned to create the conditions that will enable them to take responsibility for their lives and actions.

In this technologically advanced world, the non-education and malformation of male youth has disastrous consequences. They become burdens not only to themselves but also to their families and the society at large. Such young men can be easily enticed and lured by opportunists and mercenaries. Some of the social consequences of young men being on the margins of the church and society may include:

- Not being fit for any meaningful employment which can swell the rate of unemployment in the country.

- An increased incidence of juvenile delinquencies and serious crimes like armed robbery and assault.

- High percentage of absentee and irresponsible fathers.

- Increase in streetism

- Women's emancipation and empowerment are not complimented resulting in their goals not being achieved. This can negatively affect marriage and family lives in Africa.

- Vocations to the priesthood and religious life are greatly affected since quality young men may not be entering the houses of formation. Even in situations where they manage to go through the formation process, they may not be well-formed. This can affect adversely the church in particular and the continent in general.

The social need to guarantee the proper formation of male youth is evident. To achieve this goal, the Roman Catholic church in Africa cannot be left out or remove itself from responsible engagement.

As noted in the book, Ghana has enjoyed a relative peace compared to other countries in the sub-region. It has made a significant progress in reducing poverty and it has seen improvement in the socio-economic development, good governance, youth and gender empowerment. According to the 2007 United Nations Development Program (UNDP) Report, Ghana is the first country in Africa to achieve Millennium Development Goal 1. It has managed to reduce the people living in the extreme poverty by half from 36% in 1991/1992 to 18.2% in 2005/2006. The overall poverty incidences declined from 51.75% in 1991/1992 to 28.5% in 2005/2006.[11] These are laudable achievements. However, more needs to be done. There is the need to maintain vigilance, promote peace at all times and forge ahead in order to continue to improve upon the standard of living of the citizens. For these to be realized, young men,

---

[11] United Nations Development Programme, "Human Development Report 2007/2008 – Ghana", http://hdrstats.undp.org/countries/country_fact_sheets/cty_fs_GHA.html (accessed February 14, 2008). See also, Ghana Home Page, "2007 UNDP Report commends Ghana" http://www.ghanaweb.com/GhanaHomePage/NewsArchive/artikel.php?ID=139229 (accessed February 14, 2008).

especially those on the margins of the church and society cannot be left behind. They must be brought on-board so that they do not slip behind to derail all the gains that have been made so far.

Cultural Values and Christian Virtues:
The Challenge of Appropriation

As noted earlier on, the church is a sacrament of Christ. Its mission cannot be uncoupled from the mission of Christ. The mission of Christ was "to bring good news to the poor; to proclaim release to the captives and recovery of sight to the blind, to let the oppressed go free, to proclaim the year of the Lord's favor." (Lk. 4:18-19) It was to enable people to "have life and have it abundantly." (Jn. 10:10b) The church must, therefore, be very interested in all the aspects of the human person, with particular reference to male youth. In view of the negative consequences that marginalized male youth may have on the society, the Roman Catholic church must educate and form male youth in the areas of honesty, responsibility, integrity and positive self-image. This will assist young men to achieve self-confidence.[12]

Furthermore, self-discipline must be the backbone of the church's teaching to male youth in Africa. If they are well-educated and properly formed, young men will be strong in character, they will have belief systems, principles and values to live-by. The cultivation of such character traits will help them not to be so easily manipulated and led astray.

With regard to male youth being formed to become ambassadors, disciples and a witnesses of the Lord Jesus, the Emmaus story in the Lukan Gospel (cf. Lk. 24:13-35) may be instructive. After the resurrection, two disciples were traveling to Emmaus. They were talking about what the women had come to tell the other disciples when they (women) went to the tomb that morning. They did not see the body of Jesus. An angel had told them that he had risen from the dead. As the disciples continued the discussion a stranger joined them on the way. He asked them what they were talking about that had made them so sad. They on their part asked him whether he was the only stranger in Jerusalem who had not heard the news at that time. The three continued the discussion as they went on the journey. Night was fast approaching and the

---

[12] Refer Donal Dorr, *Spirituality of Leadership: Inspiration, Empowerment, Intuition and Discernment* (Blackrock, Co. Dublin: The Columba Press, 2006). See also Everett L. Worthington, Jr. "Virtue Orientations", in *Jesus and Psychology*, ed. Fraser Watts (London: Darton, Longman and Todd Ltd., 2007), 116-136.

two disciples were near to their destination. The stranger was bent on continuing his journey. They prevailed upon him to stay since it was getting too late. At supper time, the stranger took bread, said a blessing, broke the bread and gave it to them. Immediately, their eyes were opened and they recognized Jesus. At that very moment, he vanished from their sight. The evangelist goes on to tell us that when Jesus disappeared from their sight the two disciples, in hind-sight, began to ask themselves whether their hearts were not burning within them when Jesus opened the scriptures to them on the way.

The Significance of the Emmaus Narrative
for Those who Minister to Male Youth

One meaning that may be taken from the Emmaus narrative is that Jesus is the key to understanding the scriptures. Male youth must, therefore, be helped to cultivate the habit of reading and reflecting on the scriptures if they want to know Jesus more deeply and follow him more closely. This is captured eloquently by Jerome in the saying that "Ignorance of scriptures is ignorance of Christ."[13]

Another important insight from the story is that after the resurrection, Jesus cannot be possessed and controlled. He can only be experienced in the breaking of bread. For this reason, young men must be taught to seek Christ through the mediation of the church. As Louis-Marie Chauvet notes, "you cannot arrive at the recognition of the risen Jesus unless you renounce seeing/touching/finding him by undeniable proofs. Faith begins precisely with such a *renunciation of the immediacy* of the see/know and the assent to the mediation of the church."[14] He goes on to say, "In order to accede to faith, the two disciples of Emmaus have had to overturn their own Jewish convictions and accept something monstrous for any good Jew, a Messiah who would have to go through death. You too must convert your desire for immediacy and assent to the mediation of the church."[15]

The story indicates that Jesus joined the two disciples as a total stranger. When they reached their destination, the two disciples reached out to him and even invited him for supper. Young men in Africa need to be helped to discover that membership in the church, is not a matter between the individual

---

[13] Jerome, "Ignorance of Scripture is ignorance of Christ" *The Liturgy of the Hours*, Vol. IV, 1447.
[14] Louis-Marie Chauvet, *The Sacraments: The Word at the Mercy of the Body* (Collegeville, MN: The Liturgical Press), 25.
[15] Ibid., 28.

Christian and his God. It also includes communion and relationship with others. The Christian life, therefore, has vertical and horizontal dimensions. The young man is never an individual who is unconnected and without responsibility. As Pope Benedict XVI observes, "no human being is closed in upon himself or herself and that no one can live of or for himself or herself alone."[16] He goes on to say, "human beings are relational and they possess their lives—themselves—only by way of relationship."[17]

When the two disciples recognized Jesus in the breaking of bread and later on he vanished from their sight, they returned to Jerusalem and recounted their experience to the rest of the disciples. Male youth must be helped to recognize that any encounter or experience with Jesus always has the sense of mission attached to it. One does not become a Christian for oneself. To be a Christian is to bring Jesus Christ to others. As noted by Juan Luis Segundo, "to be a Christian is to belong to a community that has been sent."[18] The same opinion is shared by Chauvet when he said, "to be a Christian is not to belong to a "clan"; it is to become a sister and brother in Jesus Christ to every human being."[19] As authentic Africans and authentic ambassadors, disciples and witnesses of Jesus Christ, young men must be helped to inculcate non-attachment to material things, to learn the importance of human freedom, self-reflection, faithful discipleship, and self-sacrifice for the sake of love and justice.

In sum, the Roman Catholic church in Africa must be concerned about young men in the church but not to the exclusion of those who are outside the church, most especially, young men who have fallen on the wrong side of the laws in the country as it endeavors to respond to the crises facing male youth. In this way, the Church will demonstrate its concern and hope for young men whose "beards are on fire." By urging and encouraging them to become good citizens and authentic Christians and witnesses of the Christian faith, the Church may also create the conditions for their 'hearts to be on fire' so as to be eager to promote peace, development and good will for and among themselves, their people, the Church and the society.

---

[16] Joseph Ratzinger, *"In the Beginning..." A Catholic Understanding of the Story of Creation and The Fall,* trans. Boniface Ramsey (Grand Rapids, MI: William B. Eerdmans Publishing Company, 1995), 72.

[17] Ibid.

[18] Juan L. Segundo, *The Community Called Church* (Maryknoll: Orbis, 1973), 8.

[19] Louis-Marie Chauvet, *Sacraments: The Word at The Mercy of the Body,* 194.

BIBLIOGRAPHY

Abba, Chimeka JoeBarth. *The Need for Basic Pastoral Formation for Youths in Africa of The Twenty-First Century.* Aachen: Shaker Verlag, 2005.

Acts and Declarations of The Third Synod of The Catholic Archdiocese of Kumasi. Kumasi, Ghana: Kumasi Catholic Press, 2004.

Adamo, David Tuesday. *Africa and the Africans in the Old Testament.* San Francisco: International Scholars Publicans, 1997.

——. *Africa and Africans in the New Testament.* Lanham, Maryland: University Press of America, Inc. 2006.

Addai-Mensah, Peter. *Doing Christian Religious Education in Ghana Today: A Personal Approach.* Takoradi: Ghana, St. Francis Press, Ltd., 1998.

——. *The Church and its Evangelizing Ministry in the World.* Takoradi: Ghana, St. Francis Press, Ltd., 2000.

Aelred. "True, Perfect and Eternal Friendship". In *The Liturgy of the Hours.* Vol. III. New York: Catholic Book Publishing Co., 1975.

Agbeti, Kofi J. *West African Church History: Christian Mission and Church Foundations: 1482–1919.* Leiden: E. J. Brill, 1986.

——. *West African Church History II: Christian Missions and Theological Training 1842–1970.* Leiden, Netherlands: E. J. Brill, 1991.

Al-Ghazali. *Faith in Divine Unity and Trust in Divine Providence.* Trans. David B. Burrell, Louisville, NY: Fons Vitae, 2000.

Anatolios, Khaled. *Athanasius: The Early Church Fathers.* New York: Routledge, 2004.

——. *Athanasius: The Coherence of His Thought.* New York: Routledge, 2005.

Anderson, Allan. "Demons and Deliverance in African Pentecostalism". In *Angels and Demons: Perspectives and Practice in Diverse Religious Traditions.* Eds. Peter G. Riddell and Beverly Smith Riddell. Nottingham: Inter-Varsity Press, 2007.

Anselm. "Cur Deus Homo". In *Anselm: Basic Writings.* Ed. and Trans. Thomas Williams. Indianapolis: Hackett Publishing Company, Inc. 2007.

Appiah-Kubi and Sergio Torres. Eds. *African Theology En Route.* Maryknoll, NY: Orbis Books, 1979.

Aquinas, Thomas. *Summa Theologiae: Questions of God.* Eds. Brian Davies and Brian Leftow. Cambridge: University Press, 2006.

Arinze, Francis. *Sacrifice in Ibo Religion.* Ibadan, Nigeria: Ibadan University Press, 1970.

Arrupe, Pedro. "Letter to the Whole Society on Incarnation". In *Studies in the International Apostolate of Jesuits,* 7. June 1978.

Asamoah-Gyadu, J. Kwabena. *African Charismatics: Current Developments Within Independent Indigenous Pentecostalism in Ghana.* Leiden: E. J. Brill, 2005.

Asante, Kete Molefi and Emeka Nwadiora. *Spear Masters: An Introduction to African Religion.* New York: University Press of America, Inc., 2007.

Association of Episcopal Conferences of Anglophone West Africa. *Take Heart! AECAWA Bishops Speaks.* Takoradi, Ghana: AECAWA Publications, 1996.

Atiemo, Abamfo Ofori. *The Rise of the Charismatic Movement in the Mainline Churches in Ghana.* Accra: Asempa Publishers, Christian Council of Ghana, 1993.

Augustine. "On the Grace of Christ and On Original Sin". In *Augustine: Later Works.* Trans, John Burnaby. Philadelphia: The Westminster Press, 1945.

———. "Ten Homilies on The First Epistles General of John". In *Augustine: Later Works,* Trans. John Burnaby. Philadelphia: The Westminster Press, 1945.

———. *De Catechizandis Rudibus (The First Catechetical Instructions).* Trans. Joseph P. Christopher. Westminster, Maryland: The Newman Bookshop, 1946.

———. "The Teacher". *In Augustine: Earlier Writings.* Vol. I. Trans. John H. S. Burleigh. Westminster: Knox, 1953.

———. *On Christian Teaching.* Trans. R. P. H. Green. Oxford: University Press, 1977.

———. *Confessions.* Trans. Henry Chadwick. Oxford: University Press, 1991.

———. *De Trinitate (The Trinity).* Trans. Edmund Hill. Hype Park, NY: New City, 1991.

———. "City of God". In *ST. 208: Saint Augustine: Course Pack.* U. S. A.: University Readers, Inc. 2006.

———. "On Grace and Free Will". In *ST. 208: Saint Augustine: Course Pack.* U. S. A.: University Readers, Inc. 2006.

Ayaga, Augustine M. *Common Values, Contradictory Strategies: A Study of Church, State and NGO Relations in Ghana.* Accra: SonLife Printing Press and Services, 2000.

Baeta, G. C. *Prophetism in Ghana: A Study of "Some" Spiritual Churches.* London: SCM Press, 1962.

———. *The Rise of Independent Churches.* Accra, Ghana: Asempa Publishers, 1990.

Baker, Grimenko Dori and Joyce Ann Mercer. *Lives to Offer: Accompanying Youth on Their Vocational Quests.* Cleveland: The Pilgrim Press, 2007.

Baldovin, John. "Participation: What is at Stake? *Celebration.* January, 1994.

Bane, Martin J. *Catholic Pioneers in West Africa.* Dublin: Cahill and Co Ltd., 1956.

Banzikiza, R. Constance. *Consolidating Unity and Peace in Africa.* Eldoret, Kenya: AMECEA Gaba Publications, 2004.

Barnes, R. Michael and Daniel H. Williams. Eds. *Arianism after Arius: Essays on the Development of the Fourth Century Trinitarian Conflicts.* Edinburgh: T & T Clark, 1993.

Bartels, F. L. *The Roots of Ghana Methodism.* Cambridge: Cambridge University Press, 1965.

Bedouelle, Guy. *The History of the Church.* Germany: Lit Verlag Munster, 2003.

Bediako, Kwame. *Christianity in Africa: The Renewal of a Non-Western Religion.* Maryknoll, NY: Orbis Book, 1995.

———. *Jesus and The Gospel in Africa: History and Experience.* New York: Orbis Books, 2004.

Benedict XVI. "In the Beginning… ", *A Catholic Understanding of the Story of Creation and The Fall.* Trans. Boniface Ramsey. Grand Rapids, Michigan: William B. Eerdmans Publishing, 1995.

———. *Called to Communion: Understanding The Church Today.* Trans. Adrian Walker, San Francisco: Ignatius Press, 1996.

———. *Milestones: Memoirs 1927–1977.* San Francisco: Ignatius Press, 1998.

———. *Many Religions—One Covenant: Israel, The Church and The World.* San Francisco: Ignatius Press, 1999.

———. *The Spirit of The Liturgy.* Trans. John Saward. San Francisco: Ignatius Press, 2000.

———. *On The Way to Jesus Christ.* Trans. Michael J. Miller. San Francisco: Ignatius Press, 2005.

——. *Christianity and The Crisis of Culture*. Trans. Brian McNeil. San Francisco: Ignatius Press, 2006.

——. *God is Love*. Vatican City: Libreria Editrice Vaticana, 2006.

——. *God's Revolution: World Youth Day and Other Cologne Talks*. San Francisco: Ignatius Press, 2006.

——. *Values in a Time of Upheaval*. Trans. Brian McNeil. San Francisco: Ignatius Press, 2006.

—— and Marcello Pera. *Without Roots: The West, Relativism, Christianity and Islam*. Trans. Michael F. Moore. New York: Basic Books, 2006.

Bequette, P. John. Christian *Humanism: Creation, Redemption and Reintegration*. Revised Edition. Lanham, Maryland: University Press of America, Inc. 2007.

Biney, Moses. "Singing the Lord's Song in a Foreign Land: Spirituality, Community, and Identity in a Ghanaian Immigrant Congregation". In *African Immigrant Religions in America*. Eds. Jacob K. Olupona and Regina Gemignani. New York: New York University Press, 2007.

Blount, Reginald. "Journeying with Youth toward Living Waters". In *The Princeton Lectures on Youth, Church and Culture 2005: Longing for God: Youth and The Quest for a Passionate Church*. Eds. Kenda Creasy Dean et al. Princeton, NJ: Princeton Theological Seminary, 2005.

Bogle, Joanna. *The Pope Benedict Code*. Melbourne, Australia: Freedom Publishing Pty. Ltd. 2006.

Bequette, P. John. *Christian Human: Creation, Redemption, and Reintegration*. Revised Edition. New York: University Press of America, Inc. 2007.

Brakel, Van J. *The First Twenty-Five Years of SMA Missionary Presence in The Gold Coast: 1880–1905*. Drunkkeskellechef Guelle, Nymegen, 1992.

Brodie, L. Thomas. *Genesis as Dialogue: A Literary, Historical and Theological Commentary*. New York: Oxford University Press, 2001.

Busia, Kofi Abrefa. *Africa in Search of Democracy*. New York: Praeger, 1967.

Butler, Grace L. Chavis. *Africa: Religious and Culture with a Focus on the Ashanti People*. Pittsburgh, PA: Dorrance, 1994.

Burton, Augustus Keith. *The Bible and African Christianity: The Blessing of Africa*. Downers Grove, IL: InterVarsity Press, 2007.

Cahill, Sowle Lisa. "Bioethics, AIDS, Theology and Social Change". In *Reflecting Theologically on AIDS: A Global Challenge*. Ed. Robin Gill. London: SCM Press, 2007.

Calvin, John. *Institutes of The Christian Religion*. Vols. 1 & II. Louisville, KY: Westminster John Knox Press, 1950.

Catechism of The Catholic Church. Vatican City: Libreria Editrice Vaticana, 1994.

Chauvet, Louis-Marie. *The Sacraments: The Word at the Mercy of the Body*. Collegeville, MN: The Liturgical Press, 2001.

Chunney, Kow Joseph, Joanne Marie Greer and John Allen. "African Spiritual Worldview: It's Impact on Alcohol and other Drug Use by Secondary School Students in Ghana". In *Research in the Social Scientific Study of Religion: A Research*. Vol. 10. Eds. David O. Moberg and J. M. Greer, Greenwich, Conn: Brill, 1999.

Coleman, A. John. Ed. *Christian Political Ethics*. Princeton, New Jersey: Princeton University Press, 2008.

Collins, S. Francis. *The Language of God: A Scientist Presents Evidence for Belief*. New York: Free Press, 2007.

Cooper, D. Terry. *Sin, Pride and Self-Acceptance: The Problem of Identity in Theology and Psychology.* Downers Grove, ILL: InterVarsity Press, 2003.

Cyprian. *The Lapsed: The Unity of The Catholic Church.* Trans. Maurice Bevenot. Westminster, MD: Newman Press, 1957.

Dale T. Irvin and Scott W. Sunquist, Eds. "Controversy and Crisis in Christendom". In *History of the World Christian Movement.* Maryknoll, NY: Orbis Books, 2001.

Daly, J. Robert. "Sacrifice". In *The New Dictionary of Theology.* Eds. Joseph A. Komonchak, Mary Collins and Dermot A. Lane, Wilmington: Michael Glazier Press, Inc., 1987.

Day, M. James. "Personal Development". In *Jesus and Psychology.* Ed. Fraser Watts. London: Darton, Longman and Todd Ltd. 2007.

Debrunner, H. W. *A History of Christianity in Ghana.* Accra, Ghana: Waterville Publishing House, 1967.

Desai, Ram. Ed. *Christianity in Africa as Seen by Africans.* Denver: Swallow, 1962.

Dicken, Kwesi. *Theology in Africa.* Maryknoll, NY: Orbis Books, 1984.

Dolvo, Elom. "Christianity, Nation-Building and National Identity in Ghana: Religious Perspective". In *Uniquely African? African Christian Identity from Cultural and Historical Perspectives.* Eds. James L. Cox and Gerrie ter Haar. Trenton, NJ: Africa World Press, 2003.

Dorr, Donal. *Spirituality of Leadership, Empowerment, Intuition and Discernment.* Blackrock, Co. Dublin: The Columba Press, 2006.

Dulles, Avery. *A Church to Believe In.* New York: Crossroad, 1982.

———. *Models of The Church.* Garden City, NY: Double, 2002.

Dunston, Alfred. *The Black Man in the Old Testament and Its World.* Trenton, NJ: Africa World Press, 1992.

Dykstra, C. Robert, Allan Hugh Cole Jr. and Donald Capps. *Losers, Loners, and Rebels: The Spiritual Struggles of Boys.* Louisville, KY: Westminster John Knox Press, 2007.

Dzobo, N. K. "African Symbols and Proverbs as Sources of Knowledge and Truth". In *Person and Community: Ghanaian Philosophical Studies*, 1. Eds. Kwasi Wiredu and Kwame Gyekye. Washington, D. C: The Council for Research in Values and Philosophy, 1992.

Ecclesia in Ghana: On the Church in Ghana and Its Evangelizing Mission in the Third Millenium. Accra: National Catholic Secretariat, 1997.

Edie, P. Fred. *Book, Bath, Table, and Time: Christian Worship as Source and Resource for Youth Ministry.* Cleveland: The Pilgrim Press, 2007.

Einstein, Mara. *Brands of Faith: Marketing Religion in a Commercial Age.* New York: Routledge, 2008.

Ela, Jean-Marc. *My Faith as an African.* Trans. John Pairmon Brown. Maryknoll, NY: Orbis Books, 1998.

Elorm, Dovlo. "Christianity, Nation-Building and National Identity in Ghana: Religious Perspectives". In *Uniquely African? African Christian Identity from Cultural and Historical Perspective.* Eds. James L. Cox and Gerrie ter Haar. Trenton, NJ: African World Press, 2003.

Erickson, H. Erik. *Childhood and Society.* New York: Norton, 1993.

Esposito, L. John. *Unholy War: Terror in the Name of Islam,* Oxford: University Press, 2002.

Ezekwonma, C. Ferdinand. *African Communitarian Ethic: The Basis for the Moral Conscience and Autonomy of the Individual: Igbo Culture as a case Study.* Berlin: Peter Lang, 2005.

Fee, D. Gordon. *Pauline Christology: An Exegetical-Theological Study*. Peabody, Massachusetts, Hendrickson Publishers, Inc. 2007.

Ferdinando, Keith. "The Spiritual Realm in Traditional African Religion". In *Angels and Demons: Perspectives and Practice in Diverse Traditions*. Eds. Peter G. Riddell and Beverly Smith Riddell. Nottingham: Inter-Varsity Press, 2007.

Flannery, Austin. Ed. "Ad Gentes" In *Vatican Council II*. Dublin: Dominican Publications, 1975.

———. Ed. "Christus Dominus" In *Vatican Council II*. Dublin: Dominican Publicans, 1975.

———. Ed. "Dignitatis Humanae" In *Vatican Council II*. Dublin: Dominican Publications, 1975.

———. Ed. "Gaudium et Spes" In *Vatican Council II*. Dublin: Dominican Publications, 1975.

———. Ed. "Optatam Totius" In *Vatican Council II*. Dublin: Dominican Publications, 1975.

———. Ed. Presbyterorum Ordinis". In *Vatican Council II*. Dublin: Dominican Publications, 1975.

———. Ed. "Unitatis Redintegratio" In *Vatican Council II*. Dublin: Dominican Publications, 1975.

Fisher, B. Robert. *West African Religious Traditions: Focus on The Akans of Ghana*. Maryknoll, NY: Orbis Books, 1998.

Foli, Richard. *The Church in Ghana Today*. Accra, Ghana: Methodist Book Depot Ghana Ltd., 2001.

———. *The Future of the Church in Ghana*. Accra, Ghana: Methodist Book Depot Ghana Ltd., 2001.

———. *The Ghanaian Church in Retrospect*. Accra, Ghana: Methodist Book Depot Ghana Ltd., 2001.

Forrest, Jim. *The Road to Emmaus: Pilgrimage as a Way of Life*. Maryknoll, NY: Orbis Books, 2007.

Gadzekpo, S. K. *History of Ghana*. Madina, Ghana: Royal Gold Publishers, 1988.

Gennep, van Arnold. *The Rites of Passage*. Trans. Monika B. Vizedom and Gabrielle L. Caffee. Chicago: The University of Chicago Press, 1960.

Ghana Bishops Speak: A Collection of Communiqués, Memoranda and Pastoral Letters. Accra, Ghana. National Catholic Secretariat, 1999.

Gibb, Richard. *Grace and Global Justice: The Socio-Political Mission of the Church in an Age of Globalization*. Waynesboro, GA: Paternoster, 2006.

Gifford, Paul. *Ghana's New Christianity: Pentecostalism in a Globalizing African Economy*. Bloomington, IND: Indiana University Press, 2004.

Goehring, E. James and Janet A. Timbie. Eds. *The World of Early Egyptian Christianity*. Washington, D. C: The Catholic University of America, Press, 2007.

Golka, W. Friedemann. *The Leopard's Spots: Biblical and African Wisdom in Proverbs*. Edinburgh: T & T Clark, 1993.

Gower, Christopher. *Sacraments of Healing*. London: SPCK, 2007.

Graham, C. K. *The History of Education in Ghana*. London: Frank Cass and Company Ltd, 1971.

Gros, Jeffrey and Daniel S. Mulhall. Eds. *The Ecumenical Christian Dialogues: The Catechism of The Catholic Church*. New York: Paulist Press, 2006.

Groves, C. P. *The Planting of Christianity in Africa*. London: Lutterworth, 1948.

Guider, Eletta Margaret. "From the Ends of the Earth: 'International Minister' or Missionary? Vocational Identity and the Changing Face of Mission in the USA: A Roman Catholic Perspective". In *Antioch Agenda: Essays on the Restorative Church in honor of Orlando E. Costas*. Eds. Daniel Jeyaraj, Robert W. Pazmino and Rodney L. Petersen. New Delhi: Academy Press, 2007.

Gyekye, Kwame. "Person and Community in Akan Thought". In *Person and Community: Ghanaian Philosophical Studies*, 1. Eds. Kwasi Wiredu and Kwame Gyekye. Washington, D. C: The Council for Research in Values and Philosophy, 1992.

——. "Traditional Political Ideas, Their Relevance to Development in Contemporary Africa". In *Person and Community: Ghanaian Philosophical Studies*, Eds. Kwasi Wiredu and Kwame Gyekye. Washington, D. C: The Council for Research in Values and Philosophy, 1992.

——. *An Essay on African Philosophical Thought: The Akan Conceptual Scheme*. Revised Edition. Philadelphia: Temple University Press, 1995.

——. *Tradition and Modernity: Philosophical Reflections on The African Experience*. Oxford: Oxford University Press, 1997.

Haight, Roger. "Historical Ecclesiology" In *Science et Esprit XXXIX* (1987).

Hamilton, Adam. *Christianity and World Religions: Wresting With Questions People Ask*. Nashville: Abingdon Press, 2005.

Harrington, J. Daniel. *The Gospel of Matthew*. Collegeville, MN: The Liturgical Press, 1991.

——. *Who is Jesus? Why is He Important?: An Invitation to The New Testament*. New York: Rowman and Littlefield Publishers, Inc. 1999.

——. *The Church According to The New Testament: What The Wisdom and Witness of Early Christianity Teach Us Today*. Franklin, Wisconsin: Sheed and Ward, 2001.

——. *Jesus: A Historical Portrait*. Cincinnati, OH: St. Anthony Messenger Press, 2007.

Hayes, Zachary. *Visions of a Future: A Study of Christian Eschatology*. Collegeville, MN: The Liturgical Press, 1989.

Hearne, Brian. "The Church in Africa". In *A New Missionary Era*. Ed. Padraig Flanagan. Maryknoll, NY: Orbis Book, 1982.

Hendrix, Scott. "Martin Luther, Reformer". In *The Cambridge History of Christianity: Reform and Expansion: 1500-1660*. Vol. 6. Ed. R. Po-Chia Hsia. Cambridge, U. K: Cambridge University Press, 2007.

Hinchliff, Peter. *Cyprian of Carthage and the Unity of The Church*. London: Geoffery Chapman Publishers, 1974.

Hinze, E. Bradford. *Practices of Dialogue in The Roman Catholic Church: Aims and Obstacles, Lessons and Laments*. New York: Continuum, 2006.

Hock, Klaus. *The Interface between Research and Dialogue: Christian-Muslim Relations in Africa*. Ed. New Brunswick. U. S. A.: Transaction Publishers, 2000.

Holmes, F. Arthur. Ed. *War and Christian Ethics*. 2nd Edition. Michigan: Grand Rapids, 2006.

Humphreys, Lee W. *Joseph and His Family: A Literary Study*. Columbia. South Carolina: University of South Carolina, 1988.

Idowu, E. Bolaji. *Olodumare, God in Yoruba Belief*. London: Longman, 1962.

Ikuenobe, Polycarp. *Philosophical Perspectives on Communalism and Morality in African Traditions*. New York: Lexington Books, 2006.

Ipgrave, Michael. *Trinity and Inter Faith Dialogues*. Germany: Plenitude and Plurality, 2003.

Isichei, Elizabeth. *A History of Christianity in Africa*. Grand Rapids: Lawrenceville, NJ: Africa World Press, 1995.

John Paul II. *Laborem Exercens*. Vatican City: Libreria Editrice, 1981.

——. *Pastores Dabo Vobis*. Vatican City: Libreria Editrice, 1992.

——. *Veritatis Splendor*. Vatican City: Libreria Editrice, 1993.

——. *Ecclesia in Africa*. Vatican City: Libreria Editrice, 1995.

Johnson, D. Kenneth. "Five Theses on the Globalization of Thug Life and 21st Century Missions". In *Antioch Agenda: Essays on the Restorative Church in honor of Orlando E. Costas*.

Eds. Daniel Jeyaraj, Robert W. Pazmino and Rodney L. Petersen. New Delhi: Academy Press, 2007.

Kamaara, Eunice. Gender, *Youth Sexuality and HIV/AIDS: A Kenyan Experience*. Eldoret, Kenya: AMECEA Gaba Publications, 2005.

Karris, J. Robert. "The Gospel According to Luke". In *The New Jerome Biblical Commentary*. Eds. Raymond E. Brown, Joseph A. Fitzmeyer and Roland E. Murphy, Englewood Cliffs, NJ: Prentice Hall, 1990.

Keen, Sam. *Fire in The Belly: On Being A Man*. New York: Banton Books, 1991.

Keenan, James. "AIDS and a Casuistry of Accommodation". In *Reflecting Theologically on AIDS: A Global Challenge*. Ed. Robin Gill. London: SCM Press, 2007.

Keith, D. Lewis. *The Catholic Church in History: Legend and Reality*. New York: The Crossroad Publishing Company, 2006.

Kilby, Karen. *Karl Rahner: Theology and Philosophy*. New York: Rutledge, 2004.

Kim, Kirsteen. *The Holy Spirit in the World: A Global Conversation*. Maryknoll, NY: Orbis Books, 2007.

Korgen, Odell Jeffry. *Solidarity will Transform the World: Stories of Hope from Catholic Relief Services*. Maryknoll, NY: Orbis Books, 2007.

Kudadjie, J. N. "Towards Moral and Social Development in Contemporary Africa: Insights from Dangme Traditional Moral Experience". In *Person and Community: Ghanaian Philosophical Studies*, 1. Eds. Kwasi Wiredu and Kwame Gyekye, Washington, D. C: The Council for Research in Values and Philosophy, 1992.

Lara, Raphael. "Migration from Africa to Spain". In *Concilium*. Vol. 5. Eds. Andres Torres Queiruga, Luiz Carlos Susin and Jon Sobrino. London: SCM Press, 2006.

Lathrop, W. Gordon. *Holy People: A Liturgical Ecclesiology*. Minneapolis: Fortress Press, 1999.

Lennan, Richard. *The Ecclesiology of Karl Rahner*. Oxford: Claredon Press, 1995.

Lindberg, Carter. *A Brief History of Christianity*. India: Replika Press, 2006.

Long, G. Michael and Tracy Wenger Sadd. Eds. *God and Country? Diverse Perspectives on Christianity and Patriotism*. New York: Palgrave Macmillan, 2007.

Longrace, E. Robert. *Joseph: A Story of Divine Providence*. 2nd Edition. Winona Lake, Indiana: Eisenbrauns, 2003.

Luther, Martin. "The Small Catechism". *In Creeds of the Churches*. Ed. John H. Leith. Atlanta: John Knox Press, 1982.

Mackey, P. James. *The Scientist and the Theologian: On the Origin and Ends of Creation*. Blackrock, Co. Dublin: The Columba Press, 2007.

Macmurray, John. *Search for Reality in Religion*. London: Headley Brothers Ltd. 1965.

——. *Freedom in the Modern World*. New York: Humanity Books, 1992.

——. *A Challenge to the Churches: Religion and Democracy*. London: Butler and Tanner Ltd. 1999.

——. *Persons in Relation*. New York: Humanity Books, 1999.

——. *The Self as Agent*. New York: Humanity Books, 1999.

MacNamara, Vincent. "On Having a Religious Morality". In *Contemporary Irish Moral Discourse*. Ed. Amelia Fleming. Blackrock, Co. Dublin: The Columba Press, 2007.

Maly, H. Eugene. "The Birth of Esau and Jacob". In *Jerome Biblical Commentary*. Eds. Raymond E. Brown, Joseph A. Fitzmeyer and Roland E. Murphy. Englewood Cliffs, NJ: Prentice Hall, INC., 1968.

———. "Cain and Abel". In *Jerome Biblical Commentary*. Eds. Raymond E. Brown, Joseph A. Fitzmeyer and Roland E. Murphy. Englewood Cliffs, NJ: Prentice Hall, INC., 1968.

Mann, E. Williams. Ed. *Augustine's Confessions: Critical Essays*. New York: Rowman and Littlefield Publishers Inc. 2006.

Martinson, Roland. "Engaging the Quest: Encountering Youth and God in Their Longing". In *The Princeton Lectures on Youth, Church and Culture 2004: Longing for God: Youth and The Quest for a Passionate Church*. Eds. Kenda Creasy Dean et alii. Princeton, NJ: Princeton Theological Seminary, 2004.

Massaro, Thomas. *Living Justice: Catholic Social Teaching in Action*. Franklin, WI: Sheed and Ward, 2000.

——— and Thomas A. Shannon. *Catholic Perspectives on Peace and War*. New York: Rowman and Littlefield Publishers, Inc. 2003.

May, G. Gerald. *Addiction and Grace. Love and Spirituality in the Healing of Addiction*. New York: HarperCollins Publishers, 1988.

May, E. William. "Sin". In *The New Dictionary of Theology*. Eds. Joseph A. Komonchak, Mary Collins and Dermot A. Lane. Wilmington: Michael Glazier, Inc., 1987.

Mbiti, John. *An Introduction to African Religion*. London: Heinemann Educational, 1975.

———. *African Religions and Philosophy*. New York: Praeger, 1996.

———. "The Hen knows when it is dawn, but leaves the crowing to the cock: African Religion looks at Islam". In *Religions View Religions: Explorations in Pursuit of Understanding*. Eds. Jerold D. Gort et all. Amsterdam: Editions Rodopi B. V., 2006.

McDonagh, Enda. "A Discourse on the Centrality of Justice". In *Contemporary Irish Discourse*. Ed. Amelia Fleming. Blackrock, Co. Dublin: The Columba Press, 2007.

McKee, Anne Elsie. Trans. *John Calvin: Selections from His Writings*. San Francisco: HarperCollins Publishers, 2006.

McLaughlin, R. Emmet. "The Radical Reformation". In *The Cambridge History of Christianity: Reformation and Expansion: 1500-1660*. Vol. 6. Ed. R. Po-Chia Hsia, Cambridge, U. K: Cambridge University Press, 2007.

Meilaender, Gilbert. *The Way That Leads There: Augustinian Reflections on The Christian Life*. Grand Rapids, MI: Wm. B. Eerdmans Publishing Co., 2006.

Mitchell, D. Nathan. *Meeting Mystery: Liturgy, Worship, Sacraments*, Maryknoll, New York: Orbis, 2006.

Mitchem, Y. Stephanie. *Name It and Claim It: Prosperity Preaching in the Black Churches*. Cleveland: The Pilgrim Press, 2007.

Moltmann, Jurgen. *The Church in the Power of the Spirit*. New York: Harper and Row, 1977.

Morrill, T. Bruce et al. Eds. *Practicing Catholic: Ritual, Body and Contestation in Catholic Faith*. New York: Palgrave Macmillan, 2006.

Muller, A. Richard. "John Calvin and Later Calvinism—The Identity". In *The Cambridge Companion to Reformation Theology*. Eds. David Bagchi and David C. Steinmetz, Cambridge, U. K.: Cambridge University Press, 2004.

Muller, Z. Jerry. "Three Hundred Years of Positive Moral Effects of the Market". In *Markets, Morals and Religion*. Ed. Jonathan B. Imber. New Brunswick, U. S. A: Transaction Publishers, 2008.

Naaeke, Y. Anthony. *Kaleidoscope Catechesis: Ministry Catechesis in Africa Particularly in The Diocese of Wa in Ghana*. New York: Peter Lang Publishing, 2006.

Nasir, Hossein Seyyed. *The Heart of Islam: Enduring Values for Humanity*. San Francisco: HarperCollins Publishers, 2002.

Nasir, Khan. *Perceptions of Islam in The Christendoms: A History Survey*. Oslo: Sohum Forlay, 2006.

Nazir-Ali, Michael. *Conviction and Conflict: Islam, Christianity and World Order*. London: Continuum, 2006.

Neusner, Jacob. Ed. *Religious Foundations of Western Civilization: Judaism, Christianity and Islam*. Nashville, TN: 2006.

Nichols, Aidan. *The Thought of Benedict XVI: An Introduction to The Theology of Joseph Ratzinger*. New York: Burns and Oates, 2005.

Nkrumah, Kwame. *Conscience: Philosophy and Ideology for Decolonization and Development with Particular Reference to the African Revolution*. London: Heinemann, 1964.

Norman, Solomon et al. Eds. *Abraham's Children: Jews, Christians and Muslims in Conversation*. London: T & T Clark, 2005.

Nutu, Ela. *Incarnate Word, Inscribed Flesh: John's Prologue and the Postmodern*. Sheffield, U. K: Sheffield Phoenix Press, 2007.

Obeng, Pashingston. *Asante Catholicism: Religious and Cultural Reproduction among The Akan of Ghana*. New York: E. J. Brill Seiden, 1996.

Odamtten, S. K. *The Missionary Factors in Ghana's Development up to the 1880's*. Accra, Ghana: Waterville Publishing House, 1978.

O'Donohue, John. *Eternal Echoes: Celtic Reflections on our Yearning to Belong*. New York: HarperCollins Publishers Inc. 1999.

Oduyoye, Amba Mercy. "Christian Engagement with African Culture: Religious Challenges". In *Uniquely African? African Christian Identity from Cultural and Historical Perspective*. Eds. James L. Cox and Gerrie ter Haar. Trenton, NJ: Africa World Press, 2003.

Okoledah, D. K. Norbert. *Problems and Prospects of the Search for a Catholic Pastoral Ministry*. Piscataway, NJ: Transaction Publishers, 2005.

Olsen, Christian Peter. *Youth at Risk: Ministry to The Least, The Lost and The Last* Cleveland, Ohio: The Pilgrim Press, 2003.

Omenyo, Cephas Narh. *Pentecost Outside Pentecostalism: A Study of the Development of Charismatic Renewal in the Mainline Churches in Ghana*. Zoetermeer, The Netherlands: Boekencentrum, 2002.

Onwubiko, A. Oliver. *African Thought, Religion and Culture*. Enugu, Nigeria: Snaap Press Ltd., 1991.

Opoku, Asare Kofi. "Aspect of Akan Worship". In *The Black Experience in Religion*. Ed. C. Eric Lincoln. New York: Doubleday, 1974.

——. "Changes within Christianity: The Case of the Musama Disco Christo Church". In *The History of Christianity in West Africa*, ed. O. A. Kalu, Hong Kong: Sing Cheung Printing Co. Ltd., 1980.

Ositelu, O. O. Rufus. *African Instituted Churches: Diversities, Growth, Gifts, Spirituality, and Ecumenical Understanding of African Initiated Churches*. Piscataway, NJ: Transaction Publishers, 2002.

Ott, Martin. *African Theology in Images*. Zomba, Malawi: Kachere Series, 2007.

Owusu, Robert Yaw. *Kwame Nkrumah's Liberation Thought: A Paradigm for Religious Advocacy in Contemporary Ghana*. Trenton, NJ: Africa World Press, 2006.

Parrinder, E. G. *Religion in Africa*. Penguin: Hammondsworth, 1969.

——. *African Traditional Religion*. Third Edition. London: Sheldon Press, 1974.

Paul VI. *Africae Terrarum*. Vatican City: Libreria Editrice, October 29, 1967.

——. *Populorum Progressio*. Vatican City: Libreria Editrice, 1967.

——. *Evangelii Nuntiandi*. Vatican City: Libreria Editrice, 1974.

——. *Catechesi Tradendae*. Vatican City: Libreria Editrice, 1979.

Pegis, C. Anton. *Introduction to St. Thomas Aquinas: The Summa Theologica. The Summa Contra Gentiles.* New York: Random House Inc. 1948.

Percy, Anthony. *Theology of The Body Made Simple: An Introduction to John Paul II's 'Gospel of The Body'.* England: Gracewing Publishing, 2005.

Peters, E. Ronald. *Urban Ministry: An Introduction*. Nashville: Abingdon Press, 2007.

Pfann, H. *A History of The Catholic Church in Ghana*. Cape Coast, Ghana: Catholic Mission Press, 1965.

Phou, Dafue. *Peace in Troubled Cities: Creative Models of Building Community amidst Violence.* Geneva: WCC Publications, 1998.

Pickthall, Marmaduke Mohammed. *The Meaning of the Glorious Koran*. Multan, Pakistan: Maktaba Jawahar al Uloom, n.d.

Plummer, L. Robert. *Paul's Understanding of the Church's Mission: Did The Apostle Paul Expert The Early Christian Communities to Evangelize?* Milton Keyes, U. K: Paternoster, 2006.

Pobee, John. *Toward An African Theology*. Nashville: Abington, 1979.

——. *Kwame Nkrumah and The Church in Ghana 1949-1966: A Study in the Relationship between the Socialist Government of Kwame Nkrumah, The First Prime Minister and First President of Ghana, and The Protestant Christian Churches of Ghana.* Accra: Asempa Publishers, 1988.

—— and Gabriel Ositelu II. *African Initiatives in Christianity: The Growth, Gifts and Diversities of Indigenous African Churches: A Challenge to the Ecumenical Movement.* Geneva: WCC Publications, 1998.

Quinones, J. Ricardo. *The Changes of Cain*. Princeton, NY: Princeton University Press, 1991.

Rahner, Karl. "Anonymous Christianity and The Missionary Task of The Church". In *Theological Investigations* 5, New York: Herder and Herder, 1972.

——. "Christianity and Non-Christian Religions". In *Theological Investigations* 5, New York: Seabury, 1979.

——. *Foundations of Christian Faith: An Introduction to The Idea of Christianity*. Trans. William V. Dych. New York: Crossroad, 2005.

——. *The Trinity*. Trans. Joseph Donceel. New York: The Crossroad Publishing Company, 2005.

Reath, Mary. *Rome and Canterbury: The Elusive Search for Unity*. New York: Rowman & Littlefield Publishers, Inc. 2007.

Report from Seminar on The Social Teaching of The Catholic Church. Accra, Ghana: National Catholic Secretariat, 1999.

Rise, Svein. *The Academic and The Spiritual in Karl Rahner's Theology*. Frankfurt: Peter Land, 2000.

Rombs, J. Ronnie. *St. Augustine and The Fall of The Soul*. Washington: The Catholic University of America Press, 2006.

Rogerson, John. *Genesis 1-11*. New York: T & T Clark International, 2004.

Ruddy, Christopher. *The Local Church: Tillard and The Future of Catholic Ecclesiology*. New York: The Crossroad Publishing Company, 2006.

Sackey, M. Brigid. *New Directions in Gender and Religion: The Changing Status of Women in Africa Independent Churches.* New York: Lexington Books, 2006.

Sanneh, L. *West African Christianity: The Religious Impact.* London: Allen and Unwin, 1983.

Sarpong, Peter. *African Theology: A Simple Description.* Accra, Ghana: Cabot Publications, 1988.

———. *Some Notes on West African Traditional Religion: Advanced Level.* Unpublished Lectures Notes, 1990.

———. *Peoples Differ: An Approach to Inculturation in Evangelization.* Accra, Ghana: Sub-Saharan Publishers, 2002.

Schillebeeckx, Edward. *The Church: A Human Story of God.* New York: Crossroad, 1990.

Scotland, Nigel. "The Charismatic Devil: Demonology in Charismatic Christianity". In *Angels and Demons: Perspectives and Practice in Diverse Religious Traditions.* Eds. Peter G. Riddell and Beverly Smith Riddell. Nottingham: Inter-Varsity Press, 2007.

Segundo, Luis Juan. *The Community Called Church.* Maryknoll: Orbis, 1973.

Senghor, S. Leopold. *On African Socialism.* Trans. Mercer Cook, New York: Praeger, 1964.

Short, Rubert. *Benedict XVI: Commander of The Faith.* London: Hodder and Stoughton, 2005.

Shorter, Alyward. *African Christian Theology: Adaptation or Inculturation?* London: G. Chapman, 1975.

———. *Cross and Flag in Africa: The "White Fathers" during the Colonial Scramble (1892–1914).* Maryknoll, NY: Orbis Books, 2006.

Smalley, S. Stephen. *Hope for Ever: The Christian View of Life and Death.* Waynesboro, GA: Paternoster Press, 2005.

Soares, F. Benjamin. Ed. *Muslim-Christian Encounters in Africa.* Leiden, Netherlands: Brill, 2006.

Spencer, Nick and Robert White. *Christianity, Climate Change and Sustainable Living.* London: SPCK, 2007.

Steward, B. Robert. Ed. *Intelligent Design: William A. Dembski and Michael Ruse in Dialogue.* Minneapolis: Fortress Press, 2007.

Stow, Peter and Mike Fearon. *Youth in the City: Church's Response to Challenge of Youth Work.* London: Hodder and Stoughton Limited, 1987.

Taft, Robert. "What Does Liturgy Do? Towards a Soteriology of Liturgical Celebrations: Some These". *In Primary Sources of Liturgical Theology: A Reader,* Ed. Dwright Vogel. Collegeville: Liturgical Press, 2000.

Telle, Eugene. *Augustine.* Nashville, TN: Abingdon Press, 2006.

Tetteh, J. Wisdom. "Transnationalism, Religion, and the African Diaspora in Canada: An Examination of Ghanaians and Ghanaian Churches" In *African Immigrant Religions in America.* Eds. Jacob K. Olupona and Regina Gemignani. New York: New York University Press, 2007.

Timberg, Craig. "Circumcision offered to Africans: Part of Bush's Anti-AIDS Push". In *The Boston Globe.* Vol. 272, No. 51, August 20, 2007.

Tuffour, I. "Relations between Christian Missions, European Administration and Traders". In *The History of Christianity in West Africa.* Ed. O. A. Kalu. Hong Kong: Sing Cheung Printing Co. Ltd. 1980.

The Code of Canon Law. Grand Rapids, MI: Williams B. Eerdmans Publishing Company, 1983.

The Liturgy of The Hours. Vol. III & IV. New York: Catholic Book Publishing Company, 1975.

The National Catechetical Commission of Ghana. *Christ's Way to Life: An Introduction to The Catholic Faith.* Kumasi, Ghana: Kumasi Catholic Press, 1978.

The New Revised Standard Bible. New York: Oxford University, 1989.

The Sacramentary. New York: Catholic Book Publishing Co. 1974.

Tuffour, I. "Relations between Missions, European administrators and traders in the Gold Coast". In *The History of Christianity in West Africa,* ed. O. A. Kalu, Hong Kong: Sing Cheung Printing Co. Ltd., 1980.

U. S. Conference of Catholic Bishops. *Catholic Identity in Our Colleges and Universities.* Washington D. C.: 2006.

Walker, G. S. M. *The Churchmanship of St. Cyprian.* Richmond, Virginia: Knox Press, 1969.

White, F. David. *Practicing Discernment with Youth: A Transformative Youth Approach.* Cleveland, Ohio: The Pilgrim Press, 2005.

Wiles, F. Maurice, *Archetypal Heresy: Arianism through the Centuries.* Oxford: Oxford University Press, 1996.

Wiltgen, Ralph. *Gold Coast Mission History: 1471–1880.* Techny, IL: Divine Word Publishers, 1956.

Wiredu, Kwasi and Kwame Gyekye. Eds. "Death and the Afterlife in African Culture". In *Person and Community: Ghanaian Philosophical Studies,* 1. Washington, D. C: The Council for Research in Values and Philosophy, 1992.

—— and Kwame Gyekye. Eds. "The Ghanaian Tradition of Philosophy". In *Person and Community: Ghanaian Philosophical Studies,* 1. Washington, D. C: The Council for Research in Values and Philosophy, 1992.

—— and Kwame Gyekye. Eds. "Moral Foundations of an African Culture". In *Person and Community: Ghanaian Philosophical Studies,* 1. Washington, D. C: The Council for Research in Values and Philosophy, 1992.

Woods, Richard. "Angels". In *The New Dictionary of Theology.* Eds. Joseph A. Komonchak, Mary Collins and Dermot A. Lane. Wilmington: Michael Glazier, Inc., 1987.

Worthington, Jr. L. Everett. "Virtue Orientations". In *Jesus and Psychology.* Ed. Fraser Watts. London: Darton, Longman and Todd Ltd, 2007.

Wright, H. John. "Providence". In *The New Dictionary of Theology.* Eds. Joseph A. Komonchak, Mary Collins and Dermot A. Lane. Wilmington: Michael Glazier, Inc. 1987.

Wylie, W. Robert. *Spiritism in Ghana: A Study of New Religious Movements.* Ann Arbor, MI: Edwards Brothers, Inc. 1980.

York, Joe. *With Signs Following: Photographs from the Southern Religious Roadside.* Jackson, University Press of Mississippi, 2007.

Zachman, C. Randall. *John Calvin as Teacher, Pastoral Theologian.* Grand Rapids, MI: Oaker Academic, 2006.

Ziauddin, Sardar. *What Do Muslims Belief?* London: Granta Books, 2006.

Websites

http://allafrica.com/stories/200512130662.html

http://books.google.com/books?id=yUJAAAAIAJ&pg=PA&238&dpg=PA238&dq=sir=marshall&source=web&ots=wW

http://devdata.worldbank.org/external/CPProfile.asp?CCODE=ghaPTYPE=CP

http://diamondsfacts.org/

http://en.wikipedia.org/wiki/Ghana

http://news.bbc.co.uk/2/hi/africa/6500539.stm

http://www.anglicandioceseofaccra.com/index.php?option=com_content&talk=viewed&id=5&
        Itemid=34

http://www.anglicansonline.org/resources/

http://www.africanexecutive.com/modules/magazine/articles.php?article

http://www.africa-union.org/roots/ua/Conference/2007/juin/PA/20%/20juin/Meeting.htm

http://www.aidsuganda.org

http://www.antonius.org/article/009.php

http://www.archcapeghana.org/

http://www.avert/aidssouthafrica.htm

http://www.catholic-hierarchy.org/country/schghl.html

http://www.centraluniversity.org

http://www.christianpost.com/article/20070717/28483_Cathoolic_Pride_in_in_%5_True_Chur
        ch%5_Makes_Enemies

http://www.crise.ox.ac.uk/pubs/workingpaper5.pdf

http://www.dacb.org/stories/liberia/legacy_harris.html

http://www.daughtersofstpaul.com/johnpaulpapacy/meejp/thepope/jpworldyouthdays.ht

http://www.devdata.worldbank.org/external/CPPProfile.asp?CCODE=gha&PTYPE=CP

http://www.diamondsfacts.org/facts/fact-09.html

http://www.divineword.org

http://www.ecowas.info/liberia.htm

http://www.ecowas.info/sleecon.htm

http://www.ethnologue.com/show_map.asp?name=GH&seq=10

http://www.etwn.com/new_evangelization/africa/history/continent

http://www.experiencefestival.com/a/Ashanti_Confederacy_-_History/id/4810583

http://www.gcatholic.com/dioceses/data/countryGH.htm

http://www.ghanacast.com/About%20Ghana.htm

http://www.ghanacbc.org/Directory%0202.pdf

http://www.ghanaeview.com/Gcons 7.html

http://www.ghanaweb.com/GhanaHomePage/NewsArchive/artikel.php?ID

http://www.guttmacher.org/pubs/2006/06/01/fb_ghana_adolescents.pdf

http://www.infoplease.com/ipaA0107584.html

http://www.islamicug.com

http://www.kasnet.com/heroesofjamaica/mg/g6/g6.htm

http://www.liberia-leaf.org/reports/trial/war/index.htm

http://www.mafrwestafrica.net/content/view/97/81/lang,en/

http://www.methodistchurch-gh.org/projects.htm

http://www.minelonks.com/alluvial/gold 1.html

http://www.mucg.edu.gh

http://myjoyonline.com/news/read.asp?contentid

http://www.pc-ghana.org

http://www.pc-ghana/detail/htm#begunning

http://www.pentvars.gh.org/pucmision.htm

http://www.sma.ie/index.php?article=sma_history

http://www.smafathers.org/smahtml/history.html
http://www.ssrc.org/fellowships/africanyouth/
http://www.thestatesmanonline.com/pages/editorial_detail-php?newsid=63&section=0
http://www.svdconsulting.com/contact.htm
http://www.un.org/apps/news/story.asp?NewsID=21588&Cr=ifad&Cr1=developme-nt
http://www.unaids.org/en/HIV_data/epi2006/default.asp
http://www.undp.org/
http://www.unic.org/index.php?option=com_content&task=view&task=view&id=45&Itemid=
       73
http://www.uspg.org.uk/
http://www.unu.edu/unupress/ops2.html
http://www.vatican.va/
http://www.visionofhumanity.com/rankings
http://www.vvu.edu.gh/
http://www.worldpress.org/Africa/2222.cfm
http://www.youthaidscoalition.org/docs/Ghana.phf